ABSOLU BEGINNER'S GUIDE

TO

Microsoft®

Windows® XP

Second Edition

Shelley O'Hara

800 East 96th Street,
Indianapolis, Indiana 46240

Absolute Beginner's Guide to Microsoft® Windows® XP, Second Edition

International Standard Book Number: 0-7897-3432-X

Library of Congress Catalog Card Number: 2005922881

Printed in the United States of America

First Printing: June 2005

08   07   06   05   4   3   2

Trademarks

All terms mentioned in this book that are known to be trademarks or service marks have been appropriately capitalized. Que Publishing cannot attest to the accuracy of this information. Use of a term in this book should not be regarded as affecting the validity of any trademark or service mark.

Warning and Disclaimer

Every effort has been made to make this book as complete and as accurate as possible, but no warranty or fitness is implied. The information provided is on an "as is" basis. The author and the publisher shall have neither liability nor responsibility to any person or entity with respect to any loss or damages arising from the information contained in this book.

Bulk Sales

Que Publishing offers excellent discounts on this book when ordered in quantity for bulk purchases or special sales. For more information, please contact

U.S. Corporate and Government Sales
1-800-382-3419
corpsales@pearsontechgroup.com

For sales outside of the U.S., please contact

International Sales
international@pearsontechgroup.com

Associate Publisher
Greg Wiegand

Acquisitions Editor
Michelle Newcomb

Development Editor
Kevin Howard

Managing Editor
Charlotte Clapp

Project Editor
Seth Kerney

Indexer
Erika Millen

Proofreader
Tonya Fenimore

Technical Editor
Greg Perry

Publishing Coordinator
Sharry Lee Gregory

Interior Designer
Anne Jones

Cover Designer
Dan Armstrong

Page Layout
Julie Parks

Contents at a Glance

Table of Contents

About the Author

Shelley O'Hara is the author of more than 100 books, mostly dealing with computers. She has written some of the all-time best-selling computer books, including *Easy Windows XP Home Edition* and *Easy Windows 98*. She also conducts computer training and teaches writing classes. In addition to tech writing, O'Hara has also published a romantic comedy called *The Marriage Trifecta*.

Dedication

To my sister, Kimberly Lynn Moore, with love.

Acknowledgments

Just like there are dream teams in sports, there are dream teams on book projects. I was fortunate enough to work with my own particular editing dream team, the people and staff who made writing this book so much easier. (You can't imagine all the work the editors do, yet it's only my name on the cover.)

My particular dream team includes Greg Wiegand for inviting me to do this project; Michelle Newcomb for negotiating the details; my favorite do-it-all team coordinator, Sharry Lee Gregory (using your full name to make your mom happy); Kevin Howard for excellent developmental advice; Greg Perry for his savvy, smart, excellent technical editing; and project editor Seth Kerney and proofreader Tonya Fenimore.

We Want to Hear from You!

As the reader of this book, *you* are our most important critic and commentator. We value your opinion and want to know what we're doing right, what we could do better, what areas you'd like to see us publish in, and any other words of wisdom you're willing to pass our way.

As an associate publisher for Que Publishing, I welcome your comments. You can email or write me directly to let me know what you did or didn't like about this book—as well as what we can do to make our books better.

Please note that I cannot help you with technical problems related to the topic of this book. We do have a User Services group, however, where I will forward specific technical questions related to the book.

When you write, please be sure to include this book's title and author as well as your name, email address, and phone number. I will carefully review your comments and share them with the author and editors who worked on the book.

Email: feedback@quepublishing.com

Mail: Greg Wiegand
Associate Publisher
Que Publishing
800 East 96th Street
Indianapolis, IN 46240 USA

For more information about this book or another Que title, visit our website at www.quepublishing.com. Type the ISBN (excluding hyphens) or the title of a book in the Search field to find the page you're looking for.

Introduction

If you are new to Windows XP or to Windows in general, this is the book for you. In easy-to-understand language and with step-by-step explanations, this book covers all the key tasks for using Windows XP, including work-related tasks as well as fun things such as playing digital music, working with pictures, playing games, and more.

Windows is an operating system. You don't need to know the hows and whys of an operating system. You just need to know there is one. The operating system is like the behind-the-scenes manager who takes care of all the basic computing tasks such as saving your work, printing a document, starting a program, and so on.

Therefore, you only need to learn how to perform these basic actions once. That is, once you learn how to print, you follow the same basic steps to print in all Windows programs. Once you learn how to start a program, you can start *any* program. Once you learn how to move or resize a window, you can perform this action for *any* window.

You'll find that learning how to use Windows is the same thing as learning how to use your computer.

Some Key Terms

To use Windows, you need to know the basic terminology used for common actions:

- *Point*—Move the mouse on the desk to move the pointer onscreen. The tip of the arrow should be on the item to which you are pointing. To open a menu or an icon, you point to the item you want.

- *Click*—Press and release the left mouse button once. You use click to select commands and toolbar buttons, as well as to perform other Windows tasks.

- *Double-click*—Press and release the left mouse button twice in rapid succession. Double-clicking opens an icon. (See the next section for exceptions or changes to double-clicking.)

- *Right-click*—Press and release the right mouse button once. You often right-click to display a shortcut menu.

- *Drag*—Hold down the mouse button and drag the pointer across the screen. Release the mouse button. Dragging is most often used for selecting text.

Some Things to Keep in Mind

You can personalize many features of Windows so that it is set up the way you like to work. That's one of the benefits of Windows. For consistency, though, this book makes some assumptions about how you use your computer. When working through steps and especially when viewing the figures in this book, keep in mind the following distinctions:

- Windows provides many ways to perform the same action. For instance, for commands, you can select a command from a menu, use a shortcut key, use a toolbar button, or use a shortcut menu. This book covers one main method (the most common for that particular task) and also mentions other methods, usually in a tip.

- Your particular Windows setup may not look identical to the one used in the figures in this book. For instance, if you use a desktop image, you see that. (The figures in this book use a plain background.) Don't let these differences distract you; Windows may look different, but it works the same way.

- Your computer setup is most likely different than the one used in this book. Therefore, you will see different programs listed on your Start menu, different fonts in your Font list, different folders and documents, and so on. Again, don't be distracted by the differences.

- To open a folder or file, you double-click the icon. You can also set up Windows to work similar to an Internet browser. That is, you can single-click to open an icon. This book assumes the double-click setup. If you use single-click, keep in mind that you single-click instead of double-click. You can read more about changing Windows's working mode in Chapter 16, "Viewing and Finding Files."

The Basic Structure of This Book

This book is divided into six parts, each centered around a certain theme. The book builds on the skills you need, starting with the basics and then moving to more complex topics such as networking. You can read the book straight through, look up topics when you have a question, or browse through the contents, reading information that intrigues you.

This section provides a quick breakdown of the parts.

Part I, "The Basics," explains all the key tasks for using your computer. If you read only this section, you will have enough skill knowledge to perform most basic computer tasks. This part covers understanding the Windows desktop and starting programs (Chapter 1), saving and print your work (Chapter 2), managing files (Chapter 3), and troubleshooting (Chapter 4).

Part II, "Communications," includes six chapters, each devoted to a particular Windows communication feature, including getting set up for communication (Chapter 5), using a wireless connection (Chapter 6), sending and receiving email (Chapter 7), browsing and searching the Internet (Chapters 8 and 9), and faxing (Chapter 10).

Part III, "Entertainment," focuses on the various ways you can use Windows as an entertainment medium, including playing music and videos and working with photographs and movies.

Part IV, "Your Own Personal Windows," explores the many changes you can make to how Windows operates. As you become more proficient, you'll find that you may want to change certain Windows elements, such as adding a desktop image (which is covered in Chapter 13 with other desktop customizing options), adding new programs (Chapter 14), and customizing email and Internet settings (Chapter 15).

Although you don't need to know the ins and outs of computer maintenance (the topic of Part V) as a beginner, you'll find that you do need a reference and guide for various maintenance tasks. Even though you won't perform these daily, you should be familiar with how to find files (Chapter 16), use security measures (Chapter 17), improve your disk performance (Chapter 18), upgrade hardware (Chapter 19), and upgrade Windows (Chapter 20).

Part VI, "Windows XP for Special Situations," covers special features for special situations. This part includes chapters on the many Windows accessory programs (Chapter 21), multiple user accounts (Chapter 22), accessibility options for those with special needs (Chapter 23), and home networking (Chapter 24).

Enjoy your learning journey!

Conventions Used in This Book

There are cautions, tips, and notes throughout this book.

caution

A *caution* will tell you to beware of a potentially dangerous act or situation. In some cases, ignoring a caution could cause you significant problems—so pay particular attention to them!

note

A *note* is designed to provide information that is generally useful, but not necessarily essential for what you're doing at the moment. Some are like extended tips—interesting, but not essential.

tip

A *tip* is a piece of advice—a little trick, actually—that helps you use software or your computer more effectively. Tips can also help you maneuver around problems or limitations.

PART i

THE BASICS

1

Getting Started with Windows XP

The Windows desktop is where all your work starts and ends. Getting familiar with the tools and features you can access from the desktop is the backbone of using a computer. Without these skills, you won't be able to do much. But with these skills, you will be able to start programs, work with files, check the status of any activities (such as printing) and more. Luckily, all these skills are easy to learn and practice.

Checking Out the Desktop

The desktop is what you see when you first start your computer and Windows XP. The desktop provides access to all the programs and files on your computer (see Figure 1.1). Here's a quick overview of what you see:

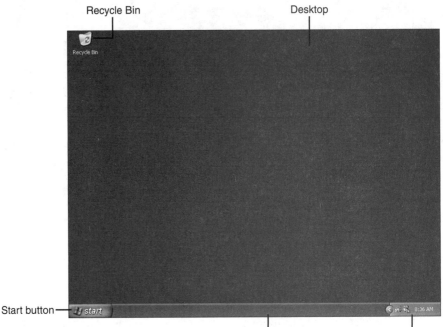

Recycle Bin   Desktop

FIGURE 1.1
The Windows XP desktop, by default, is uncluttered.

Start button — start

Taskbar   System tray

- The desktop is the background area. Think of this area as your computer "desk." You can place handy tools on the desktop.

- The only icon that appears by default on the desktop is the Recycle Bin. You can place additional icons on the desktop so that you have fast access to commonly used programs and folders. For instance, suppose that you use Microsoft Word, a word processing program, often. You can add a program shortcut icon to the desktop so that you can quickly start the program from the desktop rather than a command. For more information on adding desktop icons, see Chapter 14, "Setting Up Programs."

tip

You can change the appearance of the desktop by selecting a different set of colors or using a picture for the background. See Chapter 13, "Customizing Windows XP," for more information.

- The Start button is located in the lower-left corner and is used to display the Start menu. You learn more about this button in the "Starting a Program" and "Starting a Recent Program" sections later in this chapter.

- The taskbar displays a button for any open window or program. For instance, if you are working in a Word document, you'll see a taskbar button for the program and document (see Figure 1.2). If you are viewing files in the My Documents folder, you see a button for that folder. The taskbar provides not only information about what's currently going on, but also offers a quick and simple way to switch between tasks.

FIGURE 1.2

The taskbar gives you a view of what you are currently working on.

- The system tray includes status icons for current tasks. For instance, if you are printing, you see a printer icon. If you are connected to the Internet, you see a connection icon. For more on the system tray, see the section "Viewing the System Tray" later in this chapter.

Displaying the Start Menu

The Start menu provides a list of common programs and folder windows as well as buttons. Like its name implies, the Start menu is where you start! You can start programs or open common folders, such as My Documents, from this menu.

To display the Start menu, click the Start button. The menu is then displayed (see Figure 1.3). From this menu, you can do any of the following:

tip

You can turn off the "last used program" feature. Also, you can customize this list so that only your favorite programs appear, as opposed to the last ones used. See Chapter 14, "Setting Up Programs," for more information.

- **Start a program.** At the top of the menu, you see the programs you use for the Internet and email. You can click the appropriate program icon to start the program. Beneath the Internet and email programs is a list of several programs that you have recently used. You can click any of these programs to start them. For other programs not listed on this menu, use the All Programs command. See "Starting a Program" later in this chapter.

FIGURE 1.3

Clicking the
Start button
reveals various
commands.

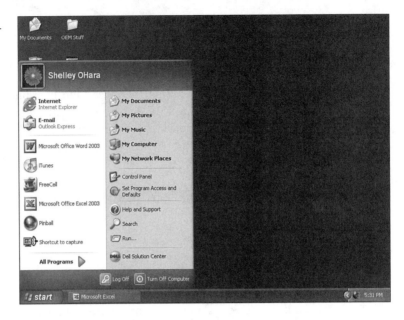

- **Access commonly used folders.** On the right side of the Start menu, you see a list of folders. You can click any of these folders—My Documents, My Pictures, My Music, My Computer, or My Network Places—to open that folder. Chapter 3 covers more on working with folders.

- **Select a command.** In addition to programs and folders, Windows XP lists commands (such as Control Panel, Connect To, Help and Support, Search, and Run) on the Start menu. You learn more about the purposes of these commands in later chapters in this book.

- **Turn off or log off the computer.** Along the bottom of the Start menu, you see some buttons: Log Off and Turn Off Computer. When you are finished working with Windows, you can turn off your computer using the Turn Off Computer button. If someone else uses the computer, you can log off so that person can log on. To do so, use the Log Off button.

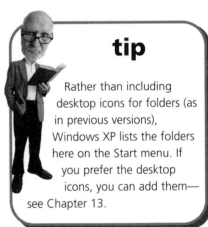

tip

Rather than including desktop icons for folders (as in previous versions), Windows XP lists the folders here on the Start menu. If you prefer the desktop icons, you can add them—see Chapter 13.

Working with Desktop Icons

You can include the icons you want, in the placement you want, on your desktop. This is like arranging your physical desk, putting the papers, pens, and other tools you need where you can find and easily access them. Likewise, you can add icons to your desktop for programs, files, folders, printers, and other hardware. Adding new icons, naming these icons, and deleting the icons are covered in Chapter 14.

When you have icons on the desktop, you can move them around so that they are positioned as you please. The simplest way to arrange the icons is to drag an icon to a new location. Follow these steps:

1. Position the mouse pointer over the icon.

2. Press and hold down the left mouse button and drag the icon to the location you want. The combination of press, hold, and drag is commonly referred to as simply "drag." That is, drag means to press and hold the mouse button while you move the mouse on the desktop.

3. When the icon is in the place you want, release the mouse button. The icon is moved to its new location.

In addition to moving the icons yourself, you can have Windows automatically align and arrange the icons on the desktop. To do so, follow these steps:

1. Right-click a blank area of the desktop.

2. Click Arrange Icons By from the shortcut menu that appears and then select an order. You can arrange the icons by name, size, type, or modification date (see Figure 1.4).

   Or

   Select Auto Arrange. Windows XP then moves icons to the upper-left corner, spacing them equally down and then in a second column (to the right of the first column of icons) if needed.

   Or

Select Align to Grid. When this command is checked, Windows XP keeps icons aligned to an underlying grid that spaces the icons automatically. To turn off

caution

If your computer freezes or if you make changes to key system features, you might need to restart. Click Turn Off Computer and then select Restart. For more information on shutting down the computer and restarting, see Chapter 4, "Troubleshooting Common Problems."

tip

You can also use the shortcut menu to turn on or off desktop items, to add and then lock Web items, and to clean up the desktop using the Desktop Cleanup Wizard. You learn more about these features later in this book.

this feature (if you want to place the icons closer together, for instance), uncheck the command.

FIGURE 1.4

From the desktop shortcut menu, you can select arrangements for the icons.

Viewing the Taskbar

The taskbar, as mentioned, contains buttons for all open windows and programs. The current window appears in a darker color. Any inactive windows use a button with a slightly lighter color than the taskbar. For instance, in Figure 1.5, the My Computer button is the active window (where you are currently working), and the Recycle Bin window is in the background.

The taskbar, then, gives you an idea of what you have running and which program or window is active (where you can work).

FIGURE 1.5

You can use the taskbar to view and change between open windows.

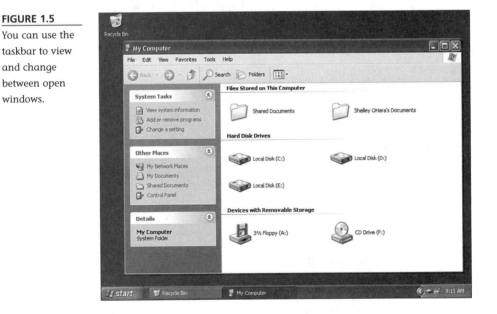

The taskbar also enables you to switch between these open windows. To display a particular program or window, click the button in the taskbar. For instance, to switch to the Recycle Bin window in Figure 1.5, click the button for Recycle Bin. That window then becomes the active window.

Viewing the System Tray

The system tray is part of the taskbar that displays the current time as well as status icons. For instance, Windows XP includes a notification icon for automatic updates. You might also see icons for hardware components, such as a scanner (see Figure 1.6).

tip

You can move the taskbar to another location and also change its appearance. See Chapter 13 for more information.

FIGURE 1.6

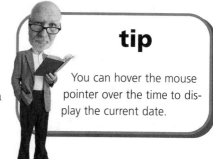

The system tray displays notification icons highlighting anything going on with your system.

Periodically, a notification message pops up from the system tray alerting you to events or suggesting actions. For instance, when a print job is successfully printed, you see a printer icon and then a message noting that the print job is complete. To close a message, click its close button.

tip

You can hover the mouse pointer over the time to display the current date.

Windows XP also may prompt you to check for new updates or to try out certain features (especially MSN Messenger, which you can use to get and send Instant Messages). To access one of the highlighted features, click in the message.

Furthermore, Windows XP can collapse the system tray to hide notification icons. To expand the area, click the left-pointing arrow next to the icons. The area will automatically return to the original view after a few seconds. You can also immediately hide the icons by clicking the now right-pointing icon.

Working with Windows

Windows XP displays all programs and content in a window on the desktop. When you start a program, for instance, you see the program window. When you open a folder, you see the contents in a window.

Part of mastering XP is learning to manipulate the windows so that you can see and work with the area you want. For instance, you might want to move windows so that you can see more than one, or you might want to maximize a window so that it fills the entire desktop area. You use the window controls, as well as other window parts (the title bar and borders) to manipulate the window. This section covers common window tasks.

Opening and Closing Windows

To open a program window, start the program (as covered later in this chapter). To open a content window, double-click the drive or folder icon from the desktop or select the folder from the Start menu. For instance, click Start and then My Computer to open this window (see Figure 1.7). The current window appears on top of any other open windows, and the title bar is brighter.

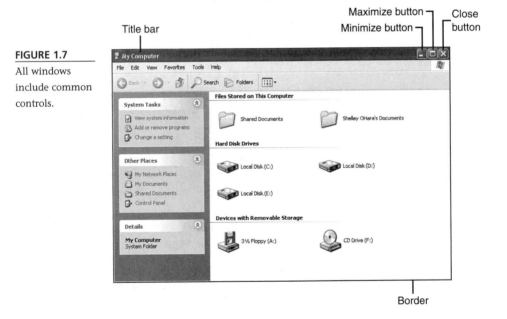

FIGURE 1.7
All windows include common controls.

When a window is open, you see the controls for the window in the upper-right corner (from left to right: Minimize, Maximize, and Close). For example, to close a window, click its Close button as shown in Figure 1.7.

The window closes and disappears from the taskbar and desktop. If you close a program window, you also exit the program. (See "Exiting a Program" later in this chapter.)

Changing the Size of Windows

In addition to opening and closing windows, you can change the size of the windows. Windows XP uses special terms to describe the various sizes of a window: maximized, minimized, and restored. The changes you can make to the size of a window are covered here.

Maximizing a Window

A maximized window fills the entire desktop and does not have borders (see Figure 1.8). You commonly maximize program windows when you want to have the maximum display area for the work. To maximize a window so that it fills the entire screen, click its Maximize button.

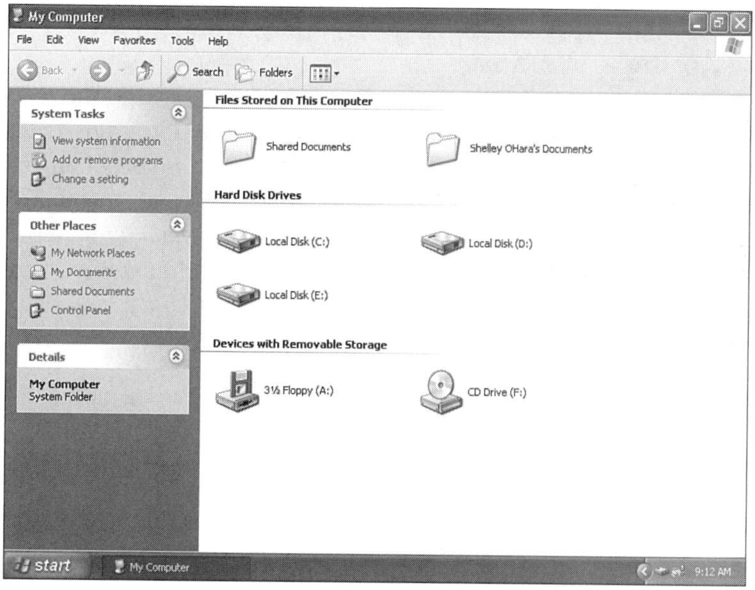

> **note**
>
> When you maximize a window, the Maximize button changes to a Restore button, which you can use to return the window to its original size.

FIGURE 1.8

Maximize a window when you want to make it as big as possible.

Minimizing a Window

A minimized window is hidden from view; it's not closed and is still available. The window is represented with a taskbar button (see Figure 1.9). To minimize a window (shrink it to a taskbar button), click its Minimize button. You can redisplay the window by clicking its button. You often minimize a window when you need handy access to it, but you don't want to use desktop space for the display of that window.

FIGURE 1.9
Minimizing a
window hides it
from view but
still keeps it
available.

Restoring a Window

When a window is open and not maximized, Windows uses the term "restore." Basically, you restore the window to its original size. To restore a maximized window, click the Restore button (see Figure 1.10). Use this size when you want to display more than one window on the desktop. For instance, if you are copying data from one program to another, you can view both windows and move between them. When a window is this size, it has borders so that you can resize it manually. You can also use the title bar to move the window (see "Arranging the Windows" later in this chapter.)

Resizing a Window

When a window is restored, you can change its size. To resize a window, put the mouse pointer on a border and then drag the border to resize the window. Remember that you can only resize restored windows. You cannot resize a maximized window.

Arranging the Windows

When you have more than one window open, you may need to arrange them on the desktop. As mentioned, you might copy data from one document or program to another. You might also open several windows when you are doing file maintenance such as copying or moving a file. In any case, you can move the windows around the desktop by dragging, or you can have Windows XP arrange the windows.

To move a window, follow these steps:

1. Put the mouse pointer on the title bar.

2. Drag the window to the location you want. The window is then moved.

To have Windows XP arrange the windows, follow these steps:

1. Right-click a blank area of the taskbar to display the shortcut menu.

2. Click one of the following commands for arranging the windows:

   Click Cascade Windows to arrange the windows in a waterfall style, layered on top of each other from the upper-left corner down (see Figure 1.11).

   Click Tile Windows Horizontally to make all the windows the same size and place them horizontally next to each other.

   Click Tile Windows Vertically to make all the windows the same size, but place them vertically in order (see Figure 1.12).

   Click Show the Desktop to minimize all open windows. If you redisplay the taskbar shortcut menu, you can select Show Open Windows to redisplay the windows.

tip

You can undo the arrangement and revert to the original placement by right-clicking the taskbar and then selecting the Undo command. The name of the command varies depending on the arrangement. For instance, if you have tiled the windows, the command is Undo Tile.

FIGURE 1.11

The cascade view shows all open windows, one on top of the other.

FIGURE 1.12

Vertically tiled windows is another arrangement choice.

Starting a Program

Most of your time on the computer will be spent working in some type of program—a word processing program to type letters, a spreadsheet program to create budgets, a database to keep track of contacts, and so on. So, one of the most important skills is learning how to start a program.

Because different people prefer different ways of working, Windows XP provides many options for starting programs. What's the best way? The way *you* like. Pick the one that is easiest for you.

When you install a new Windows program, that program's installation procedure sets up a program icon (and sometimes a program folder if the program includes several components). For example, a scanning program may include a program for executing the scan as well as a program for working with and saving the scanned document. These are listed within the Start menu.

The Start menu provides two methods for starting a program. If you recently used a program, you can select it from the left pane of the Start menu. If the program is not listed, you can display all programs and then select the program from the longer menu. This section covers both of these methods.

Starting a Recent Program

Follow these steps to start a recently used program:

1. Click the Start button. The left pane displays the last several programs you used (see Figure 1.13).

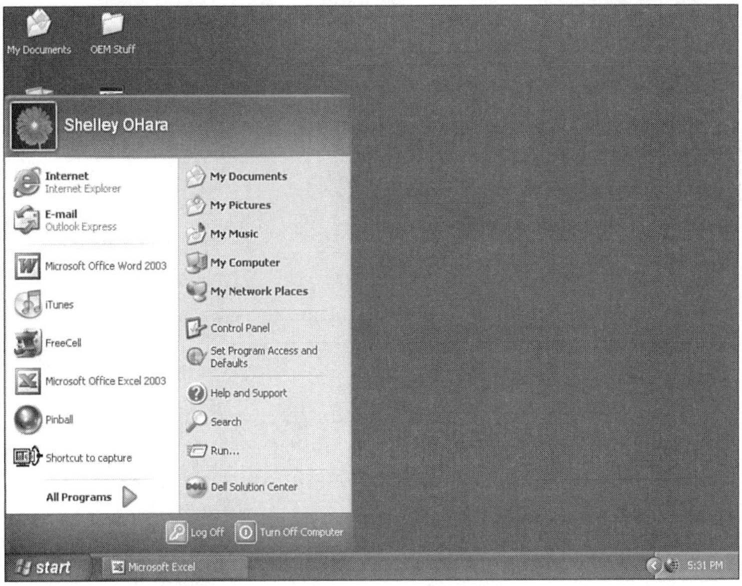

FIGURE 1.13

If you recently used a program, select it from the short list on the Start menu.

2. Click the program. That program is then started, and you see the program window.

Listing All Programs

Follow these steps to view and select from a list of all programs:

1. Click Start and then click All Programs. You'll see a list of all the program icons and program folders (see Figure 1.14).

FIGURE 1.14

You can access all installed programs by clicking the All Programs button on the Start menu.

2. If necessary, click the program folder. Any items with an arrow next to them are program folders rather than icons. When you click the program folder, you see the program icons within that folder. For instance, if you click Accessories, you see the Accessory programs included with Windows XP. Follow this step until you see the icon for the program you want to start.

3. Click the program icon to start the program. The program opens in its own window, and a button for the program appears in the taskbar. Figure 1.15 shows WordPad, a program included with Windows XP.

FIGURE 1.15
The program is opened in its own program window.

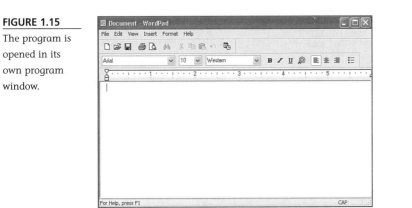

Starting a Program from a Shortcut Icon

In addition to the Start menu, you can start programs from shortcut icons. Some programs automatically create shortcut icons, placing them on the desktop. You can also add shortcut icons to programs yourself, as covered in Chapter 14, "Setting Up Programs."

Figure 1.16 shows a shortcut icon for E-mail (Outlook Express) added to the desktop. Notice the little arrow on the icon; this indicates that the icon is a shortcut to that program.

tip

As you become more proficient, you might experiment with other ways of starting a program. You'll explore these other methods in Chapter 14.

FIGURE 1.16
You can place shortcut icons to programs on your desktop and then use these icons to start the programs.

To start a program from a shortcut icon, double-click the shortcut icon on the desktop. The program starts and is displayed in its own window. A taskbar button also appears for the program.

Switching Between Programs

You often work with more than one type of program at the same time. Windows XP enables you to quickly switch from one program to another. For example, you might want to review sales figures in a worksheet while at the same time creating a sales report in a word processing program. Switching between programs enables you not only to view data from several sources, but also to share data among programs.

As mentioned, when you start a program, a button for that program is displayed in the taskbar. To switch to another program, simply click the button for that program. That program then becomes the active program.

caution

If the program doesn't start, you might not have double-clicked quickly enough. You must keep the mouse pointer in the same location and click twice. Sometimes beginners click, move, and then click the mouse. This won't work. If you continue to have problems with clicking, change the mouse speed. See Chapter 13 for more information.

Working in a Program

When a program is started, you see the program window. A great thing about Windows XP is that all program windows share similar features (see Figure 1.17). Learning to use one program helps you master key skills for almost all other programs. For example, most programs include a menu bar that works the same in all programs. This section covers some basic skills for working in programs.

Selecting Commands

The top line of the program window is called the *title bar* and includes the name of the document (or a generic name if the document has not been saved) and the program name.

Below the title bar, you'll see the menu bar. You use this to select commands. For instance, open the File menu and select the Save command to save a document. To use a menu, follow these steps:

1. Click the menu name. The menu drops down and displays a list of commands.

2. Click the command. Depending on the command you select, one of the following happens:

Toolbar   Menu bar

FIGURE 1.17

Get familiar
with the basic
program window
features.

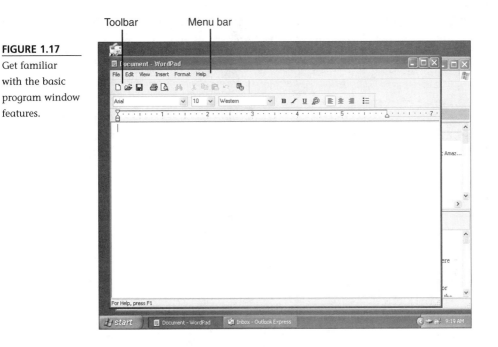

The command is executed. For instance, if you select File, Exit, the program is
closed.

You see a submenu. Any commands followed by an arrow display a submenu.
Click the command in this menu to execute the selected command.

You see a dialog box prompting you for additional information about how to
execute the command. For example, if
you select File, Print, you see the Print
dialog box. Select options and confirm
the command (see Figure 1.18). When
printing, for instance, select which
printer to use and the number of copies
to print and then click Print.

You'll find that not only do the menus work the
same in most programs, but also many programs include the same commands. For example, you can commonly find a File, Save
command for saving documents and a File,
Print command for printing documents (both of
which are covered in Chapter 2, "Saving and
Printing Your Work"). The Edit menu usually has
commands for cutting text (Cut), copying text

tip

Many commands have a
keyboard shortcut. Instead
of selecting the command,
you can press the keyboard
shortcut. For instance, the
shortcut for printing is
Ctrl+P (press and hold the
Ctrl key and then press the P key).
These shortcuts are listed next to
the command names on the
menu.

(Copy), and pasting cut or copied text (Paste). The Help menu provides access to online help; you can use the commands in this menu to look up help topics for the program. You learn more about help in Chapter 4, "Troubleshooting Common Problems."

FIGURE 1.18

The Print
dialog box.

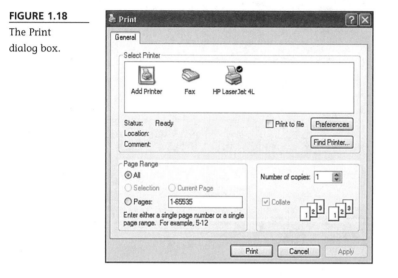

Using the Toolbar

In addition to using the menus and keyboard shortcuts, you can use toolbar buttons to select commands. Most Windows programs include toolbars, which are displayed right under the menu bar. The buttons vary depending on the program, but most of them are similar. Figure 1.19 shows the toolbar buttons in WordPad.

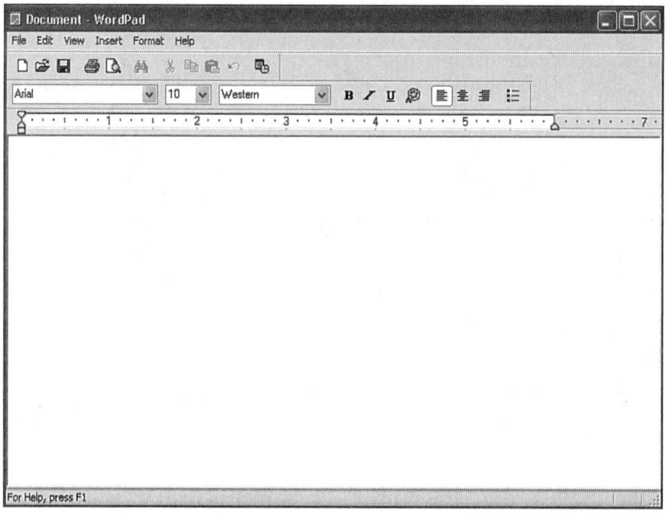

FIGURE 1.19

Look for a tool-
bar for fast
access to com-
mon commands.

The following list gives you some insight on how to work with toolbars:

- Toolbar buttons are shortcuts to commands. You can click the button instead of selecting the command. For instance, click the Save button to save a document (which is essentially the same as selecting File, Save).

- If you aren't sure what a toolbar button does, hover the mouse pointer over the edge of the button. A ScreenTip (the button name) should appear.

- Some programs have more than one toolbar. Usually, the standard toolbar includes buttons for common commands (Save, Open, New, and so on). The program may also include a toolbar with formatting options (usually called the Formatting toolbar or the Format bar). This toolbar includes buttons that let you quickly make formatting changes such as making text bold, changing the font, and so on.

- If you see a down arrow next to a command, you can click this arrow to display a drop-down list of choices. Then click the option you want to select.

- If you don't use the toolbar and you want more room for the document to be displayed, turn off the toolbar. You can also select to display more than one toolbar in some programs such as Word for Windows. Look in the View menu for a Toolbar or Toolbars command. Any toolbars that are checked are displayed (see Figure 1.20). The command is a toggle. Select the command to uncheck and hide the toolbar. To display the toolbar, select it again so that there is a check next to it.

FIGURE 1.20

Turn on or off toolbars using the View menu.

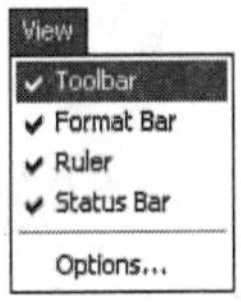

Exiting a Program

When you finish working in a program, close it to free system memory. (Your system memory is the working area of the computer where data and programs are stored temporarily while you are working within the program and on a document.) Too many open programs can tax your system's memory and slow the computer's processes.

First, save your work. (Saving is the topic of the next chapter.) Once your work is saved, you can use one of several methods to close a program:

caution

If you have not saved a file and you close the program, you will be prompted to save. To save the document, click Yes. To close the document without saving, click No. (Do this if you don't need the document or if you want to abandon any changes you made.) To return to the document without exiting the program, click Cancel.

■ Click File and then click the Exit command. The program closes.

■ Click the Close button for the program window.

■ Press Alt+F4.

THE ABSOLUTE MINIMUM

This chapter gives you a good basic framework for learning to work with Windows XP. You learn the basics of working with the desktop, manipulating windows (which display content), and starting and exiting programs. In summary, keep these points in mind:

■ The desktop is your starting place. Any programs you run or windows you open are displayed on the desktop.

■ The Start menu is what it says—your starting place! Use this menu to start programs, open folders, access commands such as Help and Support, log off, turn off, and restart.

■ To see what programs and windows are open, check the taskbar. Also, to review any system notifications or information, check the system tray at the far-right corner of the taskbar.

■ Everything you see in Windows will be displayed in a window (with a little "w"). For example, when you want to view the contents of a drive or folder or start a program, you open a window. Every window has controls so that you can place it and resize it in a way that is most convenient for the task at hand.

■ You can start a program using the Start menu or a shortcut icon.

■ In a program, you can use the menu bar to select commands. Click the menu name to display the menu and then click the command you want. You may be prompted to select additional options for the command in a dialog box. Make your selections and click the command button (usually OK).

■ When you are finished working in a program, save your work (a topic covered in the next chapter) and then exit the program. You can exit using the File, Exit command or by clicking the program window's Close button.

2

SAVING AND PRINTING YOUR WORK

The most important computer skill you can learn is saving your work. Whether you are creating a budget, typing a resume, or entering checks in a checkbook program, saving your work is key. This chapter covers the basics of not only saving a document, but also opening a saved document, creating a new document, printing a document, and more. Like the previous chapter, the skills you learn in this chapter are skills you can use throughout your computing experience. That's one of the great things about Windows XP: Basic skills, such as saving, opening, or printing a document, work the same in most Windows programs.

Saving a Document

When you work in most programs, you save your work as some type of document—a word processing file (such as a memo), a worksheet file (such as a budget), a database file (such as a list of clients), and so on. One of the most important things you should remember about using a computer is that you need to save your work and save often.

When you save your work, the program saves the file in an appropriate file format or type. For instance, if you save a document created in Word, that program saves the file as a DOC or Word file. Excel saves your spreadsheets (formally known as *worksheets* and *workbooks*) as XLS files.

caution

Don't wait until you finish a document before you save it. If something happens, such as if the power goes off or the computer gets stuck, you will lose all your work if you have not saved it. Instead, save periodically as you create and edit the document.

The first time you save a file, you must assign that file a name and location. You can include up to 255 characters for the name, including spaces. Sometimes, the program suggests a name, but it's better to replace the suggested name with a more descriptive name that you can remember.

For the location, you can select any of the drives and folders on your computer. The dialog box for saving a document has tools for navigating to and selecting another drive or folder for the file.

Follow these steps to save a document:

1. Click File, and then click the Save As command. You'll see the Save As dialog box (see Figure 2.1).

Places bar

Up One Level button

Create New Folder button

FIGURE 2.1

The dialog box for saving in WordPad. The dialog box options may vary from program to program.

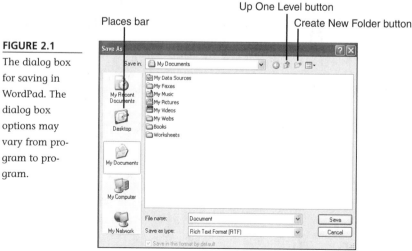

2. Type a name—for example, **Christmas Shopping List**, or something you can readily relate to as discussed previously.

3. Select the location for the file:

   To save the document in another folder, double-click that folder if it is listed.

   To select one of the common folders, click the icon in the Places Bar. For instance, click the My Computer icon to open that folder.

   If the folder is not listed, you can move up through the folder structure by clicking the Up One Level button.

   To select another drive or folder, display the Save in drop-down list and then select the drive or folder.

4. Click Save.

The document is saved, and the title bar displays the name of the document.

tip

The steps for saving a document are basically the same from program to program. Some programs offer additional options for saving. Be sure to check your program's manual for information about any additional ways to save your files.

Switching Folders

The dialog box for saving a document provides tools for selecting another folder and for creating a new folder. To save a document in another folder, you open that folder. As mentioned, you have several options for navigating to that folder. Navigating through your folders is important for saving a document and also for opening a document (covered later in this chapter).

Most computers have one or more hard drives where documents and programs are permanently stored. The default drive is named drive C:, but you may also have additional hard drives (lettered D:, E:, and so on).

note

The program adds a file extension to the file name that indicates the type of file. For instance, Word documents are saved as .DOC files. By default, these extensions don't appear, but you can display them by using the options in the Folder Options dialog box.

Windows XP sets up one main folder for documents called My Documents. To keep files organized, *subfolders* are then created (either by Windows, a program, or you) and like files are stored together. You can easily and quickly select this folder from the Start menu and from most Save dialog boxes; therefore, the My Documents folder makes a good choice as your main folder.

That said, note that you don't want to lump all your documents into one main folder. Therefore, you should create folders (sometimes called sub-folders) within the My Documents folder and place your work in one of these folders. For example, within My Documents, you might have folders for reports, worksheets, memos, and so on, or you might create a folder for each project. (As an example, I create a new folder for each book that I write.)

To keep track of where the file is stored, Windows XP uses a path. The path starts at the top (your hard drive) and then burrows down into folders and folders within folders. If you think of yourself as a groundhog tunneling through to a particular folder, you can see that if you have burrowed down one path and want to go to another branch, you have to backtrack up through the tunnels to a fork and then down to access other paths in the tunnel.

For instance, suppose that you have this folder structure:

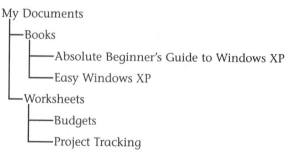

```
My Documents
  ├─ Books
  │     ├── Absolute Beginner's Guide to Windows XP
  │     └── Easy Windows XP
  └─ Worksheets
        ├── Budgets
        └── Project Tracking
```

note

Your computer may also have a floppy or diskette drive (usually drive A:) and another media drive. Your media drive may be a CD drive, a CD-R or CD-RW drive, or a DVD drive. You can insert a disk into one of these drives to open it. You can also save documents to a floppy drive and to a rewritable media drive. See Chapter 3, "Managing Files," for more information.

If you open My Documents, you see these folders: Books and Worksheets. (You also will see any other subfolders, including some additional folders, such as My Pictures and My Music, that Windows XP has set up.) You can double-click either of these folders to open that folder (refer to Figure 2.1).

If you open Books, you have two additional folders that you can open: Absolute Beginner's Guide to Windows XP and Easy Windows XP. Again, you can double-click either of these folders to open that folder.

This process of tunneling down is straightforward because you can see listed what your options are. Where it can get confusing is when you want to move to another branch of the folder structure.

If you want to open Budgets, for instance, you need to backtrack. Specifically, you need to move back two levels to My Documents and tunnel down through Worksheets and then Budgets. In a dialog box, you use the Up One Level button to jump back a level. You can also go to the top level or to another drive using the Save in drop-down list (see Figure 2.2).

FIGURE 2.2

Use the Save in drop-down list as another way to move up through a folder and drive organization.

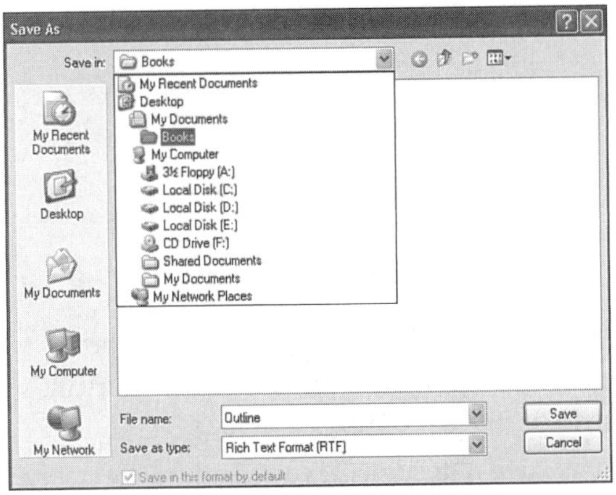

At first, navigating to folders may be confusing, but you will quickly get the hang of it. You use the same techniques for saving a document and for opening a document. It's also important to use good organization for your work (a topic covered in the next chapter) to make it easy to navigate among folders and find documents.

Creating a New Folder

You can set up a folder before you save your document and then navigate to it when you're ready to save. You also can create a new folder on-the-fly—that is, when you are saving the document. To create a new folder on-the-fly, follow these steps:

1. Click the Create New Folder button. You'll see a new folder icon with the default name New Folder (see Figure 2.3).

2. Type the new folder name and press Enter. The folder is added.

3. Open the new folder and follow the steps for saving (type a filename and click Save). The document is then saved to this new folder.

tip

You can also create folders from a file window in Windows XP as covered in Chapter 3.

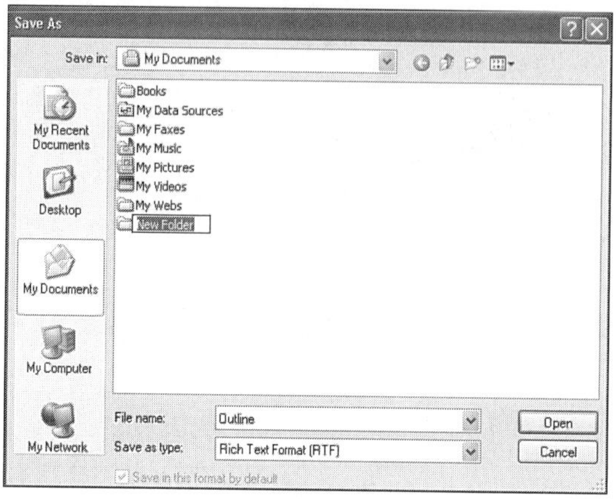

FIGURE 2.3

You can create a new folder when you save a document.

Tips for Saving a Document

Because saving is critical, most programs provide many shortcuts and safeguards for saving. Review the following list of tips for saving:

■ The first time you save a document, you see the Save As dialog box even if you do not select the Save As command. This dialog box is displayed automatically to remind you to type a filename and select a location for the file.

■ After you've saved and named a file, you can click File and select Save to resave that file to the same location with the same name. When you save again, the disk file is updated to include any changes or additions you made to the file.

■ Instead of the Save command, you can use a toolbar shortcut (look for a Save button) or a keyboard shortcut (most often Ctrl+S).

■ If you close a document or exit a program without saving, that program prompts you to save (see Figure 2.4). You can click Cancel to return to the document, No to close the document without saving, or Yes to save the document. If you have saved previously, the program saves the document with the same filename in the same location. If you have not yet saved, you see the Save As dialog box for entering a name and location.

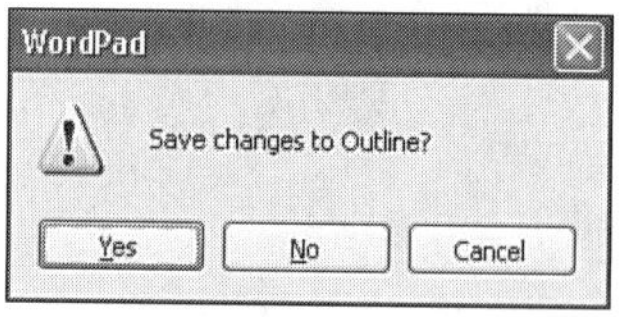

FIGURE 2.4

Most programs remind you to save if you close the document or exit the program without saving.

■ Just because the program reminds you to save doesn't mean that you should rely on this reminder. Get in the habit of saving before you exit. It is easy to whiz past the reminder prompt and possibly lose your work.

■ Some programs save your work automatically. For instance, a database is saved each time you add a new record. You do not have to select a particular command to save the data. The same is also true of check-writing programs such as Quicken or Microsoft Money. Again, think "save" first and then check out any automatic save features to be careful.

Saving Backup Copies

You often want to have more than one copy of a document. For instance, you might save a backup copy to another drive or disk. You also might use one document to create a new, similar document. You learn more about backing up files in Chapter 17, "Securing Your PC." You can also use the File, Save As command to create a duplicate document.

For instance, you might have a cover letter that you want to reuse, changing the address or other information. Instead of retyping the letter, you can open the original letter, save it with a different name (thereby creating a new document), and then edit and resave this copy. To use the Save As command to create a new document, follow these steps:

1. Click File and then the Save As command. You'll see the Save As dialog box (refer to Figure 2.1).
2. Type a new name.
3. Select a different location for the file if you want to store the new file in another location.
4. Click Save.

A new document is then created and saved. This document remains open so that you can continue working. The original document remains on disk, intact and unchanged.

Saving in a Different File Format

Another common saving task is to save a document in a different format. Sometimes, you share your work with someone who doesn't have the same version of a particular program that you have or perhaps uses a different program entirely. Because sharing data is common, most programs enable you to select from several basic file formats. For instance, in most word processing programs, you can save a document in a plain vanilla format (as a text file), as a document with some formatting changes (rich text format—RTF), as another popular program file type, or as a previous version of the same program.

To save a document in a different file format, follow these steps:

1. Click File and the Save As command. You'll see the Save As dialog box (refer to Figure 2.1).

2. Type a new name, if necessary.

3. Select a different location for the file, if needed.

4. Display the Save as type drop-down list (see Figure 2.5).

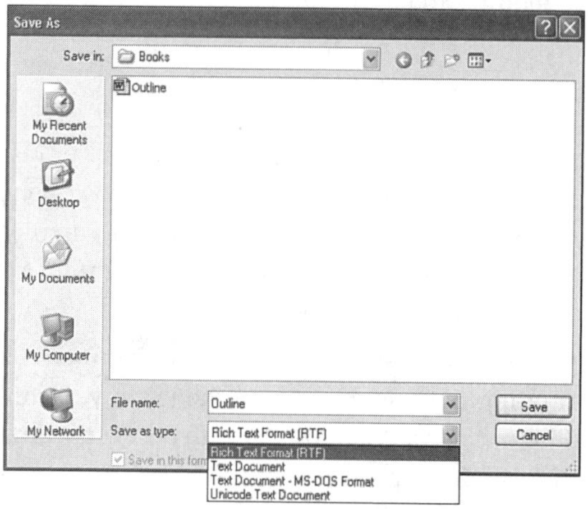

FIGURE 2.5

You can select different file formats in which to save a document.

5. Select the appropriate file type and click Save.

A new document is then created and saved using the filename, location, and type you selected. This document remains open so that you can continue working. The original document remains on disk, unchanged.

Closing a Document

When you are finished working with a document, close it to free up system resources. Most programs, with the exceptions of WordPad and Paint, include a Close command and a Close button for the document window. To close the document, select File, Close or click the Close button for the document window. In WordPad, Notepad, and Paint, you must open another document, create a new document, or exit the program to close the document.

Note that closing a document is not the same as exiting the program. To close the document and exit the program, select File, Exit or click the Close button for the program window (see Figure 2.6).

FIGURE 2.6

Use the document window's Close button to close the document; use the program window's Close button to close the document and exit the program.

Program Close button

Document Close button

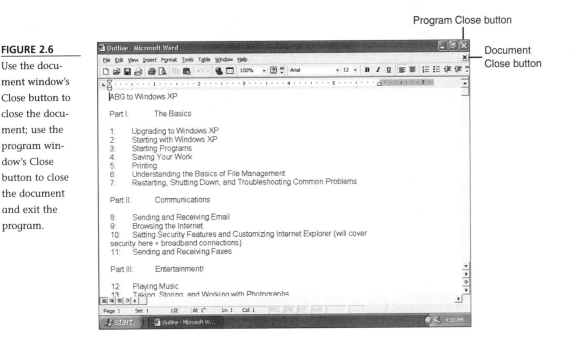

Opening a Document

When you save a document, the information is saved in a file at the location (folder and drive) you selected. When you want to work on that file again—to make changes, to print the file, and so on—you open the file.

Follow these steps to open a document:

1. Start the program you used to create the file.

2. Click File and the Open command. You'll see the Open dialog box (see Figure 2.7). If you see the file you want to open, skip to step 4.

3. If necessary, change to the location where the file was stored by doing any of the following:

   Double-click the folder that contains the file. For instance, in Figure 2.7, double-click the Books folder icon to view files within that folder.

tip

In addition to the File, Open command, look for shortcuts for opening files. You can click the Open button in the toolbar or use the keyboard shortcut (usually Ctrl+O). Some programs also list the last few files that were opened at the bottom of the File menu. You can click the filename to open that document.

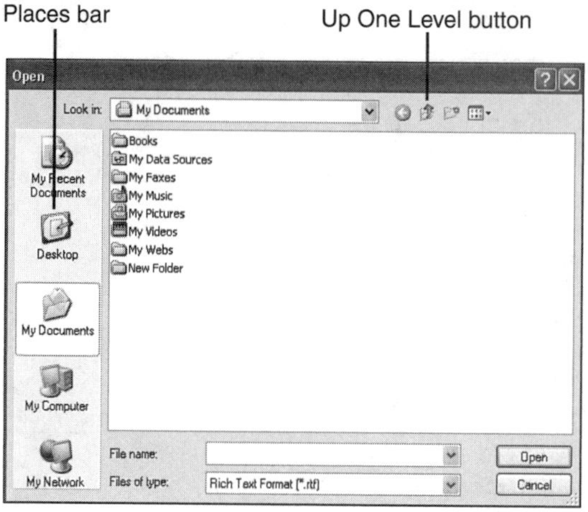

Places bar   Up One Level button

FIGURE 2.7

Use the Open dialog box to display and then open the document you want to work with.

If you don't see the folder listed, click the Up One Level button to move up through the folders and display other folders.

To find another drive or folder, display the Look in drop-down list and select the drive or folder.

To display one of the common folders, click its name in the Places Bar. For instance, to open the My Documents folder, click the My Documents button in the Places Bar.

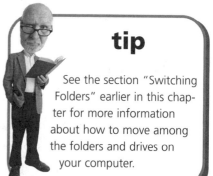

tip

See the section "Switching Folders" earlier in this chapter for more information about how to move among the folders and drives on your computer.

4. When you see the file you want to open, double-click its name to open the file. For example, in Figure 2.8, you can double-click the Outline file to open that document. The document is displayed onscreen.

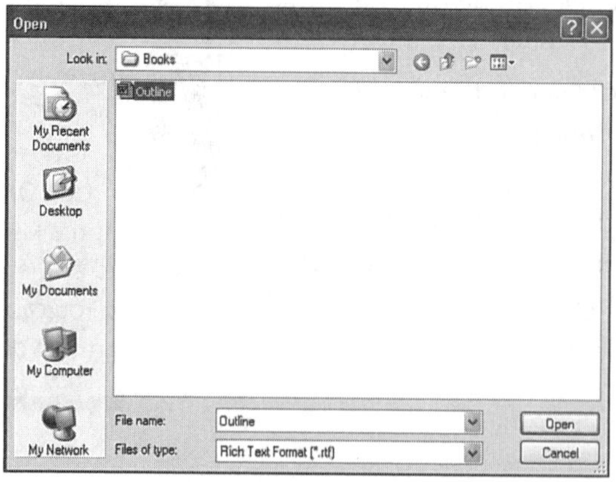

FIGURE 2.8

Navigate to the folder that contains the file and then double-click the file icon to open the document.

Creating a New Document

When you start most programs, a blank document is displayed. If you want to create another new document, you don't have to exit and restart. You can create another new blank document at any time from within the program.

In addition to a blank document, many programs enable you to select a template on which to base the new document. A *template* is a predesigned document that may include text and formatting. To get a head start on content or formatting, you can select a template for the new document—if the program has a template that matches your needs.

To create a new document, follow these steps:

1. In the program, click File and then click the New command.

2. If you see a New dialog box, click the type of document you want to create and then click the OK button. For instance, in WordPad, you can select from several document types (see Figure 2.9). When you click OK, a new document is displayed. You can use any of the program tools to create and save this new document.

tip

If you can't find the file you want, it could be because you did not save it where you thought you did. Try looking in a different drive or folder. If you still can't find it, try searching for the file. For more information about searching for files, see Chapter 16.

tip

In addition to the File, New command, look for a New icon in the toolbar or a shortcut key (usually Ctrl+N).

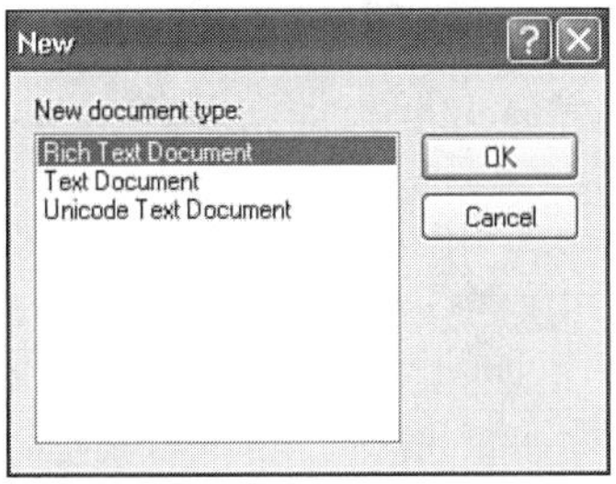

FIGURE 2.9

If the program includes templates or document types, you are prompted to select the template or document type from the New dialog box.

New	? X
New document type:	
Rich Text Document Text Document Unicode Text Document	OK Cancel

After the blank document is displayed, you can start entering data. Entering data in most programs is pretty straightforward. For example, in a word processing program, you just start typing. In a worksheet, you select the *cell* (intersection of a row and column) and type the entry. Instructions for more complex programs—for example, a database program—may require more upfront work. For the exact instructions on how to use a program to create a document, check the program's documentation.

Printing a Document

Often, when you create a document, you will print the end results. (You may also print and proofread as you create, edit, and format the document.) Like saving and opening, printing is a common task, and most programs follow the same basic procedures for printing.

To print a document, follow these steps:

1. Click File and then click the Print command. As a shortcut, look for a Print button in the program's toolbar or use a shortcut key combination (usually Ctrl+P). You'll see the Print dialog box, shown in Figure 2.10.

2. Make any changes to the print options. Most programs enable you to select a printer, what is printed (for instance, a particular page range), and the number of copies to print. Note that the available options vary from program to program.

3. Click the Print button. The document is then printed.

> **note**
>
> You most often set up a printer when you first purchase a new computer or a new printer. If your printer is not set up on your computer, you must complete this action before printing. Setting up a printer is covered in Chapter 19, "Upgrading Your Computer."

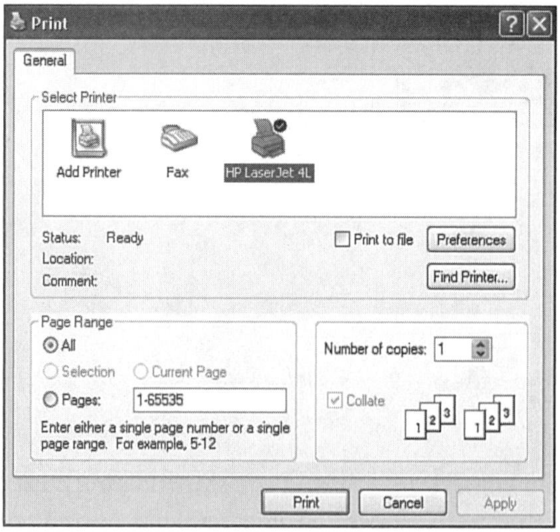

FIGURE 2.10

The Print dialog box for WordPad.

Viewing and Canceling Print Jobs

When you are printing a document, you may need to stop or cancel the print job. To do so, you start by displaying the print queue, which lists the documents that have been sent to a printer as well as how far along the printing is. Using the print queue, you can pause, restart, or cancel print jobs. For instance, you might need to pause a print job to change paper. You might also need to cancel a print job that you started by mistake.

Follow these steps to make changes to a print job in progress:

1. Click the Start button and then choose Control Panel.

2. Click the Printers and Other Hardware category.

3. Click the Printers and Faxes Control Panel icon. You'll see a list of all the installed printers and faxes (see Figure 2.11).

tip

Most programs enable you to preview a document to check the margins, heads, graphics placement, and so on before you print.

Previewing can save time and paper because you can make any needed adjustments before you print. Click File and select the Print Preview command. After you finish viewing the preview, click the Close button.

FIGURE 2.11

You can view the installed printers when you want to view the print queue.

4. Select the printer you want to view and click See what's printing in the Task pane. You'll see the print queue (see Figure 2.12). You can also display the print queue by double-clicking the Printer icon in the system tray of the

taskbar (on the far left side). The Printer icon appears whenever you are printing a document.

5. Do any of the following:

   To cancel all print jobs, click Printer and then click the Cancel All Documents command. Click Yes to confirm the cancellation.

   To pause printing, click Printer and then click Pause Printing. To restart after pausing, click Printer and then click Pause Printing again.

   To cancel, pause, resume, or restart a particular print job, click the print job in the list. Then click Document and select the appropriate command (Pause, Resume, Restart, or Cancel).

6. Click the Close button to close the queue.

Printing Tips

When you are printing, keep in mind the following tips:

- To print a document within a program, use the File, Print command. You can also look for a Print toolbar button or press Ctrl+P (the shortcut key for printing in most programs).

- Before you print in a program, preview the document. Most programs have a Print Preview command (or something similar). Look for this command in the File or View menu. You can also often find a toolbar button for Print Preview.

- You are not limited to printing from just within a program. You can also print from a file window. To do so, select the file and then click the Print this file link in the Tasks list.

note

If the print queue window is empty, either the print job never made it to the queue or it was already processed by the printer. Short print jobs are printed quickly, so you might not have time to stop the job. If the printer hasn't started printing yet, press the printer's Cancel button to stop printing.

- As another option for printing, if you have added a printer shortcut icon to your desktop, you can drag a file to this printer icon to print the document.
- To create a printer shortcut icon, open the Printers and Faxes window and then drag the icon from the printer window to your desktop. Windows XP then creates a shortcut printer icon.

THE ABSOLUTE MINIMUM

This chapter covers the main skills you need to save, open, close, and print documents. In summary, keep these points in mind:

- You should save the work that you create and save often. The first time you save, you enter a filename and select a location for the document.
- You can save a copy of a document or save a document in a different file format as needed.
- When you want to work on a document that you have previously saved, use the File, Open command.
- When you are finished working on a document, close the document. If you are finished with that program, close the document and exit the program.
- To create a new document, use the File, New command.
- Printing works the same in most programs: Select File and then Print. The Print dialog box enables you to make selections such as what to print and which printer to use.
- You can view the print queue to modify any print jobs in progress. For instance, you can cancel a print job you didn't intend, or if you need to change paper, you can pause a print job.

3

MANAGING FILES

As you work with a computer creating more and more documents, you need to find a way to keep this information organized. Without a good organizational method, all your files are lumped together in one place. This is the equivalent of shoving all your files into one filing cabinet.

Keeping your files organized provides many benefits. First, you can more easily find the folder or file you want. Second, you can keep your disk running in good shape by periodically weeding out old files. Third, with a good setup, backing up files is easier. (Chapter 17 covers backing up files.)

Good file management does not take that long and involves just a few key ideas. This chapter covers these ideas as well as explains the important tasks for working with files.

Opening My Computer

Windows XP includes many tools for file management, and the most commonly used tool is My Computer. My Computer is an icon that represents all the drives on your system. After you open this window, you can then open any of your drives to see the folders and files contained on those drives.

Follow these steps to open My Computer:

1. Click Start and My Computer. You'll see icons for each of the drives on your computer as well as system folders (see Figure 3.1).

To help you keep your documents organized, Windows sets up several special folders in addition to My Computer. These include My Documents, My Pictures, and My Music. You can view the contents of any of these folders by clicking Start and then clicking the folder you want to open.

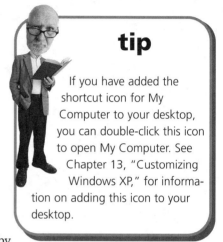

tip

If you have added the shortcut icon for My Computer to your desktop, you can double-click this icon to open My Computer. See Chapter 13, "Customizing Windows XP," for information on adding this icon to your desktop.

FIGURE 3.1

When you want to work with the folders or files on your computer, you can start with My Computer.

To help you keep your documents organized, Windows sets up several special folders in addition to My Computer. These include My Documents, My Pictures, and My Music. You can view the contents of any of these folders by clicking Start and then clicking the folder you want to open.

Opening Drives and Folders

In addition to your hard drive (drive C:), you may have a floppy drive (drive A:). Your computer may also have additional drives including other hard drives or additional media drives (such as CD or DVD drives). If you have more than one drive, they are named D:, E:, and so on. If you have a CD drive or a DVD drive, it also is named with a letter.

By default, Windows XP groups the drives by type, as shown in Figure 3.1. Opening a drive is easy: Double-click the icon representing the drive you want to open (see Figure 3.2).

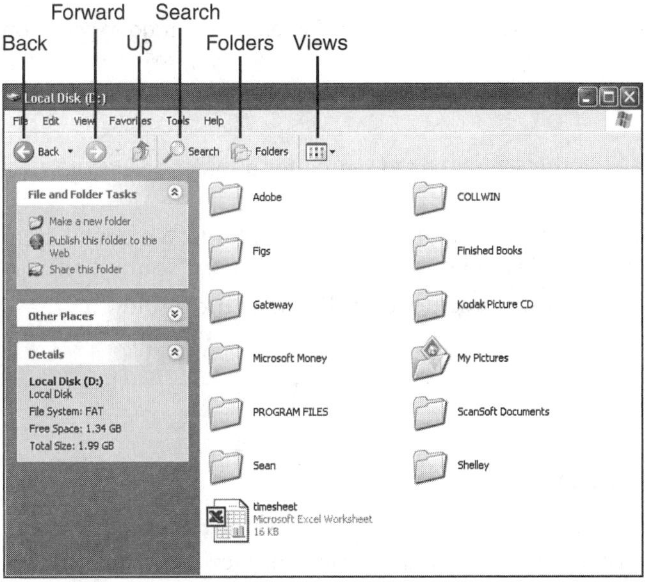

FIGURE 3.2

The contents of the hard drive D:. Note the different icons for folders and files.

Each page icon represents a document (file). Each folder icon represents a folder on your hard drive. You can nest folders within folders to organize the contents of your hard drive. To open a folder, double-click its icon. You can continue opening folders until you see the file or folder you want to work with. To close a window, click the Close button.

Navigating Folders

Each folder window includes a toolbar that you can use to navigate from folder to folder. You can go back and forth among previously viewed content windows. You can also move up one level in the folder structure to the containing folder. For instance, you might move up to the desktop level and then open drives and folders to move to another branch of the folder structure. Table 3.1 identifies each toolbar button and its purpose.

tip

You can search for a file, sort the contents, change what is displayed, group icons, and more in the folder window. For information on these tasks, see Chapter 16, "Viewing and Finding Files."

Table 3.1   Folder Window Toolbar Buttons

Button	Click to...
Back	Go back to a previously viewed folder.
⊙	Return to a previously viewed folder. You can go forward only if you have clicked Back to go back a step.
↱	Display the next level up in the folder structure.
🔍 Search	Display the Search bar to search for a folder or file.
📁 Folders	Display a hierarchical folder list (similar to Windows Explorer in previous versions of Windows). See the next section "Using the Folders Bar."
▦ ▾	Change how the contents of the folder are displayed.

Using the Folders Bar

If you want to see a hierarchical listing of all the folders on your system, you can display the Folders bar. You might prefer this view when working with folders and files because it allows you to see the contents of the selected folder as well as all the other drives and folders on your computer. The Folders bar makes it easier to move and copy by dragging, for instance. Click the Folders button to display the Folders bar (see Figure 3.3).

FIGURE 3.3

Displaying the Folders bar lets you view all the drives and folders on your computer.

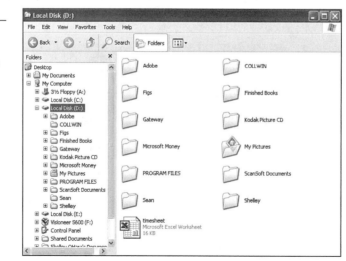

The top level is the desktop. Beneath that, you see the drives and folders on the desktop. You can expand or collapse any of the folders and drives in the list by clicking the plus or minus sign next to the drive or folder. For instance, click the plus sign next to My Computer. When you click a plus sign to expand the folder or drive, the icon changes to a minus sign. Likewise, you can click the minus sign to hide the contents of that item. For instance, you might hide content that isn't relevant to the task you are performing.

To close the Folders bar, click the Folders button again or click the Close button for the bar.

Using the Task Pane

Windows XP also displays a task pane with common tasks as well as Other Places and Details areas. When you click an icon, you can see information about the icon in the Details area. For instance, in Figure 3.4, you can see information about the selected file. You also see commands related to working with the selected item. This chapter covers using these commands for common tasks.

FIGURE 3.4
Check the Task pane for common tasks as well as information about the selected item.

Creating a New Folder

Finding, saving, and opening documents are made easier if you group related files into folders. For example, you might want to create a folder for all your word processing documents, or you might create folders for each person who uses your computer. Creating a folder enables you to keep your documents separated from the program's files so that you can easily find your document files.

You can create a folder within any of the existing folders on your computer. Follow these steps:

1. Open the folder in which you want to create the new folder.

2. In the Task pane, click Make a new folder. The new folder appears in the window, and the name is highlighted (see Figure 3.5).

3. Type a new name and press Enter. The folder is then added.

tip

Windows XP includes several shortcuts to the My Documents folder. Therefore, you might want to set up all your document folders within this one key system folder.

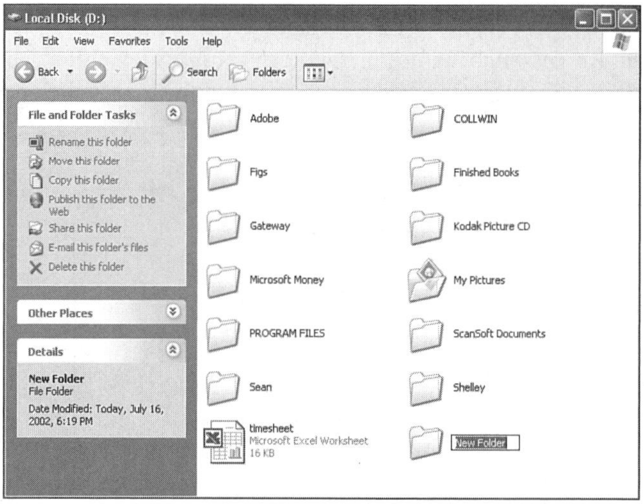

FIGURE 3.5

You can add a new folder to your hard drive.

Displaying and Selecting Files

When you want to perform some file- or folder-related tasks, you start by selecting that file or folder. You can select a single file or multiple files. For instance, if you wanted to delete a group of files, you could select the ones to delete and then give the command to delete them.

For any task, the first step is to open the drive and folder where the file is stored. After you display the file or files you want to work with, you then select them by doing any of the following:

caution

If you do not see the Make a new folder option listed, you probably have a file or folder selected in the window. Click in a blank part of the window.

- To select a single file, click it.
- To select several files next to each other, click the first file of the group that you want to select and then hold down the Shift key and click the last file. The first and last files and all files in between are then selected. Figure 3.6 shows multiple files selected.

FIGURE 3.6

Note that when several files are selected, Windows XP displays the number of items selected, as well as the approximate size of all the selected files, in the Details area of the Task pane.

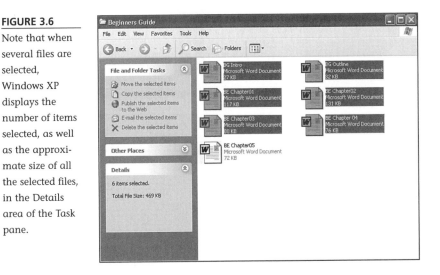

- To select several files that are not next to each other, hold down the Ctrl key and click each file you want to select.
- To select all the files, click the Edit menu and then click the Select All command, or press Ctrl+A.
- To deselect a file, click outside the file list.

Deleting and Undeleting Files and Folders

Eventually, your computer will become full of files, and you'll have a hard time organizing and storing them all. You can delete any files you no longer need. You can also delete entire folders. When you delete a folder, the folder and all its contents are moved to the Recycle Bin.

tip

When you select a single file, you can view details about the file in the Task pane. If the Details area is not displayed, click the down arrow next to the heading. If multiple files are selected, this area displays the number of files selected as well as the total file size.

Windows XP doesn't really delete a file or folder; instead, it moves it to the Recycle Bin. If needed, you can retrieve the file or folder from the Recycle Bin. This common task is also covered in this section.

Deleting a File or Folder

Follow these steps to delete a file or folder:

1. Select the file or folder you want to delete.

2. Click Delete this file. You are prompted to confirm the deletion (see Figure 3.7).

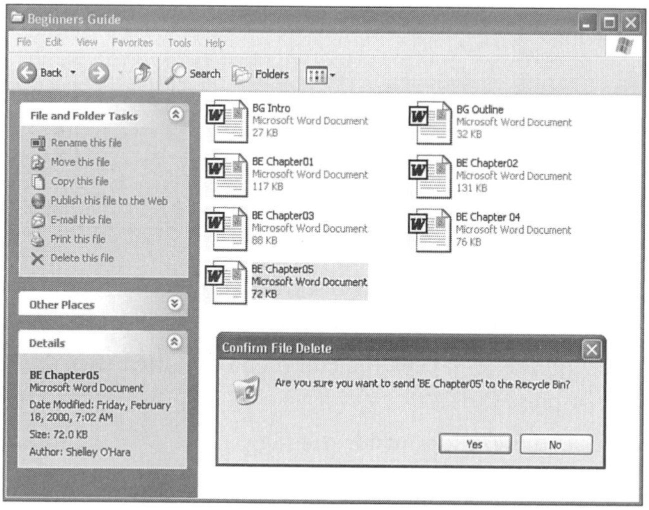

> **tip**
>
> You can have Windows clean up files as part of your maintenance routine. See Chapter 18 for information on using the Disk Cleanup wizard.

FIGURE 3.7
Before deleting, Windows XP prompts you for confirmation.

3. Click Yes to confirm the deletion. Windows removes the file or folder, placing it in the Recycle Bin.

Undeleting a File

Sometimes, you will delete a file or folder by mistake. If you make a mistake, you can retrieve the file or folder from the Recycle Bin (as long as the Recycle Bin has not been emptied) and return the file or folder to its original location. Usually, Murphy's Law goes into effect: The minute you delete an old

> **tip**
>
> You can also press the Delete key to delete a selected file or folder. As another option, right-click the selected file or folder and then select Delete from the shortcut menu.

file is a minute before you determine you need it. Don't fret, though, you can undelete a file.

To undelete a file or folder, follow these steps:

1. Double-click the Recycle Bin icon on your desktop. You'll see the contents of the Recycle Bin, including any folders, icons, or files you have deleted (see Figure 3.8).

FIGURE 3.8

The Recycle Bin includes any files and folders you have deleted.

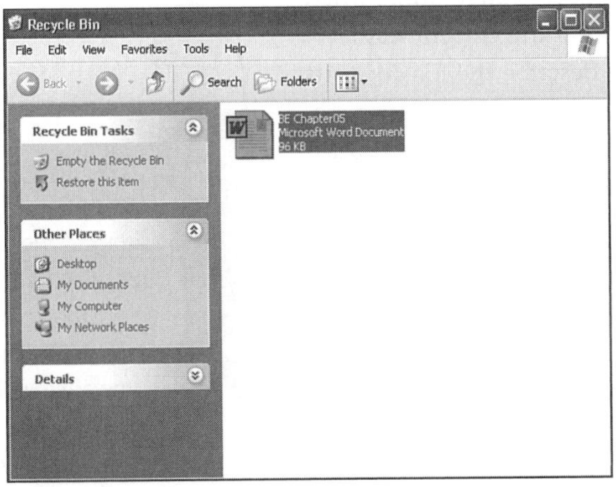

2. Select the file or folder you want to undelete.

3. Click Restore this item in the Task pane. The file or folder is then moved from the Recycle Bin back to its original location.

4 Click the Close button to close the Recycle Bin.

Emptying the Recycle Bin

The contents of the Recycle Bin take up disk space, so you should periodically empty it. The icon changes if it contains something, so you can tell by looking at it whether or not it is empty. You can permanently delete the contents by emptying the Recycle Bin. However, be sure that it doesn't contain any items you need. Follow these steps:

1. Double-click the Recycle Bin icon.

2. Check the contents of the Recycle Bin and undelete any files or folders you need.

tip

If you are sure the Recycle Bin doesn't contain anything you need, you can also right-click the Recycle Bin icon and then select the Empty Recycle Bin command from the shortcut menu. (It's usually best to open and check the contents of the Recycle Bin first, before emptying it.)

3. Click Empty the Recycle Bin in the Task pane. Windows displays the Confirm Multiple File Delete dialog box, prompting you to confirm this action.

4. Click Yes to empty the Recycle Bin.

Renaming a File or Folder

If you did not use a descriptive name when you saved the file or if the current name doesn't accurately describe the file contents, you can rename it. You can also rename a folder you created, selecting a more descriptive name as needed. You can rename only a single item at a time.

Follow these steps:

1. Select the file or folder you want to rename.

2. Click Rename this file in the Task pane. The current name is then highlighted (see Figure 3.9).

3. Type the new name and press Enter. The file or folder is renamed.

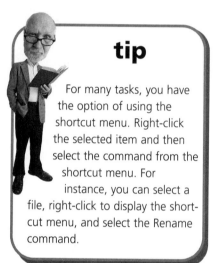

tip

For many tasks, you have the option of using the shortcut menu. Right-click the selected item and then select the command from the shortcut menu. For instance, you can select a file, right-click to display the shortcut menu, and select the Rename command.

FIGURE 3.9

To rename a file, type a new name for the highlighted file.

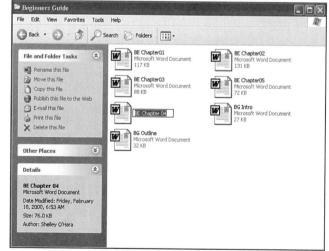

Reorganizing Folders and Files

As you create more and more documents, you may need to do some rearranging. For example, say you have several documents all within one folder, and you decide it would make sense to create subfolders to further organize and categorize the files. You can create a new folder and then move files (or folders) to this new folder.

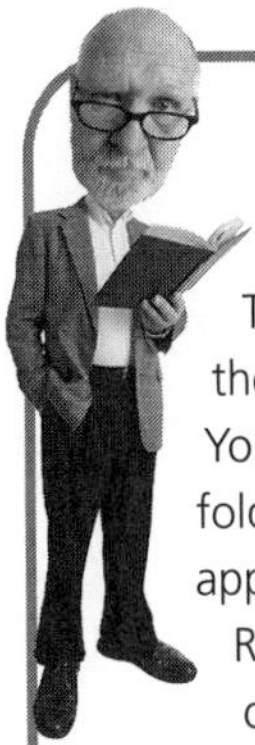

tip

This section covers using the Task pane commands. You can also right-click a folder or file and select the appropriate command (Copy, Rename, Delete, and so on). Furthermore, you can select a folder or file and then use the commands in the Edit menu (Copy To Folder, Move To Folder, and so on).

To move a file or folder, follow these steps:

1. Select the file or folder you want to move.
2. Click the Move command. The name of the command varies depending on what you have selected. For folders, click Move this folder. For a single file, click Move this file. For several files and/or folders, click Move the selected items. You'll see the Move Items dialog box (see Figure 3.10). This dialog box lists all the drives and folders on your system.

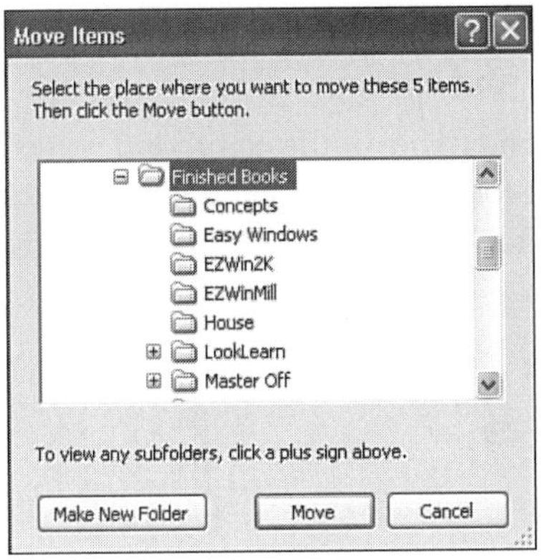

FIGURE 3.10
Select the drive and folder to which to move the selected item(s).

3. Display the folder or drive you want. If an item has a plus sign beside it, that item (the drive or folder) contains other folders. You can click the plus sign to expand the list to show subfolders.
4. Click the folder from the list and click Move. The selected items are then deleted from the original location and are moved

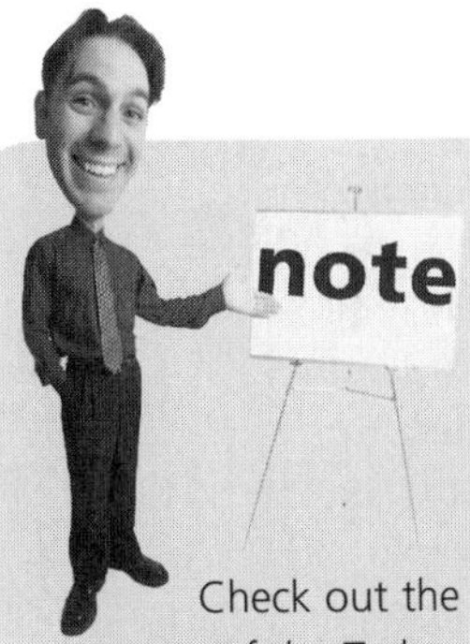

Check out the Details area of the Task pane. It shows the number of items selected as well as the total file size.

to the new location. Keep in mind that if you move a folder, you move not just the folder, but its contents as well.

Copying Folders and Files

In addition to moving folders and files, you can copy them. You may want to keep extra copies of files or folders. Rather than using a backup program (covered in Chapter 17), many users simply copy files or folders to create a backup copies. As another example, you may copy files to a floppy disk or a CD, for instance, to share with others or to bring home from your office.

Windows XP provides several methods for copying files and folders. If you want to copy files or folders to other folders, consider using the Copy command. If you want to copy files or folders to another drive, consider using the Send To command. Both methods are covered in this section.

Copying with the Copy Command

To copy a file or folder, follow these steps:

1. Select the file or folder you want to copy.

2. Click the Copy command. The name of the command varies depending on what you have selected. For folders, click Copy this folder. For a single file, click Copy this file. For several files and/or folders, click Copy the selected items. You'll see the Copy Items dialog box (see Figure 3.11). This dialog box lists all the drives and folders on your system.

FIGURE 3.11

The Copy Items dialog box is the same as the Move Items dialog box (from the previous section), only you are copying the items to the selected drive or folder rather than moving them.

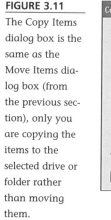

3. Display the folder or drive you want. If an item has a plus sign beside it, that item (the drive or folder) contains other folders. You can click the plus sign to expand the list to show subfolders.

4. Click the folder from the list and click Copy. The selected items then remain both in the original location and the new location. Keep in mind that if you copy a folder, you copy not just the folder, but its contents as well.

Copying Files to a Floppy Disk

Because it's common to copy a file to another disk, Windows XP also provides the Send To command. You can use this command to copy a file or folder to a floppy disk.

1. Select the file or folder you want to copy.

2. Right-click any of the selected items and select the Send To command. You'll see the Send To options (see Figure 3.12).

3. Select the drive from the shortcut menu. The file or folder is then copied.

> **tip**
>
> You can also use the Send To command to compress files. (See Chapter 18 for more information.) You can create a desktop shortcut, send the files via email, or send them to the My Documents folder.

FIGURE 3.12

For a fast way to copy files or folders to a floppy disk, use the Send To command.

Copying Files to a CD

Most new CD drives enable you to both read and write information to the CD drive. Because a CD drive can hold a lot of information, it makes a good medium for making a copy of files you want to save. Copying files to a CD disc is often called "burning" a CD. You must have a CD-R drive (which stands for CD Recordable—you can only write data to this disc once) or a CD-RW drive (which stands for CD-Rewritable—you can read and write to the disc) to copy files. If you have a CD-ROM drive, you can only read information from the drive; you cannot record information.

To copy a file or folder to a CD disc, follow these steps:

1. Select the file or folder you want to copy.

2. Do one of the following:

   Display the Folders bar by clicking Folders. Then, drag the selected file or folder to the CD drive icon.

   Right-click the selected item, select Send To, and select your CD drive from the submenu.

   You'll see a message saying that you have files waiting to be written to the CD.

3. Click this message. The files are listed, and in the task pane, you'll see a command for writing the selected files to the CD disc (see Figure 3.13).

4. Click Write these files to CD. The files are then copied to the disc.

caution

Because reading files from a CD drive is slower, don't use this as a primary storage device. Use it for big files you want to keep. It's a great way to make backup copies of important files without having to use a ton of floppy or zip disks. Also, note that some disks created on CD-RW drives can't be read in some CD players.

caution

You may have other programs you can use to copy files to a CD (including music files, which are covered later in this book). If you have another program, you may be prompted to use it to copy the files to the CD. Follow the specific instructions for your particular program.

FIGURE 3.13

You can copy the files from the temporary storage folder to the CD disc.

The Absolute Minimum

This chapter provides the basics of file management, including the following concepts:

- You have at least one hard drive on your system, and this is drive C:. You might have additional drives, which are lettered consecutively.

- To view the drives, folders, and files on your computer, open the My Computer icon. You can then navigate to and open any of the drives, files, and folders on your system.

- To keep your files organized, you can create folders. Windows XP starts with a system folder called My Documents. Consider storing all your work in subfolders within this one main folder. You can create new folders as needed.

- When you want to perform an action on a file (such as deleting it), you select it. You can select a single file, multiple files, or all files within a window.

- Delete files you no longer need. If you delete a file by accident or find that you really do need it, you can undo the deletion by retrieving the item from the Recycle Bin.

- If you did not use a descriptive name for a file or a folder, you can rename it.

- If you need to change the location where a file or folder is stored, you can move the file or folder.

- You can copy a folder or file to keep an extra copy, or to take a copy to another location.

4

TROUBLESHOOTING COMMON PROBLEMS

This chapter covers some common, simple-to-fix problems as well as explains how to restart your computer (when it gets stuck), how to get help, and how to protect your computer. You should have a good understanding of these common troubleshooting techniques in your "toolkit" of computer skills. Later in this book, you'll build on some of these skills. For instance, you'll learn more about making backup copies in Chapter 17.

Closing Stuck Programs

Encountering problems is part of working with any sophisticated piece of equipment, especially one as complex as a computer. But, Windows XP makes it easier than previous versions to pinpoint and deal with problems. One common problem is dealing with a program that is stuck (or as Windows XP says, "is not responding"). If this happens, you can follow the suggestions in this section to see whether you can close the program without losing your work.

Try each solution in the order listed so that you look for easy fixes first before moving on to more drastic steps (such as restarting or turning the computer off and then back on, the topic of the next section).

Is the Program Busy?

If you think a program is not responding, make sure that it is not busy with another task. Is the disk light active? Can you hear the drives moving? Does the keyboard respond? If the computer is active, you might just have to wait a few seconds to get the program to respond.

Also, make sure that the program is the active window. It is an easy mistake to have more than one window displayed and *think* you are working in one window (but it's not responding), when actually another program or window is active. Click in the program window or use the taskbar to switch to the program.

Also, make sure that the menu bar is not active. If you press Alt, the menus are activated. Then if you try to type, nothing will happen (or a menu will open). Press Esc a few times to make sure that you are actually in the working area (not in the menu bar).

> **tip**
>
> Your Esc key is just that—an escape. If you think you are stuck, try pressing Esc. You might get out of the jam, and even if you don't, pressing Esc doesn't hurt anything.

Closing a Program from the Taskbar

If the computer is not busy and you still can't get a program to respond, try closing it from the taskbar. Follow these steps:

1. Right-click the taskbar button for the program. You'll see a shortcut menu for that window (see Figure 4.1).

> **caution**
>
> If you use this method, you risk losing any work you've done, but sometimes that's the only choice you have. As mentioned, try the suggestions in the preceding section first before closing the program window.

FIGURE 4.1

Use the taskbar button to try to close a program.

2. Select the Close command. The program may then be closed. If it's not closed, Windows XP displays an error message saying that the program is not responding. You can then choose to wait or to close the program immediately.

3. Click End Now if prompted.

Closing a Program from the Task Manager

If the taskbar method doesn't work (or if you are not sure what's running on your computer), you can display the Task Manager. The Task Manager displays all the open programs (as well as any behind-the-scenes system programs that are running). From the Task Manager, you can close a program.

Follow these steps:

1. Right-click a blank area of the taskbar.

2. Select Task Manager. The Windows Task Manager appears (see Figure 4.2), listing all the programs that are running.

3. Select the program you want to close.

4. Click End Task.

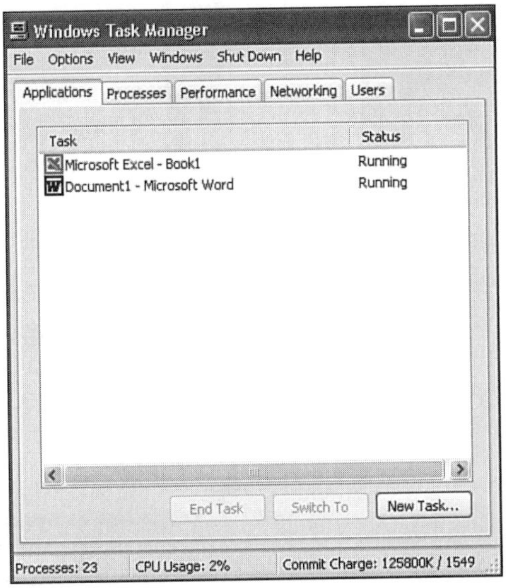

tip

These exit methods work for stuck programs. You can also use them as other ways to exit regular programs (those that aren't stuck).

FIGURE 4.2

The Task Manager displays what programs are running.

The program is then closed. If the program is "stuck," you'll see a message stating that the program is not responding. At that point, you can click End Now to close down the stuck program.

Restarting and Shutting Down the Computer

If your computer gets stuck, your first task is to close any open programs using one of the previous methods. If you get them all closed, you can then restart. If you can't get a program to close, you can restart using the menu command or by turning off the computer (the last resort).

tip

Sometimes, you can't even click the mouse. That's when you are really stuck. So are you out of luck? Not yet. Try pressing Ctrl+Alt+Del (all three keys together) and see whether that pops up the Task Manager. You can then try closing a stuck program.

Restarting with a Command

To try restarting to clear up problems, you can use the Turn Off Computer button on the taskbar. You might also need to restart if you make system changes; restarting puts such changes into effect. If you need to restart, try using the Start menu first:

1. Click the Start button.

2. Click the Turn Off Computer button. You'll see the various shutdown options (see Figure 4.3).

FIGURE 4.3
You can select to restart or turn off the computer.

3. Select Restart to restart the computer. The computer is then restarted. This usually clears up your problem.

tip

The Log Off button is used when multiple people use the computer and each has his or her own settings. See Chapter 22, "Setting Up Windows for Multiple Users," for more information on using the Log Off button.

Also, from the Turn Off dialog box, you can choose to hibernate the computer to conserve power—just select the Hibernate button. This is most commonly used for laptops.

Restarting by Turning Off the Computer

Sometimes, everything freezes, and you can't use your mouse or the keyboard. In this case, you need to do what is sometimes called a *hard reboot*. If your computer has a reset button, you can press this button to force the computer to restart. If you do not have a reset button, you need to turn off the computer by pressing the power button. You may have to hold the button for 3 to 5 seconds to get the computer to turn off.

Turn off the computer, wait a few seconds, and then turn the computer back on. Doing so is a last resort, but it does clear out any programs that are not running.

Shutting Down the Computer

To avoid problems, you need to shut down properly before you turn off your computer. Doing so allows Windows XP to perform behind-the-scenes tasks before shutting down. Normally, when you want to turn off your computer, follow this procedure:

1. Click the Start button.
2. Click the Turn Off Computer button.
3. Select Turn Off. The computer is then shut down.

Getting Help

Another useful feature for handling problems or just getting information is Windows online help. You can select from a list of help topics by browsing through a table of contents of help. You can also use the index to look up a topic or search for a topic.

The online help includes troubleshooters that help you pinpoint problems and offer suggested fixes. These troubleshooters are most often used to pinpoint problems with hardware components

tip

The power button is located in different places on different computers. You might have a reset button and a power button on the front of the computer. You might have only a power button, or the power button might be located on the back of the system unit.

tip

Should you turn off your computer each time you are finished? Different people have different opinions. Some think it's best to always turn off the computer. Some turn off just the monitor and the printer. Doing so conserves power and provides some measure of security for power surges. Others leave the computer running. This camp thinks that powering on and off the computer repeatedly degrades the power supply, and that the computer is protected (or should be) from power surges with a surge protector. You should do what is most comfortable for you.

or "devices." See Chapter 19, "Upgrading Your Computer," for information on these hardware-related troubleshooters.

Browsing Help Topics

Follow these steps to get help:

1. Click the Start button.

2. Click Help and Support. You'll see the Help and Support Center window (see Figure 4.4).

3. Click the topic on which you want help. For instance, select Windows basics. You'll see the related topics.

tip

Your computer manufacturer may also provide help features and access to its online help on your help page. For instance, in Figure 4.4, the computer displays help from Dell (the maker of this particular computer).

FIGURE 4.4

You can get extensive help from the Windows XP help guide as well as online sources.

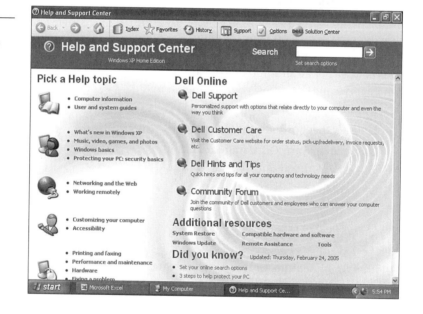

4. Click the subtopic you want. The right pane lists relevant help topics. Figure 4.5, for instance, shows the topics for protecting your computer.

FIGURE 4.5

Use Windows help to get detailed information about features.

5. Click the topic you want in the pane on the right. Windows displays the relevant help information (see Figure 4.6).

FIGURE 4.6

You can display step-by-step information on using Windows XP features.

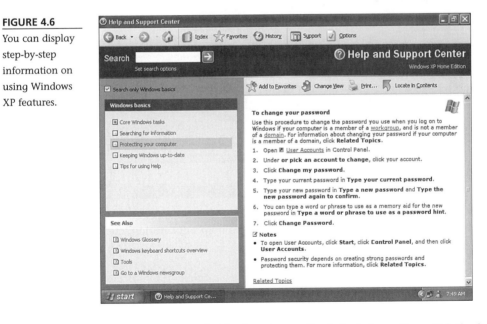

6. When you are finished reviewing the help information, click the help window's Close button.

Searching for Help

Rather than browsing for help, you can go directly to a related help topic by searching for it. To do so, follow these steps:

1. Click the Start button.

2. Click Help and Support. You'll see the Help and Support Center window (refer to Figure 4.4).

3. In the Search text box, type your question or topic and click the search button (the green arrow). Windows XP then displays related help topics.

4. Select the task you want from the list of suggested topics. Windows XP displays the related information in the help pane on the right (see Figure 4.7).

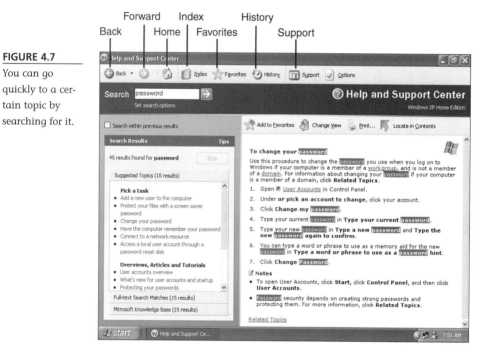

FIGURE 4.7

You can go quickly to a certain topic by searching for it.

5. When you are finished reviewing the help information, click the help window's Close button.

Using the Help Window Toolbar

In addition to browsing and searching, you can use the toolbar buttons to get help in other ways:

- If you have looked up several pages during your browsing or searching, you can return to previous pages or go forward by using the Back and Forward buttons.

- To return to the opening help page, click the Home button.

- To display an index of topics, click the Index button. Then type the keyword in the pane on the left. Windows XP then displays matching topics. Click the topic about which you want to display help information in the pane on the right.

- If you frequently refer to the same help pages, you can set up a list of favorite pages. Use the Favorites button to go to favorite pages.

- If you recently used help and want to return to a topic you know you looked up, use the History list to display a list of recently viewed help pages. You can then select the relevant page from this list.

- To access online support, click the Support button. Your options are displayed in the left pane and include sending an email to a friend for help, getting help from Microsoft, or visiting a Windows Web site forum. For more information about online browsing (including help options), see Chapter 8, "Browsing the Internet."

- To customize the help options, use the Options button. You can change such options as the font size and what appears in the navigation bar (also known as the toolbar).

Handling Printer Problems

Printing is supposed to be straightforward, but there can be times when the printer just won't give you what you want. In such cases, you can fix common problems by reviewing this list:

- Windows XP should display error pop-up messages in the system tray (the far right of the taskbar) when the printer is not functioning correctly. If the printer isn't connected or is out of paper, check for printer messages from Windows to locate the problem.

- If you missed the error message, start with the basics: If a document won't print, make sure that the printer is plugged in and turned on. Also, check the printer cable—is it solidly connected to the printer and the computer? A loose cable is easy to fix and overlook.

■ Check the printer for error messages. Usually, these are displayed as flashing lights. More sophisticated printers may display actual messages. On my particular printer, I have lights for paper and error. Paper means a paper jam. Error means something else, usually something simple like the paper drawer isn't pushed in all the way, or I didn't clear the paper jam correctly. If you get an error message from the printer and you don't know what it means, check your printer manual.

■ You can tell whether the printer and computer are communicating because the printer should display some type of indication when it is receiving data. (Mine flashes the data light.) If you see this light, you know the data is getting to the printer, but the printer just isn't printing.

■ Some printers can "choke" on documents that are too complex. In some instances, the computer may not have sufficient memory to print such a complex document. If you are trying to print a complicated layout or complex graphics and the print job never comes out of the printer, you might not be able to print that document. Instead, try printing a single page. If that works, print the pages in batches. If it doesn't, you might need to make some modifications to the layout and formatting (or get a better printer).

■ For additional troubleshooting advice on printers, click Start, select Control Panel and click Printers and Other Hardware. From this window, under Troubleshooters, click Printing. Select your problem from the list of problems and then click Next to use the Troubleshooter to check out the problem and recommended solutions.

Dealing with Viruses and Other Security Problems

Computers provide connectivity with others, which is great, but this also brings with it some security issues that need to be handled. If you are connected to the Internet, if more than one person uses your computer, or if you share work (perhaps by bringing work home from the office or collaborating on a project and sharing files), you need to protect yourself.

Security has become a big issue, and you should take these risks seriously. While a computer is replaceable, you may find that the data you stored on it is not. For instance, suppose that you just finished writing the next great American novel, and you have only your disk files from the hard drive. If something happens to those files, poof, your entire novel and all your writing may be lost. Or, suppose that you store all of your financial records on your laptop, and the laptop is stolen.

Because security affects many various aspects of using a computer, security issues are covered throughout this book, with the information included where it is most relevant. This section gives you an overview of the key security risks and where you can find additional information. It's best to think about security at the beginning—before you have problems. Spend some time reviewing this list and making sure you have an adequate plan for each of the following security issues:

- **Protection against viruses.** Just like you can get a virus, so can your computer. Computer viruses range from simple, mischievous programs that might display stupid messages to really dangerous ones that can wipe out all the data on a drive. You can get a virus from any number of sources, including the Internet, email attachments, and opening a file that happens to be infected from a floppy disk or other removable media (like a CD drive). To protect yourself, you should get and use a virus scan program. You learn more about viruses in Chapter 17, "Securing Your PC."

- **Blocking annoying ads (called pop-ups or pop-unders).** Often, when you browse the Internet, you may find that ads keep popping up. If so, you can use special software to prevent the ads from appearing. Chapter 8 covers how to deal with ads.

- **Blocking junk email (called *spam*).** Another annoying problem can be with the amount of junk email you receive. To handle spam, review the suggestions in Chapter 7.

- **Safeguarding your privacy.** In addition to security, you should be concerned about your privacy. One type of program called spyware, for instance, tracks where you go online and then relays this information back to its sponsor, often without your knowledge. To check for and prevent spyware (and to handle other privacy issues), see Chapter 8.

- **Securing your PC if you use a 24/7 Internet connection (a cable modem).** If you are always online, you need to use a *firewall* to make sure that others can't access your computer. Chapter 8 discusses how to check to see whether you have a firewall, and if you don't, how to use the Windows XP firewall feature to protect your computer.

tip

One way that you get on "junk" mailing lists is by registering at different Internet sites—for instance, if you order a product via the Internet. Look for options that say, "Yes, please send me information on upcoming sales," or "Please add me to your mailing list," or something similar. Make sure to uncheck these options when you place an order or register for something online.

■ **Making an extra copy of your data.** As mentioned previously, your data is the most valuable thing about your computer. You should make backup copies of all your data files, as well as your entire system, periodically. Chapter 17 covers protecting your data.

The Service Pack 2 Release of Windows XP includes a new Security Center, which provides you with the status of some of the preceding issues. To view Windows's evaluation of your security, display the Security Center:

1. Click Start, All Programs, Accessories, System Tools.

2. Click Security Center. You'll see an assessment of your current security (see Figure 4.8). You'll learn more information about viewing and working with the Security Center later in this book.

FIGURE 4.8

You can get an overview on many security issues using Windows XP's new Security Center.

The Absolute Minimum

Most computer problems are easily solved, and you will be surprised how disaster-proof your PC is. Common problems can usually be fixed by restarting. If not, you can use Windows XP's help system. Keep these "tools" in mind:

- If you are having problems, try exiting all your programs. (Save your work first.) You can exit using the program's File, Exit command. If that doesn't work, try exiting from the taskbar button. Still no luck? Try using the Task Manager to exit.

- You might have to restart your computer. You might have to do this if the computer gets stuck or if you make changes to your computer (such as adding a new hardware component or a new software program). To restart, use the Turn Off Computer button on the Start menu. If that doesn't work, you can turn off the computer by pressing its reset button or power button.

- Make a habit of shutting down the computer properly. To do so, use the Turn Off Computer button and select the Shut Down option.

- Windows provides extensive assistance in its help system. You can look up topics by browsing, searching, or using one of several other tools including Web support and an index.

- If your printer won't print, check the obvious things first: Is it connected? Does it have power? Does it have paper? You can also check Windows or your printer for any printer error messages.

- To make sure your data is safe and your online experience is not hampered by unwanted email or advertisements, you need to take some security precautions. In this chapter, you learn the key security issues you need to consider to safeguard your computer, as well as where to find more information on these topics.

PART II

COMMUNICATIONS

5

GETTING WIRED FOR COMMUNICATION

One of the most exciting things you can do with a computer is connect to the Internet. The Internet provides a vast source of information, communication, entertainment, and more. This chapter covers the equipment you need to get connected, as well as provides an understanding of the basics of setting up that equipment. You also get a quick overview of some of the many things you can do once connected. Other chapters in this section provide more how-to information on Internet topics.

Understanding the Internet

The Internet is a network of networks all loosely connected through phone lines or network hookups. You can connect to one network (your service provider) and then gain access to the entire network via a connection (usually a phone line or a cable connection). When connected, you can navigate from one network system to another network; this process is called *browsing* or *surfing*.

You don't need to know a lot about the details of how the Internet works or is organized. All you need to worry about is how to set up your connection the first time and then how to get connected thereafter. If you are curious about how the Internet was developed, or if you want more technical details on the Internet, consider reading *How to Use the Internet, Eighth Edition* (ISBN# 0-7897-2813-3) by Que Publishing.

When connected, you can do any of the following:

- **Send and receive email.** You can send email messages to anyone with an email address. You can also receive email. Email is covered in Chapter 7, "Sending and Receiving Email."

- **Communicate live online by typing messages.** You can type instant messages to others who are online at the same time you are, thereby having a live conversation through these typed words. You can also participate in *chats*. Again, in a chat, you type your messages, but the conversation involves a group of people—everyone within a particular *chat room,* and anyone can see and respond to your typed messages. You can find informal chats as well as scheduled and monitored chats with famous people, such as authors, actors, and other individuals.

- **Post messages and review responses in a newsgroup.** Another way to connect with other users is through a *newsgroup*. (Newsgroups have little to do with news, even though they are called *news*groups.) Rather than a live conversation, you post messages to an electronic bulletin board. Then, anyone who visits that newsgroup can

note

Often the Internet is called the World Wide Web or the Web for short. The World Wide Web is not a physical part of the Internet; instead, it is a way of presenting information. Initially, the Internet was all text based, but someone came along and developed a new method that allowed for graphics and other media elements (sounds, animation, and so on). Sites that were set up in this multimedia format were part of the World Wide Web. As more sites became graphical, the Internet and the World Wide Web became pretty much synonymous.

read and respond to your messages. You can find newsgroups on topics as diverse as Elvis sightings to molecular biology.

■ **Browse Web sites.** You can go to other sites on the Internet (see Figure 5.1). You can go directly to a site by typing its address, you can search for sites, or you can browse from site to site by using links. For more information on browsing, see Chapter 8, "Browsing the Internet."

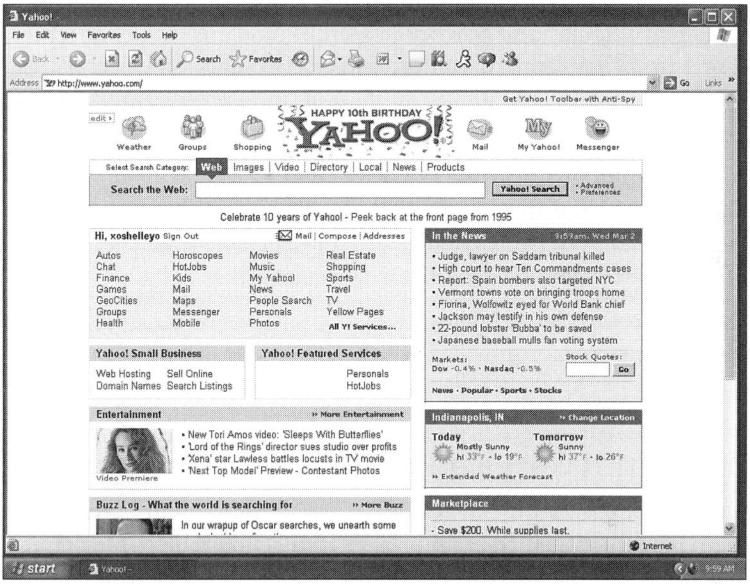

FIGURE 5.1

The first site you see is your home site. From this site, you can go to other Web sites.

Getting the Right Equipment

To access the Internet, you need certain hardware components. You also need some additional items such as an Internet provider and a way to get connected. Basically, you need the following:

■ A modem

■ An Internet service provider (often abbreviated to ISP)

■ A connection

■ A program for browsing the Internet

■ A program for handling mail

This section describes each of these items.

Describing Modems

A *modem* is a device used with a telephone line or cable wire and your computer. The modem enables your computer to connect to and communicate with other computers via the phone line or a cable line. Regular phone-connection modems are often referred to as *dial-up modems*. Faster connections, including cable modems, are often called *broadband connections*.

Most new computers come with a modem, which is most often stored inside the computer. You can also purchase external modems that connect to your computer with a cable and sit on your desk. One of the newer ways to get connected is through a cable connection (usually provided by your cable TV company). To use a cable connection, you need a cable modem; you can purchase one, or sometimes the cable company provides one when you subscribe to its service. You can also connect through a special phone line called a DSL connection. This type of connection is similar to a cable connection; it provides fast access and its pricing is somewhat similar. (More on connection types later.)

You plug in the phone line or cable line to the modem. Then you can connect to your Internet service provider, which allows you to access email and browse the Web.

Finding an Internet Service Provider

An Internet service provider (ISP) has one or more high-powered networks that your computer calls to get connected. Your connection type (which is covered next) determines how you get connected and also which provider you use. For instance, if you decide to use a cable modem, you need to select a cable provider. If you decide to get a DSL hookup, you need a provider for DSL.

In addition to providing online browsing, your ISP also serves as your mailbox. When someone sends you an email message, it is sent to your provider's network and stored there. When you get connected, you can then *download* or transfer any messages from your ISP to your computer.

You pay a monthly fee for this service; the fees and services vary from company to company. Usually, you can shop around for an ISP that meets your needs.

Windows XP provides links and even free trials for popular Internet providers such as America Online (AOL) and Microsoft Network (MSN). Some providers are nationwide; some are local. Picking a local provider does not limit your connection to local sites; it just means that the company that provides the service is local.

If you do not have a provider, or if you are thinking of upgrading or changing your provider, do some research first by asking the following questions:

- **Does the company provide service for your type of connection?** That is, if you want to use a cable connection, does that company have cable hookups? If you want DSL, do they provide DSL? Some areas may not have cable, for instance.

- **What is the cost?** Expect a monthly fee around $20 for basic service and up to $50 or more for high-speed access. Fees also vary from one area of the country to another. Furthermore, fees vary depending on the type of connection. You may, for instance, choose a DSL connection because the pricing is better than it is for a cable connection.

- **What other services are provided?** As you become more proficient, you might want to expand your Internet skills. If you think that down the road you might want to create your own Web site, see whether your provider has Web hosting services. If so, what is the fee? Also, if more than one person uses your computer, consider multiple email addresses, one for each person. Check to see whether your ISP provides (and what they charge) for multiple addresses.

- **What is the top connection speed?** Speed is measured in bits per second (bps) or kilobytes per second (Kbps). Regular modems max out at about a speed of 56,000 bps or 56K. Cable and DSL lines are much, much faster. DSL lines and cable connections include speeds ranging from 128K to 768K on up to 1500K. Check out the various speeds for providers in your area. A great Web site for reviewing broadband speeds is BroadbandReports.com.

tip

You can search for a provider using the New Connection Wizard. See "Getting Connected" later in this chapter for information on this wizard. Another great site for finding an ISP is a site called The List at www.thelist.com.

Selecting a Connection Type

Most users connect to the Internet through a phone line, but it is becoming more popular to hook up through your cable provider or through a special phone line such as DSL. (Again, these connections are called broadband connections.) These methods often cost more, but provide faster connections. Common connection types include

- **Cable**—You can connect to the Internet through the same company that provides your cable television. Usually, the cable company provides the modem and runs the cable line for you for a setup fee. You then pay a monthly fee for the service. (Prices vary. Comparison shop among the various high-speed or broadband connections to get the best speed *and* price.)

■ **Phone line**—You can get connected through a high-speed phone line such as a DSL line. Again, this provides a faster connection but may require a special phone line and a higher service fee. You may also be able to get connected through your regular phone line as long as you use the filters set up by the DSL company. Check with your local phone company for information about this connection option.

■ **Network connection**—Businesses often use a network connection as their access to the Internet. The network is often directly connected to the Internet through a networking line.

■ **Wireless connection**—One of the newer popular methods of getting connected is through a wireless network. Chapter 6 covers this method of hooking up to the Internet.

Selecting Browser and Email Programs

In addition to the service provider and hardware equipment, you need programs for browsing the Internet and for sending and receiving mail.

Windows XP includes a mail program called Outlook Express. This program suits the needs of most users. (Sending and receiving email is the topic of Chapter 7.) Figure 5.2 shows the Outlook Express window.

Some users may prefer another mail program. For instance, your company may use a different mail program for interoffice email, or you may prefer a full-featured mail program. For instance, if you use Microsoft Office, you can use Outlook, a personal information manager program that includes mail, calendar, and contact features.

caution

Cable and DSL modems are usually connected 24/7 (24 hours a day, 7 days a week). To protect your computer, you need to turn on a safety device called a *firewall*. You can find more on this topic in Chapter 8.

note

Many DSL providers (for instance, Verizon) can now use your regular phone line rather than a special phone line. You have to put filters on the jacks you don't want to use for DSL, but the filters are easy to install. They plug into the jacks, and you plug your phone into the filters. If you are looking into DSL as your connection type, check into all your options.

FIGURE 5.2

You can access
your email with
Outlook Express.

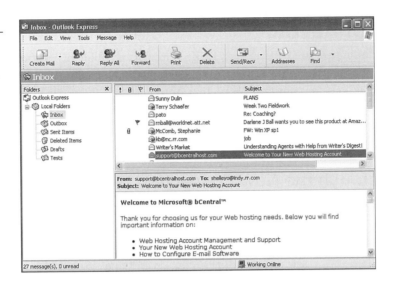

Windows XP also includes a browser program called Internet Explorer. Browsing the
Internet is covered in Chapter 8 and in Chapter 9, "Searching the Internet." Figure 5.3
shows Internet Explorer. Again, different users may prefer to use different programs.
Initially, Netscape Navigator was the most commonly used browser program. Some
users still use this program. You can get more information and download this browser
from www.netscape.com. Picking a browser is simply a matter of preference (and sometimes price, given that Internet Explorer is included with Windows XP and that you
might have to pay for software for other browser programs).

FIGURE 5.3

The most popu-
lar Internet
browser program
is Internet
Explorer, which
is included with
Windows XP.

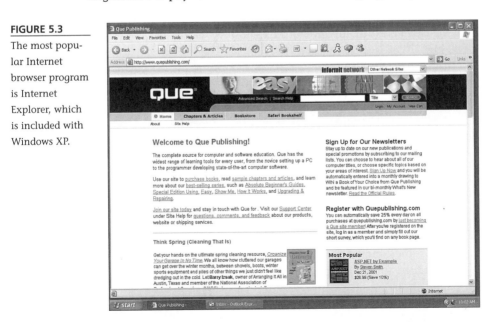

Getting Connected

To summarize so far, you need certain hardware components, software, and a provider to access the Internet. After you have these lined up, your first task is to set up Windows for your new connection. You only have to do this once. After that, starting your email program or going to a Web site is as simple as clicking an icon. But, the first time, you need to enter some technical information about your connection and provider.

Stepping Through the New Connection Wizard

Windows XP provides the New Connection Wizard, which leads you step by step through the process of getting connected. Using information supplied by your provider, this setup wizard gets you up and running in no time. If you have any problems or questions, contact your Internet service provider.

Follow these steps to start the New Connection Wizard and get connected:

1. Click the Start button and then click All Programs.

2. Click Accessories, Communications, New Connection Wizard.

3. Complete each step of the wizard, clicking Next to advance to the next step. Click Back if you need to change one of your selections. Keep in mind that the steps vary depending on the type of connection. You can get a rough idea of setting up a dial-up account from the following:

   Select the connection type—dial-up modem, broadband connection (DSL or cable), or network broadband (DSL or LAN).

   Enter the name of your ISP.

   Enter the connection information. For instance, for a dial-up account, you type the phone number your computer dials to connect with the Internet service provider.

caution

The other chapters in this part of the book assume that you have set up your Internet connection and email account. Because the process varies from provider to provider, this book cannot list the exact steps. Use the New Connection Wizard to help you get set up. If you have problems, try Windows help or contact your Internet service provider for help.

note

You can also use this wizard to set up a home network. See Chapter 24, "Setting Up Windows XP on a Home Network."

Type your account information (username and password). Use the information provided to you by your ISP.

4. When you have completed all your steps, click the Finish button. You are set!

Starting Your Connection

After you finish with the wizard, you connect to the Internet or email by clicking Start and then clicking Internet or E-mail from the Start menu. You'll see your connection prompt (see Figure 5.4). For dial-up accounts, you normally type your username and password. Then, Windows XP dials your provider and connects you to the Internet.

> **tip**
>
> You also need to set up your mail accounts. The first time you start Outlook Express you are prompted to do so. You learn more about mail programs in Chapter 7, "Sending and Receiving Email."

FIGURE 5.4

Follow the steps to log on to your provider.

> **tip**
>
> You can set up your connection so that Windows XP remembers the phone number to dial as well as your username and password.

You are now ready to start your Internet journey.

Exiting and Disconnecting

When you are not working online, you should exit your mail and browser programs and log off (if you have a dial-up account). To do so, click the Close button for the program window. You are prompted to log off if you have a dial-up connection. If you are prompted to log off, select Yes or Disconnect.

If you are not prompted to log off, right-click the connection icon in the taskbar and select Disconnect (see Figure 5.5).

FIGURE 5.5

Use the connection icon in the system tray to log off or display connection information.

THE ABSOLUTE MINIMUM

This chapter explains what you need to access the Internet for mail, Web browsing, or both. In particular, this chapter covers these key points:

- To get connected, you need a modem, an Internet service provider, a connection (usually a phone line or cable line), and software for email and Web browsing. You can use two programs included with Windows XP for email and Web browsing: Outlook Express and Internet Explorer.

- To set up a new connection, use Windows XP's New Connection Wizard, completing each of the required steps by entering specific information about your provider and connection.

- After you have set up your Internet account, you can log on to the Internet and check and send email as well as browse the Internet.

6

Setting Up Wireless Connections

Many people have more than one computer and want to share resources, such as a printer or an Internet connection. To do so, you could set up a regular network, physically connecting the different components (using phone lines, for instance). Networking in this method is covered in Chapter 24. For more convenience, though, you might set up a wireless network.

As another example, if you use a laptop computer and want to be able to connect to the Internet from anywhere in your house or office, you might consider a wireless network. With a laptop and wireless connections, you can also connect to the Internet at cafés, airports, hotels, educational institutes, and other places.

This section gives you an overview of how wireless networks operate and explains the equipment you need to get set up. If you are interested in a wireless network, you can get a good idea of what you need to accomplish to set up this type of network in your home.

Understanding How Wireless Networking Works

Wireless networking is what its name implies—networking without wires. Instead of communicating through physical connections (such as cables or phone lines), a wireless network uses radio signals (much like walkie-talkies, only much more sophisticated).

The radios used in a wireless network can convert 1s and 0s (computer data) into radio waves. The receiving component can then convert the radio waves back into 1s and 0s (much like a telephone modem works to convert 1s and 0s to analog signals for transmission through telephone wires).

The radios also can change frequencies (called frequency hopping) so that multiple components can talk to each other at the same time without interference. This means that

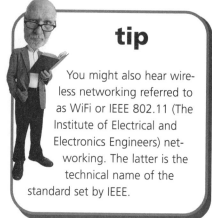

tip

You might also hear wireless networking referred to as WiFi or IEEE 802.11 (The Institute of Electrical and Electronics Engineers) networking. The latter is the technical name of the standard set by IEEE.

you can print a document (which involves communicating to your printer) and also connect to the Internet (which involves communicating with your online Internet connection).

Wireless networking offers many advantages. It is relatively simple, fast, and cost-effective. It's perfect for connecting laptops (as well as desktop computers) or for setting up a network where physical connections would be cumbersome. The next section discusses the components you need to set up a wireless network.

What You Need To Set Up a Wireless Network

If you want to install a wireless network in your home or office, you need wireless network cards and a Wireless Access Point Router. This section covers these components.

Wireless Network Cards

To enable your computer(s) to connect to the wireless network, you need to install a wireless network card on each of the computers you want to be able to access the network. If you purchased a new laptop, it may already include a wireless network card. Many new systems do. If not, you can purchase and install a card. For laptop computers, you can add a card (called a PCMCIA card) that you slide into a PCMCIA port, or you can purchase a card that plugs into your computer via a USB port. For desktop computers, you can install a card into a slot inside your system unit or, again, add an external card that plugs into your computer through a USB port.

Wireless cards have somewhat confusing names and vary in transmitting and receiving speeds. Common cards include the following:

- 802.11b, the first card introduced. This is the slowest and cheapest card. It can transmit at speeds around 2.4 GHz (gigahertz) and receive at 11 megabits per second. The speed factor comes into play when you want to share files and is especially important when sharing big files, such as video files. (You don't really have to remember the speeds. Just use the speeds for comparison, noting that some cards are faster than others.)

- 802.11a, the second card introduced. This card is significantly faster than the 802.11b card: It can transmit at 5 GHz and can receive at 54 megabits per second.

- 802.11g combines features of the a and b cards. It's cheaper than and has a better range than the a card, transmits at the speed of the b card (2.4 GHz), and receives at the speed of the a card (54 megabits per second).

Wireless Access Point Router

For the connection, you need to set up a *hotspot*, the connection point for the wireless network. You create a hotspot by adding a Wireless Access Point Router, a small box that contains the radio used to send and receive signals. The Wireless Access Point Router also includes a port to which you can connect your cable or DSL modem. When you connect your modem, you then provide access to the Internet from any computers on the wireless network.

You can also create software access points. For this type of configuration, you install the software on a computer with a wireless network card and Internet-sharing software. For this type of wireless network, you create a peer-to-peer network. (You can find more information about peer-to-peer networks in Chapter 24.)

tip

You can also find hotspots at restaurants, hotels, schools, libraries, airports, and other places. If you have a wireless card on your laptop, you can connect to the Internet using these hotspots. Note that some may charge a fee for access.

Setting Up a Wireless Network

Setting up a wireless network requires you to be able to install hardware components and troubleshoot problems if the wireless connection doesn't happen automatically. This section gives you a quick overview. You should consult more detailed instructions based on your particular hardware, network configuration, and software. (You can find additional information about regular networks and Windows XP's Home Networking wizard in Chapter 24.)

If you want to set up a network in your home, follow these basic steps:

1. Purchase the equipment you need (as described in the preceding section).

2. Install the network card(s) on your computer(s) and install the drivers for the card(s). Your network card should come with a disk with the driver as well as a program you can run to set up and install the driver. If the disk doesn't have an installation program, you can use Windows XP's Add New Hardware wizard to search for and install the driver. See Chapter 19, "Upgrading Your Computer" for more information on adding new hardware.

3. Set up your hotspot. If your computers are already networked, you can simply add a Wireless Access Point (WAP) to that network. If you are setting up a new network, you need to buy and install a Wireless Access Point Router.

4. Configure the network. In most cases, you simply need to turn on the WAP and your computer(s). On newer systems, the network cards will find and automatically connect to the network. If the automatic connection doesn't happen, you need to run the software for the card, searching for the network connection and then accessing the connection. Check the specific steps for your particular network card and WAP.

> **tip**
>
> You can also find cell phones and personal digital assistants (PDAs) that provide wireless access to the Internet. These also connect using radio signals. Note that only very few Web sites are available through these types of connections. They usually only include text (because of the connection speed, as well as the size of the display area). Finally, navigating may be more difficult using these devices because you don't have as many keys to use to scroll through information.

How To Ensure Wireless Network Security

Some hotspots are open, meaning that anyone can access them. For instance, if an airport or a restaurant provides open wireless network access, anyone within the range of the network can access the hotspot. Ranges indoors are usually 150 to 300 feet, but can be shorter if the building interferes with the radio signals. Outdoor ranges can be as high as 1,000 feet, but can also vary.

If you set up a wireless network in your home or office, you should secure the hotspot so that others cannot access the connection (and any hardware or files on the network). To do so, you need to add a WEP (Wired Equivalent Privacy) key. This encryption system requires that you enter this key to access the network.

THE ABSOLUTE MINIMUM

If you have more than one computer or if you use a laptop, you may want to look into setting up a wireless network. Doing so enables you to connect to the Internet from anywhere within the range of your wireless network (usually 150–300 feet indoors). The following list includes the key points for wireless networking:

- If you want to set up a wireless network, you need to install wireless network cards on each of the computers you want to connect. You also need to purchase a Wireless Access Point Router.

- For the connection, you need to create a hotspot. For this, you need to purchase and set up a Wireless Access Point Router.

- You can connect your modem to the Wireless Access Point Router. Then, when your computers connect to the wireless network (through radio signals), they can also connect to the Internet.

- To ensure security on your wireless network, you can set up a WEP (Wireless Equivalent Privacy) key. Then, to get connected, you must enter the key.

7

Sending and Receiving Email

Electronic mail (or *email*) is a fast, convenient, and inexpensive way to stay connected. You can send a message to anyone with an email address, and it is sent immediately. You can send a message to a friend down the street or to a colleague across the world! The recipient can then, at his or her convenience, respond to your message.

In addition to typing messages, you can send pictures or other documents. For instance, you may want to submit an expense report to your home office, or send pictures of your new puppy to your family.

Windows XP includes a mail program called Outlook Express. You can use this program to create new mail as well as handle mail you have received. This chapter covers the basics of sending and receiving email with Outlook Express.

Setting Up Your Email Account

Before you can use Outlook Express, you need to set up your Internet connection and email account information. Setting up an Internet connection is covered in Chapter 5, "Getting Wired for Communication." You also need to set up information about your particular email account.

Setting Up an Outlook Express Account

The first time you start Outlook Express you are prompted to set up your email account. You should have handy all the connection information from your Internet service provider (ISP)—your username, email address, password, and technical information, such as the incoming mail server name (called the POP3, IMAP, or HTTP server) and the outgoing mail server (called the SMTP server). If you have problems or questions about this information, contact your Internet service provider.

Setting Up a Web Mail Account

If you want to be able to check your email from any location and from any computer, you can use a Web mail account. This address enables you to log on to the Internet from any site and access the mail. For instance, Hotmail (www.hotmail.com) is a popular Web mail provider.

To set up an account, go to the mail site and follow the specific instructions for that site. For example, Hotmail requires a Microsoft .NET passport account. You log on with this account and set up your mail account. You can then log on to this site and check your email by entering your user name and password to access your Web mailbox.

tip

One of the downsides of Web email is that you get a lot of junk mail; often, the site uses advertising to generate income. While you don't pay for the account, you may be bombarded with unsolicited email.

Checking Your Email

After your email account is set up, you can start Outlook Express and check your mail. To do so, follow these steps:

1. Click Start and then click E-mail (Outlook Express).

2. If prompted, connect to your Internet service provider. Outlook Express starts and checks your email server for any messages. Messages are then downloaded to Outlook Express. The number of new messages appears in

parentheses next to the Inbox in the Folders list. The message header pane lists all messages. Messages in bold have not yet been read. You can open and read any message in the message list (see Figure 7.1).

FIGURE 7.1

Start Outlook Express and then check your Inbox for new messages.

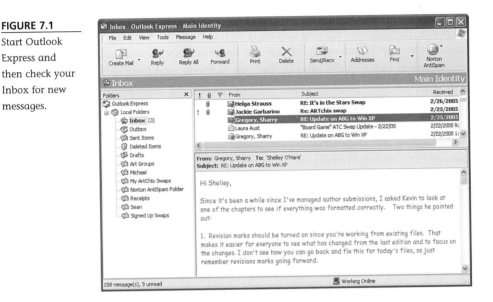

3. If necessary, in the Folders list of the Outlook Express window, select Inbox.

4. Double-click the message you want to read. The message you selected is then displayed in its own window (see Figure 7.2). You can display the previous or next message in the list with the Previous and Next buttons in the toolbar. To close the message, click the Close button.

FIGURE 7.2

You can open and review any of the messages you receive. Use the toolbar buttons to display other messages.

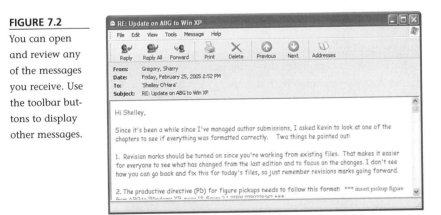

Sending Messages

In addition to reading messages you have received, you can send your own messages. You have several options for creating new mail. You can reply to an existing message. For instance, suppose that your sister emails you some dates for the upcoming family reunion. You can reply to her message. Replying is convenient because you don't have to type the email address. Also, the text of the original message is included in the reply so that the recipient understands the context of your response.

However, you aren't limited to simply replies. You can send messages to anyone with an email address. For instance, you may send a message to a family member who lives out of town, thereby keeping in touch via email, or you may email a company asking about a product or service.

As another option, you may forward a message you received to someone else. For instance, suppose that one of your co-workers sends you a funny joke. (You'll quickly get used to the many jokes that are swirling around the Internet.) You can then pass it along to your father, the joke master of the family.

This section covers how to create and send email messages.

tip

Many Web pages include email links. You can click an email link to send a message to someone at that site. You also can use Internet Explorer's toolbar buttons to send a link to a particular Web page or a copy of the Web page itself. See Chapter 8, "Browsing the Internet," for more information on these types of messages.

Responding to Email

You can easily respond to a message you've received. Outlook Express completes the address and subject lines for you and also includes the text of the original message; you can then type your response. You can reply to just the original sender or to the sender and any other recipients (anyone cc'd in the message). You also can forward the message to someone else.

To reply to a message you have received, follow these steps:

1. Display the message to which you want to reply.

note

The subject line is modified to include prefixes. Replies start with Re: in the subject line; forwarded messages start with Fw: in the subject line.

2. Do any of the following:

   To reply to just the sender, click the Reply button in the toolbar.

   To reply to the sender and any other recipients, click Reply All.

   To forward the message to another recipient, click Forward. Then type the email address for that person.

   The address and subject lines are completed, and the text of the original message is appended to the bottom of the reply message (see Figure 7.3).

> **tip**
>
> The easiest way to reply to and create new messages is by using the toolbar buttons. You can also use Message menu commands. You can select to create a new message, to reply to a sender, to forward a message, and other options.

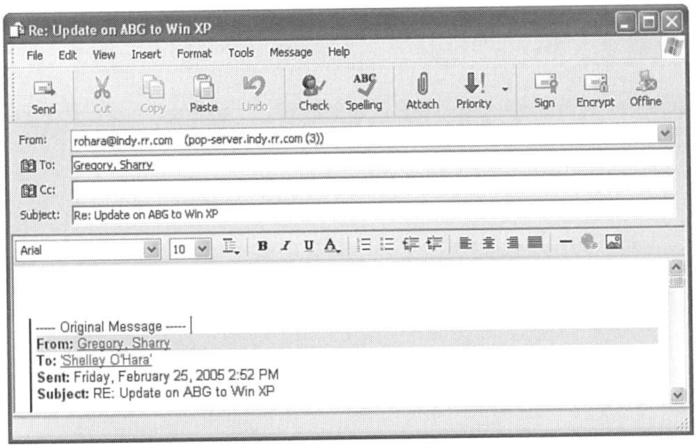

FIGURE 7.3

You can respond to a message by typing a reply and then sending the message.

3. Type your message.

4. Click the Send button. The message is placed in your Outbox and is then sent.

Depending on your email preferences, the message may be sent immediately or may be placed in the Outbox and sent when you click the Send/Recv button. Also, by default, Outlook Express saves a copy of all sent messages in the Sent Items folder. You can view this folder by clicking Sent Items in the Folders bar.

> **tip**
>
> You can customize your email setup. To change your email preferences, such as saving copies, use the Tools, Options command. See Chapter 15, "Customizing Email and Internet Explorer."

Creating New Mail

You aren't limited to replying to existing messages. You can send a message to anyone with an Internet email address. To do so, you must know that person's email address. You can type it or select it from your Outlook Express address book. In addition to the address, you can type a subject and the message.

Follow these steps to create and send a new email message:

1. In the Outlook Express window, click the Create Mail button. You'll then see a blank email message (see Figure 7.4).

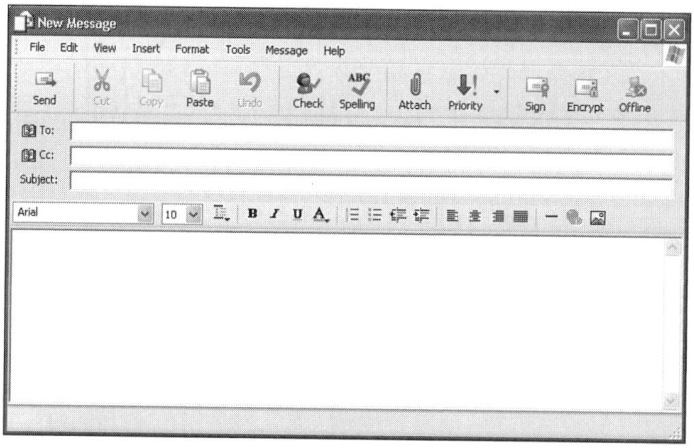

tip

Rather than typing the email address, you can set up an address book and select recipients by name (reducing the chance of a mistyped address).
See Chapter 15 for more information.

FIGURE 7.4

Create a new email message and then complete the To and Subject fields and type the message.

2. Type the recipient's address. Addresses are in the format *username@domainname.ext* (for example, sohara@msn.com). Then press Tab.

3. To send a carbon copy (cc) to another recipient, type an address for that person and press Tab. To skip the Cc field, simply press Tab again.

4. Type a subject in the Subject text box and then press Tab.

5. Type your message.

6. Click the Send button. Like when replying to a message, the message is either sent immediately or placed in your

caution

If you enter an incorrect address and the message is not delivered, you usually receive a Failure to Deliver notice. You can then check and correct the address and resend the message.

Outbox and sent when you click Send/Recv, as determined by your email preferences.

Sending New Messages

Depending on how Outlook Express is set up, your messages may be sent immediately when you click the Send button, or they may be placed in your Outbox, waiting to be sent. You might save up all your messages and send them at once. Using the Outbox also enables you to compose messages offline (when you are not connected). You can then get connected and send the messages.

Keep in mind these tips when sending messages:

- The Folders list displays the mail folders as well as information about the contents. For instance, if you have messages in your Outbox, the Outbox folder appears in bold, and the number of messages to be sent is listed in parentheses after the folder name. You can view these messages by clicking Outbox in the Folders list.

- If you have not yet sent a message, you can cancel it by opening the Outbox and deleting the message. (See "Deleting and Undeleting Messages" later in this chapter.) After you send a message, you cannot retrieve it.

- You can control what is included with a reply and a forwarded message, whether copies of your sent messages are saved, and when messages are sent. To do so, click Tools and then Options. Use the tabs in the Options dialog box. For more information on mail options, see Chapter 15.

- If your messages are stored in the Outbox, you can click the Send/Recv button in Outlook Express to send them. To send messages, you must be connected. If you are not connected, you are prompted to do so. Follow the logon procedure for your particular ISP. The messages are then sent.

tip

You can use a special pre-designed format for messages (called stationery) as well as format the text. Because some mail programs may be unable to display your formatting choices and because stationery slows down the receipt of the message, I usually recommend keeping the message plain and simple. You do have options for changing the appearance, though, and they are covered briefly in Chapter 15.

caution

If you are angry or upset and fire off a message, it's usually best to let the message sit for some time before sending it. Wait overnight or at least a few hours. Then, read your message and make any edits. Because you cannot convey tone of voice, facial expressions, or body language through typed comments, your message might not achieve your desired intent. Double-check any sensitive messages before sending them.

Sending and Handling Attachments

In addition to the text of a message, you can also attach a file. As mentioned, you might email an expense report to your home office, or perhaps you have pictures you want to share with your family and friends. (You learn more about pictures in Chapter 12, "Working with Photographs and Movies.") This section covers how to attach and send files as well as how to handle files sent to your email address.

Attaching a File to a Message

If you want to share a file with someone else, you can attach it to an email message. Keep in mind that the recipient must have the appropriate software to open and work with that file. For instance, if you email an Excel worksheet to a co-worker, that person must have Excel (or a program that can open Excel files) to access the file.

To attach a file, follow these steps:

1. Click the Attach button in the email message window. You'll see the Insert Attachment dialog box.

2. Open the folder that contains the file you want to attach. The dialog box includes tools similar to those you use for opening a document (covered in Chapter 2, "Saving and Printing Your Work"). You can use the Look in drop-down list to select another drive or folder. You can click the Up One Level button to navigate up through the folder structure. You can double-click any listed folder to display its contents.

3. Select the file to attach (see Figure 7.5).

FIGURE 7.5

Browse through the folders on your computer and then select the file(s) you want to attach.

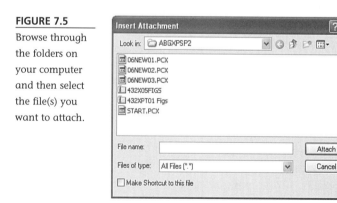

4. Click the Attach button. The file attachment is then listed in the Attach text box of the message (see Figure 7.6).

FIGURE 7.6

Your attachment is listed in the message header.

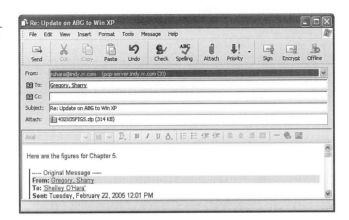

5. Click the Send button to send the message and the file attachment.

When sending attachments, keep a few pointers in mind:

■ You can attach more than one file, but keep in mind that downloading attachments takes time. Also, some ISPs have a limit to the size of file attachments. You can send files individually to get around the limit, or consider compressing the files. This topic is covered in Chapter 3, "Managing Files."

■ If you need to send a large file or several files, create a compressed folder and then send the folder. You learn more about compressing files in Chapter 18.

Opening a File Attachment

If someone sends you a file attachment, you can either open it or save it to disk. Messages with file attachments are indicated with a paper clip icon. Note that to open the attachment, you must have a program that can open and display that particular file type.

Follow these steps to open an attachment:

1. Double-click the message. The file attachment is listed in the Attach text box (see Figure 7.7).

2. Double-click the attachment icon. You'll see the Mail Attachment dialog box (see Figure 7.8).

3. Click the Open button. The attachment is then opened.

caution

One way computer viruses spread is through email attachments. Before you open any file—from strangers or people you know—scan the file for viruses. See "Checking a File Attachment" later in this section.

FIGURE 7.7

You can receive messages with attachments.

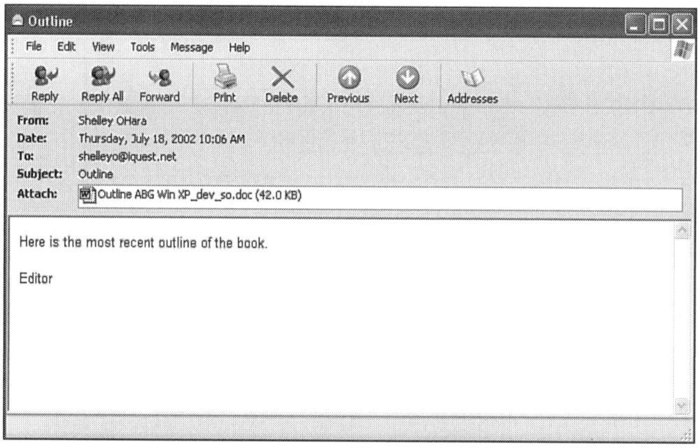

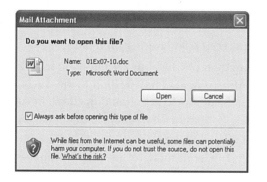

FIGURE 7.8

You are prompted to confirm opening the attachment.

Saving a File Attachment

For some attachments, you may want to save the document to your computer. For instance, if someone emails you a document to revise, you can save it to your hard drive. Like saving other documents (covered in Chapter 2), you can specify the drive and folder in which to save the file.

Follow these steps to save a file attachment:

1. Right-click the file attachment and click the Save As command. You'll see the Save Attachment As dialog box (see Figure 7.9).

2. Change to the drive and folder in which you want to save the attachment. You can use the Up One Level button or the Save in drop-down list to change to another folder or drive.

> **caution**
>
> You may set up some file types to open automatically. For instance, some forwarded email messages come with attachments that contain the forwarded message. If you have told Windows XP to go ahead and open this file type automatically, you may open the file when you double-click. To select a different option (save, for instance), right-click the attachment and then select Open or Save.

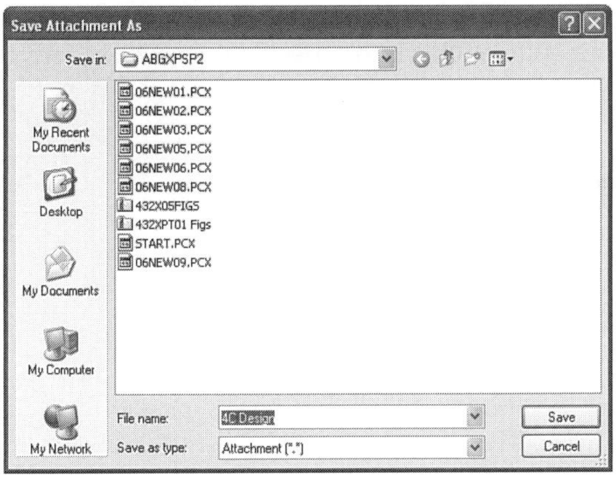

FIGURE 7.9

You are prompted to select a drive and folder in which to save the attachment.

3. Click the Save button. The file is then saved to the drive and folder, and you can access and open this file from this new location.

Checking a File Attachment

One way that viruses are spread from computer to computer is via email attachments—usually program (or .exe) files, but also through other file types. If you share files with someone, you should check each file attachment for viruses before you open the file or run the program.

Outlook Express evaluates some file attachments and warns you if it suspects a danger. Messages flagged with a yellow caution indicate an attachment type that could pose a risk. (Outlook sees if the attachment contains computer code, a possible indicator of a virus.)

You shouldn't just rely on Outlook Express, however. You should install and use a virus program such as Norton Antivirus. (You learn more about Internet Security programs in Chapter 8.)

With a virus protection program, you can set up the program to automatically scan files and check for viruses. (The program will also scan files from a removable source such as a floppy disk.) You can control how such a program handles email. For instance, Figure 7.10 shows Norton Antivirus options for dealing

tip

If you always want to open this file type, uncheck the Always Ask Before Opening This Type of File check box.

tip

If the message contains multiple attachments, you can save them all. To do so, click the Save All command. In the dialog box that appears, click the Browse button and select the drive and folder in which to save all the attachments. Select the folder from the folder list and click OK. Then click Save.

with email. You can also run the program and ask it to check the file. To set the defaults or to scan your system, check the specific instructions for your particular virus program.

FIGURE 7.10
You can set up your virus program to scan incoming and outgoing mail.

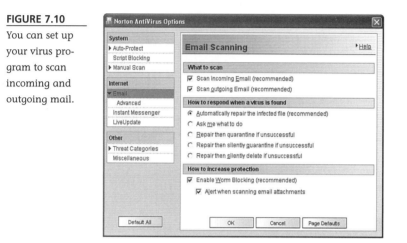

If you find a virus, often the program can safely remove it and protect your computer from harm. Follow the specific instructions for your program on handling the virus.

Handling Messages

Your Inbox will quickly fill up with messages. To keep Outlook Express streamlined, get in the habit of handling messages and then deleting them or saving them, as needed. Delete old, unneeded messages. Move messages you want to save to a special folder. This section includes some of the options you have for dealing with messages, including deleting messages, moving or copying messages, printing messages, handling junk email, and more.

Deleting and Undeleting Messages

As part of keeping your Inbox uncluttered, you can delete messages. In the Outlook Express window, select the message you want to delete or open the message you want to delete, and click the Delete button. When you delete a message, it is not deleted, but is moved to the Deleted Items folder.

If needed, you can undelete a message. Follow these steps:

1. In the Folders list, click the Deleted Items folder. You'll see the messages that have been deleted.

2. Click the message you want to undelete.

3. Drag the message from the message header pane to one of the folders in the Folders list. For instance, you can drag the message from Deleted Items to Inbox. For more information on moving and copying messages, see "Organizing Messages" later in this section.

To permanently delete a message, open the Deleted Items folder, select the message, and click the Delete button or press the Delete key. You are then prompted to confirm the deletion. Click Yes to permanently delete the message.

tip

If you want to delete all messages in this folder, click Edit and then select Empty 'Deleted Items' Folder. Confirm the deletion by clicking Yes. Be sure that this is what you want to do. When messages are deleted this way, you cannot retrieve them.

Printing Messages

On occasion, you might want to print a hard copy of a message. For instance, suppose that someone sends you directions to a party. You can print the directions and take them with you. You also might want to print and save a hard copy of a message with important information, such as an online order confirmation.

To print a message, follow these steps:

1. Select the message from the Outlook Express window or open the message.

2. Click the Print button. You'll see the Print dialog box (see Figure 7.11).

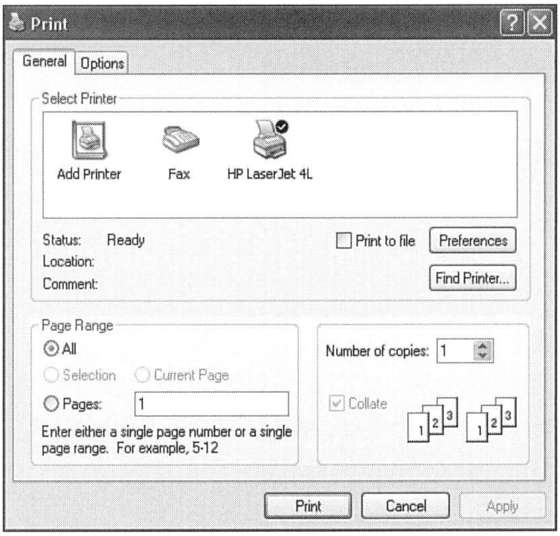

FIGURE 7.11
Select the printing options for the message.

3. Click Print to print the message.

Organizing Messages

If you think you need to keep some of your messages, consider creating a mail folder and storing the messages in that folder. Doing so keeps your Inbox uncluttered. You can just keep messages that you need to handle in the Inbox and either delete, print, or move other messages out of the Inbox folder to another folder. For instance, suppose that you have several business messages that you need to keep. You can set up a folder for these messages and then move them from the Inbox (or other folder) to the business folder. As another example, you might want to keep copies of the funny jokes you receive. You can set up a joke folder and move joke messages to that folder. You can use Outlook Express to both create a new folder and move or copy items to different folders.

tip

Outlook Express sets up several mail folders for you, including Inbox, Outbox, Deleted Items, Sent Items, and Drafts. Some messages are automatically moved or saved to these folders. For instance, when you delete a message from your Inbox, it is simply moved to the Deleted Items folder.

To create a folder, follow these steps:

1. Click Local Folders in the Folders list. Doing so ensures that the new folder will be placed at the same level as the existing folders.

2. Click File, New, Folder. You'll see the Create Folder dialog box (see Figure 7.12).

FIGURE 7.12

Type the folder name here to create a new mail folder.

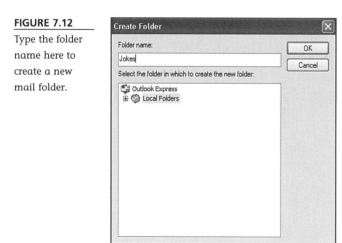

3. Type the folder name and click OK to create the folder.

After the folder is created, you can move or copy messages to it (or any other folder). To do so, follow these steps:

1. Select the message you want to copy or move.

2. Click the Edit menu and select Move to Folder or Copy to Folder. You'll see either the Move or Copy dialog box (see Figure 7.13). The dialog boxes are identical except for their names; both list the mail folders.

3. Expand the Folders list by clicking the plus sign next to Local Folders. Then click the folder in which you want to place the selected message.

4. Click OK to move or copy the message.

> **tip**
>
> You also can nest mail folders within existing folders. For instance, you can create business and personal folders within the Inbox. To do so, click the Inbox for the first step or expand the Folders list in the dialog box by clicking the plus sign next to Local Folders and then clicking the folder you want.

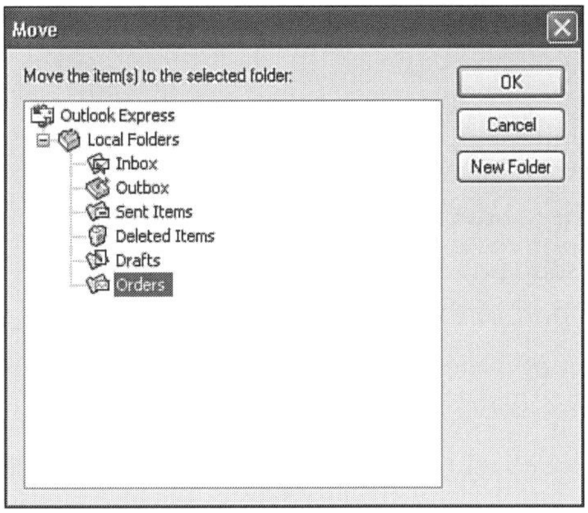

FIGURE 7.13

Select the folder to which you want to move or copy the selected message.

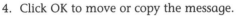

Finding Messages

If you don't (and sometimes even when you do!) organize your messages, you may find it difficult to find a message you received. For instance, suppose that you placed an order for a product via the Internet and kept the order confirmation message. Because the product has not arrived, you want to review the confirmation. Rather then sifting through various folders and messages, you can search for a message.

> **tip**
>
> You also can drag a message from the message header pane to the appropriate folder in the Folders list of the main Outlook Express window to move a message.

To help you find a message, Outlook Express includes a Find command. You can use this command to search for messages by matching the sender, the recipient, the subject, or a word or phrase in the content of the message. Follow these steps to search for a message:

1. Select the folder to search in the Folders list. If you don't know which folder contains the message, click Local Folders to search all the folders.

2. Click Edit, Find, Message. You'll see the Find Message dialog box (see Figure 7.14).

FIGURE 7.14

Enter your search requirements in this dialog box.

3. Click in the text box next to the item for which you want to search and then type or select a value. You can do any of the following:

   To search for a message based on the sender, click in the From text box and type all or part of the sender's name.

   To search for a message based on whom it was sent to, click in the To text box and type all or part of the recipient's name.

   To match the subject of a message, click in the Subject text box and type all or part of the message subject.

   If you don't know the exact sender or subject, click in the Message text box and type a unique word or phrase from the message content. (Typing a unique word or phrase helps limit the matches to those of interest.)

   If you don't know the contents or details of the message, but you know when it was sent, select a date. You can select to view messages received before or after a certain date.

   To search for messages that have attachments or that were flagged for attention, check these check boxes.

4. If you selected Local Folders for step 1, make sure that the Include subfolders text box is checked to search all the folders.

5. Click Find Now. Outlook Express then searches the messages and displays any matches in the lower half of the dialog box (see Figure 7.15). You can double-click any message to open it.

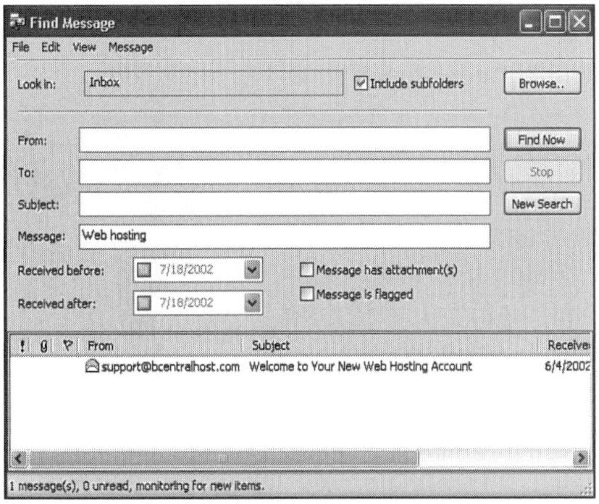

FIGURE 7.15

You can search for messages in any of your mail folders.

Handling Junk Mail

As mentioned in the section on attachments, one way that computer viruses spread is through email. You should purchase and use an antivirus program to scan and check not only email attachments, but other documents that you share (for instance, via a floppy disk).

Another downside to email is the amount of electronic junk mail (called *spam*) that you receive. You can easily get unwanted messages from people and companies. To handle this type of mail, you can block senders and use an antispam program.

Blocking Senders

Outlook Express enables you to block mail from certain senders. If you receive an email message from someone on your blocked list, it is placed in the Deleted Items folder. The message is in boldface type so that you can find and review the message. If it's not spam, you can undelete it. (Sometimes, messages get tagged as junk mail by accident.)

To block a sender, follow these steps:

1. Select a message from that sender.

2. Open the Message menu and click the Block Sender command. You are then asked how to handle existing messages in your mail folders.

3. Click Yes to delete all the messages or No to keep the messages but block the sender.

If you want to unblock a sender, you can remove him or her from your Blocked Senders List. Click Tools, Message Rules, Blocked Senders List. Select the sender and then click Remove. Click OK to close the dialog box.

Using an Antispam Program

Outlook Express's spam features are not that extensive, so you may want to use a special program for handling junk mail. Many antivirus programs or Internet security suites include features for dealing with junk mail. For instance, if you have Norton Internet Security, you can use Norton AntiSpam to handle junk mail. This program adds an icon to your mail program, and you can use this program to flag certain messages as junk mail.

When it receives messages it thinks are junk mail or that have been flagged as junk mail, Norton AntiSpam places them in a special junk mail folder. You can open this folder and review and delete messages as needed.

If you have an antispam program, follow the specific instructions for turning on and config-uring that program. Figure 7.16, for instance, shows the options for turning on Norton AntiSpam. You also can create a blocked sender list (like in Outlook Express), and you can cre-ate rules that will find and flag certain mes-sages as spam. To do so, create mail rules from the Spam Rules tab. Figure 7.17 shows the first step in creating a spam mail rule. You enter the text to match and in the subsequent steps select what to search (entire email, sender's name, sub-ject line, recipient, and/or body text) and how to classify the message (as spam or not spam).

note

It's virtually impossible to get rid of all unwanted mail. One thing you can do to keep spam at a minimum is to carefully check any information you agree to when you visit a site or purchase an item online. For instance, some sites include a check box (which is usually checked) that in effect says "go ahead and send me information about new services and products." After you are on one mailing list, your name pops up on many other lists. Uncheck any invitations for free newsletters or product infor-mation. Also, be careful when sub-mitting personal information such as your address.

Norton
AntiSpam offers
a range of spam
filtering levels.

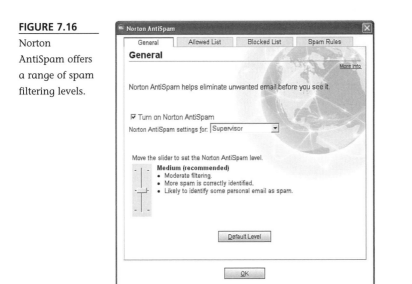

FIGURE 7.17

You can tell
Norton
AntiSpam what
phrases to look
for in your
incoming
messages.

Exiting and Disconnecting

When you are not working online, you should exit your mail program and log off (if
you have a dial-up account). To do so, click the Close button for the Outlook Express
window.

If you have a dial-up account, you should be prompted to log off the connection.
Select Yes or Disconnect. (If you are not prompted, right-click the connection icon in
the taskbar and select Disconnect.) If you have a 24/7 connection and don't log off,
you can simply exit Outlook Express to close the mail program.

THE ABSOLUTE MINIMUM

This chapter covers the basics of using Outlook Express, the mail program included with Windows XP. With this program (and an Internet provider), you can send email messages to and receive messages from all over the world. Email is quick and free! Keep in mind the following key points about Outlook Express and email features:

- The first step to using Outlook Express is to set up a mail account. Use the information from your ISP to set up your mail account. The steps vary depending on the provider and the type of provider.

- To check your mail, start Outlook Express. New mail messages are listed in your Inbox. You can open any messages by double-clicking them.

- You have several choices for creating new mail: You can respond to messages you have received, you can forward messages, and you can create new messages. The fastest way to do so is by using the toolbar buttons in the Outlook Express program window.

- In addition to typing messages, you can attach files to send, such as pictures. You may also receive email messages with attachments, which you can open or save to your computer. You should check any file attachments you receive for viruses.

- Try to keep your Inbox uncluttered. You can do so by deleting messages you no longer need, setting up folders and moving messages that you want to save to those folders, and printing and saving hard copies if needed.

- If you cannot find a message you received by looking through the various mail folders, you can search for a message using the Edit, Find, Message command. You can search by sender, recipient, subject, or content.

- One way to handle junk email (or spam) is to block certain senders. You also can use a spam program such as Norton AntiSpam.

8

BROWSING THE INTERNET

The Internet is a huge resource for information and entertainment. You can find sites with current news, financial data, online stores, music, computer articles and help information, and much, much more. You simply cannot sum up all the content you can find on the Internet. You have to experience it yourself.

This chapter covers how to log on to the Internet and then navigate from site to site using several methods.

Getting Started with Internet Explorer

To access the Internet, you need a program called a *Web browser*. Luckily enough, Windows XP includes Internet Explorer, which is a Web browser. You can use Internet Explorer to go to and view Web pages.

To start Internet Explorer, follow these steps:

1. Click Start and then click Internet.

2. If prompted, enter your username and password (some information might have been completed for you), and then click the Connect button. Depending on the type of connection, you may not need to complete this step.

   Windows then connects to your ISP and displays the Internet Explorer window. At this point, you see your start page, usually the MSN home page, in the program window (see Figure 8.1).

tip

Before you can take advantage of all the benefits of the Internet, you must set up your Internet connection. The specifics of setting this up depend on your type of connection and your provider. Therefore, follow the specific instructions you received from your Internet provider. You can learn more about getting connected in Chapter 5, "Getting Wired for Communication."

FIGURE 8.1

Take a look the various tools in the Internet Explorer program window.

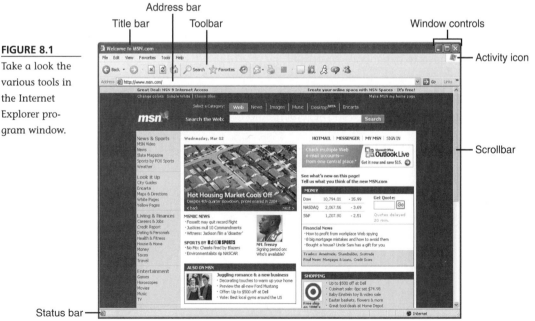

Understanding the Internet Explorer Window

Like most programs, the Internet Explorer window has a toolbar with various buttons to help you navigate from page to page. Before you start on your Internet journey, take a few minutes to look closely at the program window, including the following key items:

- **Title bar**—Like other program windows, Internet Explorer displays a title bar at the top. This title bar lists the title for the current page.

- **Window controls**—In the upper-right corner you see window control buttons for changing the size of the window. You can close the window (and exit Internet Explorer). You can minimize the window as another option. For information on changing the size of the window, see Chapter 1, "Getting Started with Windows XP."

- **Activity icon**—Right beneath the window controls, you see an icon with the Microsoft Windows XP logo. This icon moves when Internet Explorer is busy. For example, displaying some pages (especially pages with many graphics) can take a while. You may think that the program is stuck. A good way to see whether the program is stuck or just simply busy is to take a look at this icon. If the flag is moving, the program is still busy trying to display the page.

- **Toolbar**—Underneath the title bar and menu bar, you see a row of buttons. Again, like many other programs, Internet Explorer includes a toolbar with buttons for frequently used commands. See the next section, "Using the Toolbar," for a description of each of the toolbar buttons.

- **Address bar**—The address bar lists the address of the current page. You can type another address to go to a particular site. Using the address bar is covered later in "Typing a Web Address."

tip

You can select a different start page as covered in Chapter 15, "Customizing Email and Internet Explorer."

caution

If you have problems connecting—the line is busy, for example—try again. If you continue to have problems, check with your ISP.

tip

If the page is taking too long to display and you want to cancel the display, click the Stop button.

■ **Scrollbar**—If the page contains more than one screen of information (and most do), you see scrollbars along the right side of the window. You can scroll down the page by clicking the down arrow or by dragging the scroll box (the colored part of the scrollbar) up or down. To scroll up through a page, click the up scroll arrow.

■ **Status bar**—The status bar appears along the bottom of the program window. This displays link information. For instance, if you place your mouse pointer over a link (more on links later), you see the address of the linked page or site. If Internet Explorer is busy downloading data for the page, you see the status of this activity in the status bar.

tip

You can customize what appears onscreen. For instance, you may also see a Links toolbar. For more information on customizing Internet Explorer, see Chapter 15.

Using the Toolbar

The most common way to navigate from page to page is to use the toolbar buttons. To use most buttons, you simply click the buttons themselves. Other buttons have a down arrow next to them. For these buttons, you can click the down arrow and then select your choice from the button menu. For example, if you click the down arrow next to the Mail button, you see commands for mailing pages (see Figure 8.2).

FIGURE 8.2

Some buttons include a drop-down menu for making a selection.

Some buttons open a bar on the left part of the program window. You then use the options in this bar to display other pages. For instance, you can click the Media button to display a list of media sites. You can click the Search button to display a list of search tools (more on searching in the next chapter). As well as using any of the links within the bar, you can scroll through the bar (click the scroll arrows or drag the scroll box), resize the bar (drag the bar border), and close the bar (click the Close button).

Table 8.1 lists each of the buttons and provides a description of each one.

> **tip**
>
> If you are unsure what a button does, you can display its ScreenTip name. To do so, place the mouse pointer on the border of a button. The button name should pop up, but don't click it.

Table 8.1   Internet Explorer Buttons

Button	Name	Click To...
	Back	Go to the last page you visited. You can click the button several times to go back several pages. You can also click the down arrow next to the button and select a page from the drop-down list. The same is true for the Forward button.
	Forward	Go forward a page. This button is available only if you have clicked Back to go back a page.
	Stop	Stop the display of a page. Use this button if the page is taking too long to display or if you change your mind.
	Refresh	Redisplay the page, refreshing the data on that page.
	Home	Return to your home page.
	Search	Display the Search bar to search for a site. See Chapter 9, "Searching the Internet" for more information.
	Favorites	Display a list of favorite sites. See Chapter 15.
	Media	Display a Media guide with access to music, videos, and other media features.
	History	Display a list of recently visited sites. See "Using the History List" later in this chapter.
	Mail	Email a page or the link to a page. See "Emailing Web Pages" later in this chapter. For more information on all email messages, see Chapter 7, "Sending and Receiving Email."
	Print	Print the current Web page.

Table 8.1 (continued)

Button	Name	Click To...
⊠	Edit	Open the page in a Web editing program. If you are interested in Web publishing, try one of Que's many guides to this topic, including *10 Minute Guide to Microsoft FrontPage 2002*.
▭	Discuss	Join a discussion server for sharing comments about different topics.

Viewing the Page Content

Now that you are familiar with the program window, you can take a look at the page itself.

The first page you see when you log on to the Internet is your *start* or *home page*. (Both names are commonly used to refer to that first page.) Your home page will vary. Your ISP may display its opening page as your home page. For instance, if you have a cable connection, you may see your Internet cable provider's page (such as Road Runner for Time Warner's cable connections). You may see MSN, the home page for Microsoft's online service. Otherwise, you may see a page you have selected yourself. You can customize the home page by selecting the page you want (see Chapter 15).

tip

If you have Instant Messenger programs set up, such as America Online Instant Messenger (AIM) or Windows Messenger, you'll also see icons for these tools. You can click these to view and send online messages.

Regardless of what page you see, all home pages (and almost all pages you visit on the Internet) have the same basic elements. Here's what you can expect to find in the content area of the Internet Explorer window:

- **Links**—The great thing about the Internet is how information is linked. You can click a link to view other information. For instance, you may see a headline on a page. By clicking the headline, you can view the complete story. You learn more about using links in the next section.

- **Information**—You also see articles about various topics, similar to the front page of a newspaper. You can review any of the articles posted on the page.

- **Advertisements**—Nearly all Web content is provided free of charge. To finance this free information, most sites sell advertising. You may see ads at the top, bottom, or sides of the page.

- **Table of contents**—Many sites provide a quick table of contents to the site. You can jump to other pages at the site using this table. These may also be named *channels* or *categories*. For instance, in Figure 8.1, you see the MSN channels. Here, information is organized into topics such as Business, News, and so on. You can find these table of contents links along the top, side, or bottom of the page. Sometimes they appear on the page in more than one place.

- **Search button**—Because a site may include a lot of information, you may find a Search button on the page. Use this Search button to search for particular content at that site (see Figure 8.3). You may also see a Search button for searching the Internet—that is, one that is not limited to just content at the site. Chapter 9 is devoted to the topic of searching.

- **Resource features**—Many sites include useful resource features. For instance, maps are common resource tools. You can click the link for maps to get directions to a place. Directories of businesses and other listings (such as the Yellow Pages) are other common resources. You can use these directories, for instance, to find the address or phone number of a company.

caution

Don't be surprised if you see pop-up windows with advertisements when you log on. Usually, these are displayed in their own windows. You can click the Close button for that window to close the ad. Some have pop-behind ads, ads that appear behind the program window and show up when you close it. Again, you can click the Close button to close any advertisement windows. You can purchase and use software to block these intrusions. See "Ensuring Internet Security and Privacy" later in this chapter.

FIGURE 8.3

You can navigate around a site by searching for a topic or item.

Search the Web

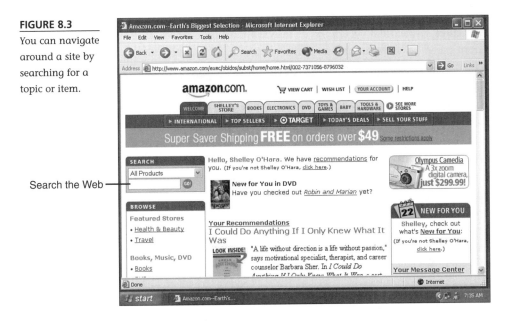

- **Entertainment**—Many sites have multimedia elements. You can listen to music, view a short video, check out animations, and more.

- **Custom information**—Many home or start pages let you customize what appears on the opening page. For example, you might display local weather or news stories. You might display your horoscope for the day. The process for customizing your home page depends on that particular site. Look for links on your home page for specific information on customizing the contents.

Now that you know what to expect on your start page, you are ready to jump from that page to other sites. Keep in mind that sites are constantly changing. Also, most sites follow a similar structure—that is, they have articles, a table of contents (sometimes called a *site map*), advertisements, and so on. The next section covers how to navigate from page to page using links.

tip

The preceding list gives you a quick overview of what you can expect. You'll find much more information and many more links at your site. Also, the content is frequently updated. The best way to get a sense of what's available is to explore and experiment with your own home page.

Using Links to Navigate

Information on the Internet is easy to browse because documents contain links to other pages, documents, and sites. A *link* is a text or graphic reference to another site. Links, also called *hyperlinks*, usually appear underlined and sometimes in a different color. Images can also be links.

Links are what makes the Internet so valuable, as you can use links to jump to related sites. For example, if you see a link for Careers (refer to Figure 8.1, which contains a Careers & Jobs link), you can click that link to view career-related pages. At the Careers page, you may see links for resume tips and job postings (see Figure 8.4). You can click one of these links to go to that page. Jumping from link to link is called different things: *navigating*, *surfing*, or *browsing*. Using links is simple and is the best way to become familiar with the wealth of information on the Internet.

You can click a link on the current page to view the page associated with that link. Sometimes the link takes you to another section in the current page. Sometimes the link takes you to another page at the current Web site. Other times, clicking a link takes you to an entirely different site. Half the fun of browsing is exploring all types of topics and levels of information using links.

FIGURE 8.4

You can click
links to jump to
different pages;
here you see
MSN's Careers
page.

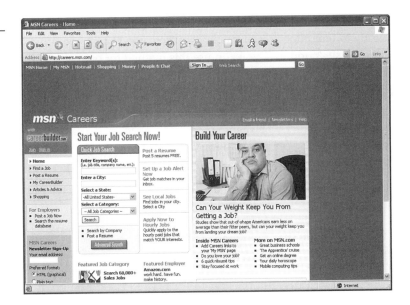

FIGURE 8.4

You can click links to jump to different pages; here you see MSN's Careers page.

To go to a link, simply click it. You can jump from link to link until you find the information you seek. If you get too far astray, remember that you can use the Back button to return to the previous page. You can click the Back button as many times as needed to return several pages back. You can also click the down arrow next to the Back button and select the site from the list.

If you have gone back to a page, you can also move forward again to pages you have viewed. Use the Forward button to do so.

tip

You can tell when text or an image is a link because when you point to it, the pointer changes to a hand with a pointing finger, and the address to that link appears in the status bar.

Finally, if you get lost or want to start over from the home page, you can click the Home button to go back to your start page.

Typing a Web Address

Browsing is a great way to explore the Internet, especially if you are not exactly sure what you are looking for. You can browse around to see what information or resources you can find. Think of browsing as flipping through the pages in a book to get a sense of the content or looking through the table of contents. Browsing is like an expedition, and you are not always sure where you'll end up!

If you don't want to browse, you can go directly to a site. Typing a site's address is the fastest way to get to that site. In keeping with the book metaphor, typing an address would be similar to looking up the page number in the index and then going directly to that page. When you know where you want to go—that is, when you know the site's address—you can use this method for accessing content on the Internet.

Every page on the Internet has an address (sometimes called a *URL* or *uniform resource locator*), and this address follows a certain naming method. For instance, the address to Que's Web site is `http://www.quepublishing.com`. The URL breaks down like this:

- The first part is the protocol (usually `http://`, *hypertext transfer protocol*) and indicates that the site is a graphical, multimedia page. This designation indicates a file site. You do not have to type that part (`http://`) of the address. Internet Explorer assumes that you want to go to an HTTP site.

- The next part of the address is the host name (usually www for Web servers). When you type this part, you usually can leave off the www.

- The most important part of the address is the domain name (which also includes the extension). The domain name is the name of the site and is usually the name or abbreviation of the company or individual. For instance, Que's domain name is `quepublishing`.

- The extension indicates the site type. Common extensions include `.com`, `.net`, `.gov`, `.edu`, or `.mil` (commercial, network resources, government, educational, or military, respectively).

- The address (or URL) might also include a path (a list of folders) to the document.

You can find Web site addresses in advertisements, newspaper or magazine articles, and other media sources.

note

Another common protocol is `ftp://` (*file transfer protocol*). This type of site is commonly used for sharing files. Also, `https://` is the protocol used for secure sites. See "Ensuring Internet Security and Privacy" later in this chapter.

tip

Most Web site names are some form of the site or company name, so often you can simply guess. For instance, to go to the NFL site, type **www.nfl.com**. If the address is incorrect, you'll see a page explaining that the site is not available. You can try another version of the name or search for the site as covered in Chapter 9.

To go to an address, follow these steps:

1. Click in the Address bar.

2. Type the address of the site you want to visit and press Enter. Internet Explorer then displays the page for that address.

Using Shortcuts for Web Browsing

To help you get to sites quickly, Internet Explorer provides several shortcuts, including using the Favorites list, the History list, and others.

tip

If you have typed a specific address before, you can type only its first few letters; Internet Explorer will display the rest. Press Enter to let Internet Explorer complete the address for you. This feature is called AutoComplete.

Setting Up a Favorites List

If you find a site that you especially like, you might want a quick way to return to it without having to browse from link to link or having to remember the address. Fortunately, Internet Explorer enables you to build a list of favorite sites and to access those sites by clicking them in the list.

To add a site to your Favorites list, follow these steps:

1. Display the Web site that you want to add to your list.

2. Open the Favorites menu and click the Add to Favorites command.

3. In the Add Favorite dialog box, shown in Figure 8.5, type a name for the page (if you're not satisfied with the default name that is provided).

FIGURE 8.5

Add favorite sites to your Favorites list.

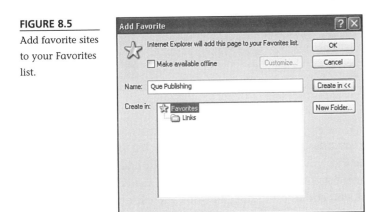

4. Click OK.

After you have added a site to your Favorites list, you can go to that site by following these steps:

1. Click the Favorites button.

2. In the Favorites bar that is displayed (see Figure 8.6), click the site you want to visit. The selected favorite site is displayed in the main window.

3. Click the Close button in the Favorites bar to close this pane of the window.

tip

Rather than having one long list of favorites, you might organize your list into folders. For instance, you might have a folder for shopping sites, and you might have a folder for sports sites. You can create and select folders when adding favorites by clicking the Create in button.

FIGURE 8.6

Use the Favorites list to go quickly to your most visited sites.

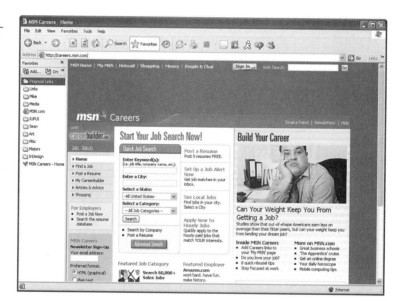

Using the History List

In addition to using the Favorites list, you can use the History list to go to a site. If you recently visited a site that you liked but can't remember its address, you can view the History list, which lists the sites and pages you have visited in the last several weeks. From this list, you can find the site you want and click the link to go to that site.

Follow these steps to view and go to a site in the History list:

1. Click the History button. The History bar is displayed.

2. Click Today to view sites visited today. Otherwise, click one of the weeks you want (last week, two weeks ago, three weeks ago). The list expands to show sites for the time period you selected (see Figure 8.7).

tip

You can also display the Favorites menu and select the site from this list. For help with organizing your Favorites list into folders as well as deleting or renaming sites in the list, see Chapter 15.

FIGURE 8.7

Use the History list to go to a site you have visited recently.

3. Click the site you want to visit. The list expands again to display pages (if applicable) you have visited at that particular site.

4. Click the specific page at that site. That page is displayed.

5. Click the Close button to close the History bar.

tip

As another shortcut, you can click the down arrow at the far right of the address bar to display a list of sites you have visited by typing the address. You can then click any listed site to go to that site.

Working with Web Pages

Usually, you go to a Web site and review the information. When doing so, you may want to email the link (or the page itself) to someone. For instance, you may email a book review to your mom. You may also print a page. For example, you may print an order form to order a product via the telephone or fax. You can also work with the text and images on a page. As an example, you can copy an image from a Web page to a document. For example, you might copy a logo to include in a report. This section covers some of the basic tasks you can do with Web pages and their contents.

Emailing Web Pages

Often in your Web browsing, you come across sites that might be of interest to others. Internet Explorer makes it convenient to send a link or the actual page to others. (You can also open your mailbox and review your mail, using the Read Mail command.)

Follow these steps to send a link or a page via email:

1. Click the down arrow next to the Mail button.

2. Click Send a Link or Send Page. Internet Explorer displays a new mail message.

3. Complete the address and click Send to send the message (see Figure 8.8).

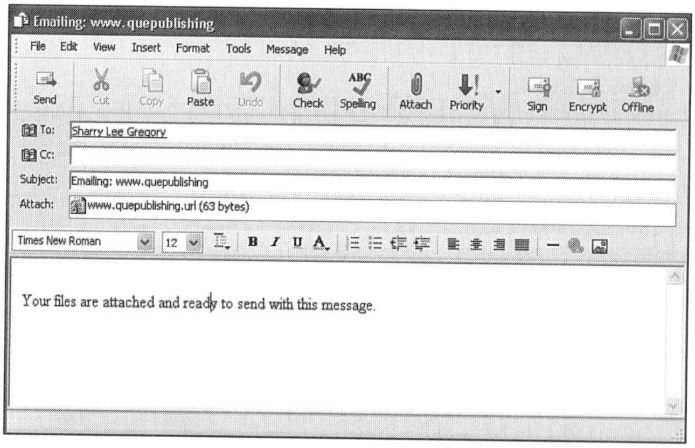

FIGURE 8.8

You can email a page or a link to a page.

If you send the page, the recipient can view the contents of the page, but usually cannot use any of the links. (This is like taking a snapshot of the page.) If you send a link, the link is included as an attachment or as a link within the message text. The recipient can open the attachment or click the link to go to that page. The recipient can then access any of the information and links at that site.

Printing Web Pages

In addition to emailing pages, you can also print Web pages. For instance, suppose that you are doing research on Leonardo da Vinci and you find a site with a detailed bibliography. Rather than reading this information onscreen, you might want to print and review the information away from your computer. To do so, you can print the page(s).

To print a Web page, follow these steps:

1. Click the Print button. The Print dialog box appears (see Figure 8.9).

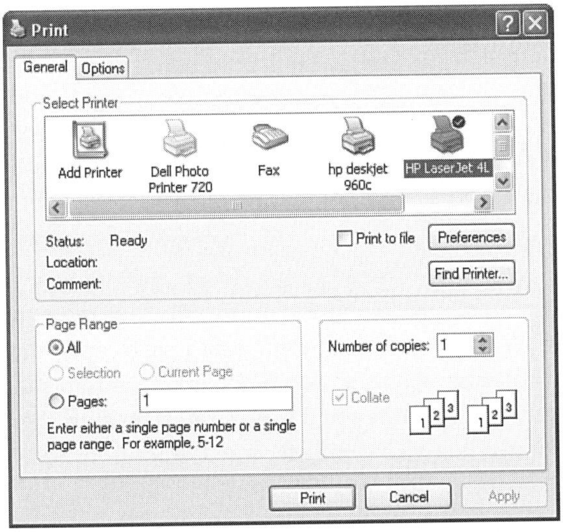

FIGURE 8.9

You can print a Web page so that you have a hardcopy of the information.

2. In the Print dialog box, make any changes to the print options and then click OK to print. The page is printed. If the right side of the page is cropped, you can print it correctly by changing the orientation to landscape.

Working with Text and Images

If you want to quote a passage from a Web site, you can retype it. Otherwise, you can copy the text from the site to a document as a shortcut. (Keep in mind that you should cite all sources and should never present someone else's ideas, images, or words as your own.) Likewise, you can copy an image from a Web site to a document.

Follow these steps to copy text or an image:

1. Select the text or click the image you want to copy.

2. Right-click the selected item and then click Copy.

3. Move to the document where you want to paste the text or image.

4. Open the Edit menu and click Paste. (Or right-click in the location where you want to paste the item and click Paste from the shortcut menu.) The text or image is pasted.

tip

You can also save an image as a file. To do so, right-click the image and select Save Image As. Then, select a drive and folder for the image and click Save.

Downloading Files

Some sites provide programs, images, documents, or other file types for you to download. You may download programs to add to your computer, such as Adobe Reader, a popular program for sharing documents. Some companies provide add-ons or updates to their programs via the Web; you can download these add-ons or updates. You may also download documents, such as an Adobe Acrobat document (or PDF file) that you can open and read using Adobe Reader. If you have Microsoft Office, you can go online and access its clipart or design gallery and download templates, images, fonts, and so on.

The specifics for downloading a file depend on the site, but most commonly, you click the link for the file and then are prompted to save or open the file. (Usually, you save it, but you can also open and run a document from a site.) If you select to save the file, you next specify a drive and folder and then start the download process. Often, a progress box shows the estimated amount of time needed to download the file, as well as the time already elapsed.

Keep in mind that sharing files is one way to get a computer virus (and potentially put your documents and computer at risk). You should use a virus program to check any downloaded files, especially program files, before you run them. You can find out more about virus programs in Chapter 17.

Ensuring Internet Security and Privacy

While browsing the Internet presents many advantages, there are a few dangers as well. You should safeguard your computer from any unauthorized use (by using a firewall, for instance). You may also set Internet security levels for sites, change the privacy controls, and use additional programs to prevent intrusions (which are harmful or simply annoying). This section discusses these security features.

Turning On Windows XP Firewall Systems

Many home users these days use cable Internet connections. Because these types of connections are always on, it's important that you protect your computer from outsiders. Both cable and DSL connections have more security issues than systems that use dial-up access. Why? Because they are connected 24/7 and usually have a static (unchanging) IP address. Dial-up access is connected only when you are online and uses a temporary IP address, making those connections much more difficult to crack into.

To protect your computer, you can use Windows firewall protection. As defined by Windows XP online help, "a firewall is a security system that acts as a protective boundary between a network and the outside world." To activate the firewall, follow these steps:

1. Click the Start button, All Programs, Accessories, System Tools, and finally Security Center. The Security Center provides information about the security of your computer.

2. To view detailed information about a firewall, click the down arrow next to the firewall setting. You'll see the current firewall settings, as well as information about using a firewall (see Figure 8.10).

> **tip**
>
> If you aren't sure how this feature protects your Internet use, you can click the link for more information. That link gives you all the technical details about how the firewall monitors incoming, unsolicited traffic from the Internet.

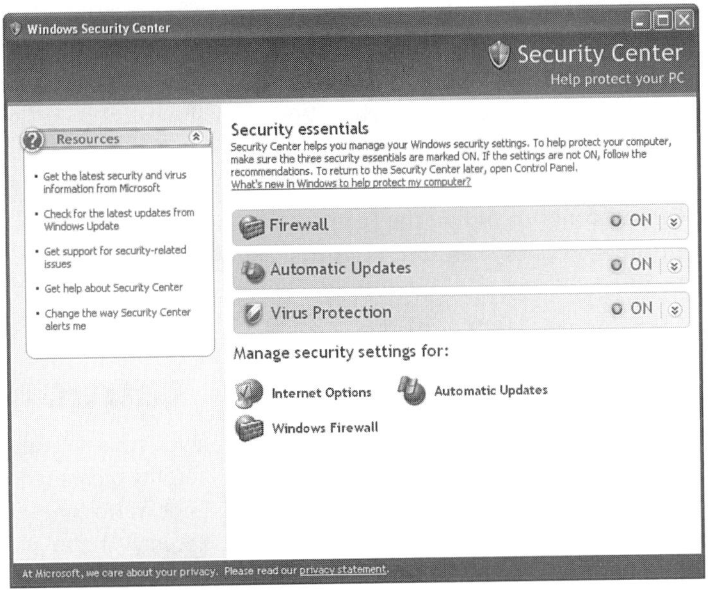

FIGURE 8.10

You can check out key security settings using the new Windows Security Center.

3. If the firewall setting isn't on or if you need to change the setting, click the Windows Firewall link at the bottom of the Security Center. You'll see the options for using Windows XP's firewall (see Figure 8.11).

FIGURE 8.11

You can turn on or turn off Windows XP's firewall using the options in this dialog box.

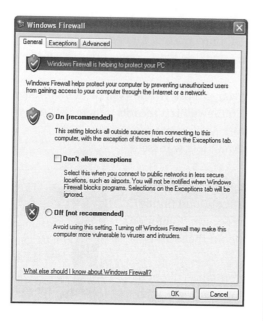

4. Make any changes and click OK.

Setting Privacy Options

Privacy is one of the key issues of debate about the Internet. How do you take advantage of all the Internet has to offer, while still maintaining some privacy? To address this concern, Windows XP includes a Privacy tab that you can use to set the level for privacy. With this tool, you have various zones including the Internet, Local intranet, Trusted sites, and Restricted sites. You can then add sites to each of these zones.

You can also make sure that the Pop-up Blocker is on, a new feature designed to block annoying advertisements that pop up (or pop under) as you navigate to a site. These ads appear in a separate browser window and may appear on top of Internet Explorer or under it. When they are blocked, Windows XP displays a message under the address bar in Internet Explorer. You can display the blocked windows by clicking the message. (Some pop-ups or pop-unders are useful.)

note

If you have a home network and used the Home Networking Wizard to set it up, Internet Connection Firewall is turned on automatically. You can get more information on home networking in Chapter 24, "Setting Up Windows XP on a Home Network."

caution

If you have an Internet Security program or suite (such as Norton Security), it may include a firewall also. In this case, you don't want to turn on both firewalls, or you will have a conflict. Use one or the other.

Follow these steps to select the level of privacy and check for pop-up blocking:

1. Open the Tools menu and click the Internet Options command.

2. Click the Privacy tab (see Figure 8.12).

3. Drag the lever to set the privacy at the level you want. As you change the level, Windows XP displays an explanation of what that privacy setting means.

4. Make sure that the Block pop-ups check box is checked.

5. To view what happens when an ad is blocked (and make any changes), click the Settings button. In the dialog box, which is shown in Figure 8.13, make any changes to the notification (such as whether a sound is played). You can also change the Filter Level by displaying this drop-down list and selecting the level you want. Click Close to close the Pop-up Blocker Settings window.

4. Click OK to close the Internet Options dialog box.

caution

If you set privacy on a high setting, you may have problems visiting or displaying information at some sites. Therefore, you may need to adjust the setting if you do want to view a blocked site.

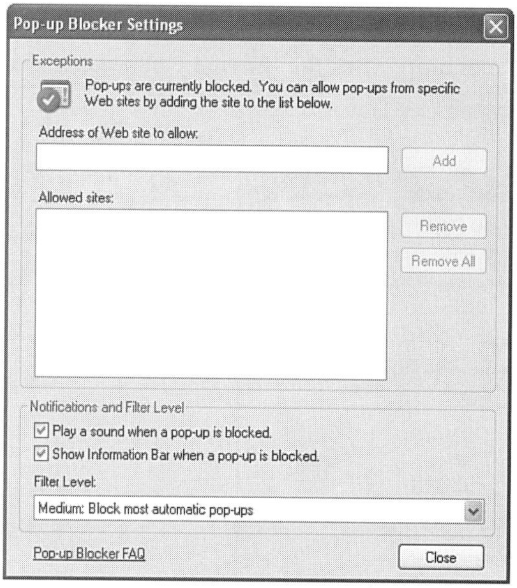

FIGURE 8.13

You can change the settings for how pop-up ads are handled in this dialog box.

If you have children, you might also use the Content Advisor on the Content tab of the Internet Options dialog box. Furthermore, you can set up special security zones (trusted sites and restricted sites). You do this from the Security tab of the Internet Options dialog box by selecting the type of site (trusted or restricted), manually typing in the addresses of the sites in that category, and then adding them to the list.

tip

If you are an online shopper, be sure to read that site's privacy statement before entering any information. Most reputable sites provide a link that specifically outlines their privacy rules. Also, watch out for check boxes for automatic alerts, new products, or joining mailing lists. Often, these are checked (turned on), and if you don't make a change, you are placed on that mailing list and receive constant messages about "special" offers "just for you!"

Dealing with Spyware

Another privacy issue that you should think about is checking for (and getting rid of) spyware. Spyware programs are installed on your computer (sometimes without your knowledge). They track what Web sites you visit and relay this information back to their sponsors. With this information, marketers and others can track what sites you frequent. They claim they want to use this information to provide customized advertising—advertising that is pertinent to your interest, but most people feel this is a violation of their privacy, especially if they don't even know the program is working.

To check for and delete spyware, you need to use an anti-spyware program such as Spybot's Search and Destroy. This program is a shareware program; you can try it and if you decide to use it, pay a small fee to the author of the program. You can also purchase and use other spyware programs, such as StopZilla or NoAdware. (Some spyware programs also include features for dealing with unwanted email or spam.)

These programs search your computer for any installed spyware and then delete it (with your consent). You should periodically run your spyware program to check for this privacy problem.

Exiting and Logging Off the Internet

When you are finished browsing the Internet, you should not only exit Internet Explorer, but also log off your dial-up account. (If you have a broadband connection that is always connected, you do not need to log off.)

To exit Internet Explorer, click its Close button or click File, Close. When you exit Internet Explorer, you may be prompted to log off your Internet provider. Click Yes or Disconnect Now. If you are not prompted, be sure to log off. To do so, right-click the connection icon in the system tray and select Disconnect.

THE ABSOLUTE MINIMUM

This chapter covers the basics of using Internet Explorer, the Web browser program included with Windows XP. With this program (and an Internet provider), you can access the many resources of the Internet. Keep in mind the following key points:

- The first step to using Internet Explorer is to set up an Internet account. Use the information from your ISP to set up this account. The steps vary depending on the provider and the type of provider.

- To start Internet Explorer, click Start and then Internet Explorer. If prompted to get connected, follow your logon procedure (which usually involves typing your username and password). The first page that is displayed is called your home page.

- You have two basic methods for displaying Web pages: You can browse from page to page using links, or you can type the page address to go directly to a page.

- Use the toolbar buttons to navigate among pages. Click Back to go back a page, Forward to go forward a page, and Home to return to your starting page.

- If you frequently visit a site, add it to your Favorites list. You can then display this list and go to any of the sites by clicking the site's name.

- You can display pages you have viewed on the current day as well as several weeks ago by displaying the History bar.

- You can print, email, or save text or images from the Web pages you view.

- You should take precautions to ensure your computer's safety and your privacy if you use the Internet. If you have a 24/7 connection, you should use a firewall to block unwanted intrusions. You can also use Internet Explorer's features (or those of other programs) to block pop-ups and control other security and privacy issues.

9

SEARCHING THE INTERNET

The Internet includes many different sites. Looking for the site you want by browsing can be like looking for the proverbial needle in the haystack. Instead, you can search for a topic and find all sites related to that topic.

You can use Internet Explorer's search tool, or you can visit and use the search features at any number of Internet search sites.

Searching with Internet Explorer

To help you get where you want to go quickly, Internet Explorer provides a Search bar. You can use the features in this pane to search for sites relating to a particular topic or interest.

To search for sites using Internet Explorer, follow these steps:

1. Click the Search button in the toolbar. You see the Search bar in the left pane of the Internet Explorer window. Your particular search may look different if you've changed your settings.

2. Type what you want to find (see Figure 9.1). Type a unique word or phrase, being as specific as possible. For instance, if you type "beads," you will find too many matches to make the search worthwhile. If you type "Mardi Gras beads," your results will more closely match what you want to find.

FIGURE 9.1

Type the topic that you want to find.

3. Click the Search button. You see the results of the search in the window on the right (see Figure 9.2). Sponsored links appear in the search bar on the right. Usually, a sponsored site in a search engine is one that has paid to get itself listed higher in the search results.

4. Scroll through the list to see information about the first set of matches.

5. To go to any of the found sites, click the link in the search results window. The page you selected appears in the right pane.

FIGURE 9.2

You can review
all the matches
found for your
topic. You can
also refine the
search using sug-
gestions in the
Search bar.

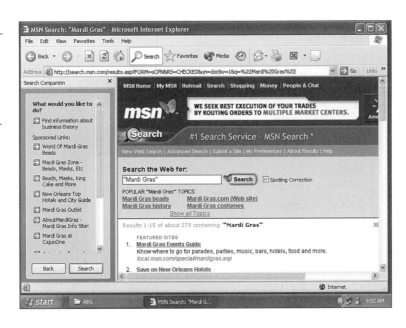

Getting the Most from the Search Results

If you use the Search button, MSN (Microsoft Network) is the search engine that is
used, unless you or someone else changed it. (You can also use other search tools,
which are covered later in this chapter, and you can change the engine used by
Internet Explorer.) MSN's search results page includes several useful features for finding the most closely matching site. Review these tips:

■ To see as many of the search results as possible, close the Search bar by clicking
   its Close button. Also, the header and the left side of the search page contain
   other MSN links (and ads). Scroll further down the page to view the actual
   matches.

■ Different search engines use different matching formulas that determine which
   sites are listed first. MSN tries to rank the most common sites related to your
   search topic. These are listed at the top.

■ To get an idea of the scope of your search, check out the number of found
   matches. For instance, in Figure 9.3, sites 1–15 out of 2,469 matches are
   displayed.

FIGURE 9.3

Review the search results and search-related information to fine-tune your search.

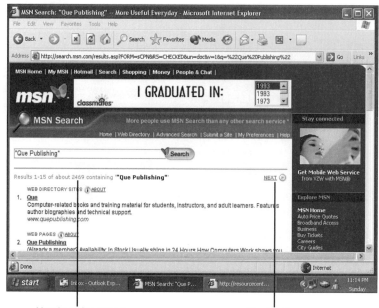

Number of matches   Next button

- If more than one set of results is found, MSN lists the most popular. You can view other matches by clicking the Next button (refer to Figure 9.3).

- The site name as well as a short description and the address for the site are listed. Use this data to determine whether a particular listed site has the information you want.

- To go to any matching site, click its link. Figure 9.4, for instance, shows the Que Publishing site, one of the matching links from the search.

- In searching, you'll find that you normally try one of the links and then go back to the results. Then, you try another link and go back to the results. You may need to go back and forth several times to find the information you need. Also, you may find valuable information at more than one site, so you can visit several.

tip

As mentioned in Chapter 8, "Browsing the Internet," many sites provide Search tools on their pages. You can use these to search for content at that site. Type the word or phrase to locate and then click the Search button. You can also use Internet Explorer's Edit, Find (on This Page) command to search for a word or phrase on the current page.

FIGURE 9.4

You can click
any of the search
matches to go to
and display that
page (here the
Que home page).

FIGURE 9.4

You can click
any of the search
matches to go to
and display that
page (here the
Que home page).

Fine-Tuning the Search

If you don't find an appropriate match, you can refine your search. The Search bar provides some suggestions for fine-tuning the search. You can also use more complex search criteria. For instance, if you are searching for the White House, most results start with listings of sites that include both words. However, the listings also include sites that have "White" or "House." You can limit the search to only those sites that contain both "White House."

To use MSN's additional search features, click the Settings link on the MSN Search page. You see the various options for refining your search criteria (see Figure 9.5). Here, you can pick and choose from among several search options, including how matches are made: all of the words, any of the words, words in the title, the exact phrase, and others. You can limit the search to particular domains (only government or .gov sites, for instance). You also can specify that the matching sites contain certain elements, such as audio or images. Make your choices and then start the search.

tip

If you are unsure about the various Help options, click the Help link next to each for an explanation.

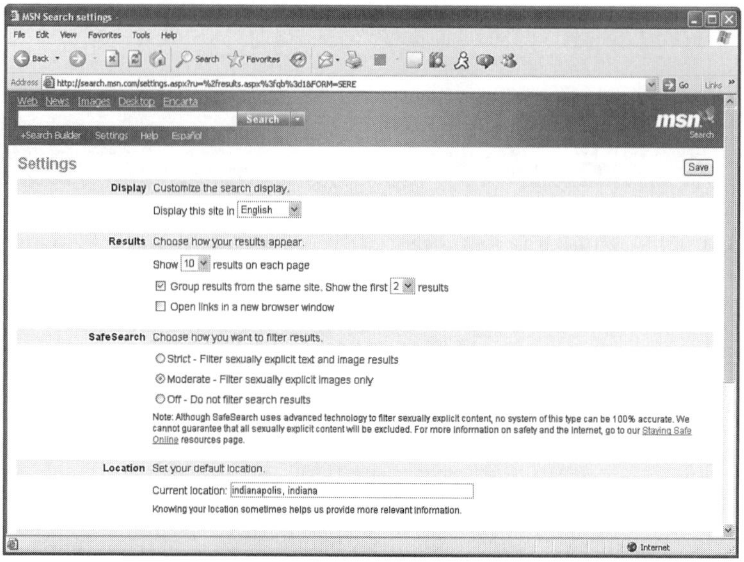

FIGURE 9.5

If you get too many matches (or none!), try changing some of search settings.

Using Other Search Sites

In addition to MSN's search tool, you can go to other sites dedicated to searching. New search sites are popping up all the time, adding to the several already established and popular ones. A search site is often called by various names, including *search tool*, *search directory*, or *search engine*. Each search site uses its own method for categorizing and cataloging the sites. They also usually provide various other research tools (such as access to maps or email searches), and the options for searching vary. However, the basics of using the services remain the same.

Follow these steps to use another search site:

1. Go to the site by typing the address and pressing Enter.

2. Type the word or phrase you want to find. Be as specific as possible.

3. Click the search button. (The name of the button varies.) You'll then see the results of the search.

Some popular search sites include

- Google—www.google.com
- Yahoo!—www.yahoo.com
- Alta Vista—www.altavista.com
- Lycos—www.lycos.com

tip

Is one search engine better than another? Not definitively so. You'll find that you just prefer one site over another, usually when you get the most success on your searches from a site. For example, I prefer Google because the start page is streamlined and doesn't include an overwhelming set of options.

■ Excite—www.excite.com

■ Teoma—www.teoma.com

■ Ask Jeeves—www.askjeeves.com

Refining Your Search

Most search sites provide many options for fine-tuning the search. Common search features may be listed on the home page. Also, look for a link named something like Advanced Search or More Search Options. For instance, Figure 9.6 shows some other options for searching using Google. These options are similar to those found on MSN's Settings page.

FIGURE 9.6

Change the search settings on the Advanced Search options page.

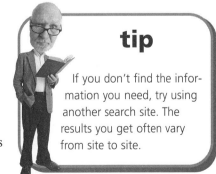

Searching for Images or News

Many sites also provide different categories to search. For instance, with Google, you can search for images or for news stories. To do so, click the appropriate link from the starting page. Then, enter a word or phrase and click the Search button to search. Figure 9.7 shows the results of searching for images of the Mona Lisa using Google. You also can search for news stories (by clicking the News link) or for user-group postings (by clicking the Groups link).

tip

If you don't find the information you need, try using another search site. The results you get often vary from site to site.

FIGURE 9.7

You can search for an image using Google's Images page.

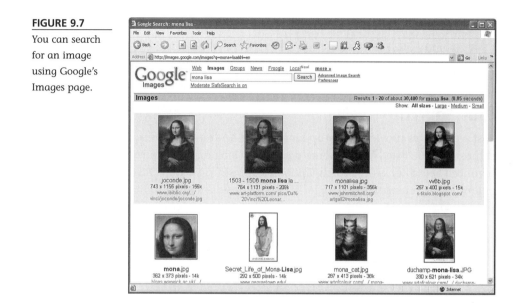

Different search sites will include different options for searching, so follow the specific steps for using the features at your site of choice.

Browsing Through Directories or Channels

In addition to search tools, many sites provide channels or directories of content. You can browse through these categories to find information. For instance, if you want to know generally what entertainment sites are available, you can view the Shopping or Health channel or category. For instance, Figure 9.8 shows the home page for Yahoo! You can click any of the channels to view sites within that topic area.

Using Other Search Site Tools

To make them as versatile as possible, many search sites include other useful features for finding information. These vary by site, but you can expect to find the following features at most sites:

- **Weather forecasts.** You can usually view current weather information, as well as forecasts specific to your area.
- **Maps.** If you need directions, you can use the Map feature to look up directions to an address (or city or landmark). Click the Map link and then follow the specific steps to view a map or print driving directions.

FIGURE 9.8

You can browse through categories or channels that group similar sites together.

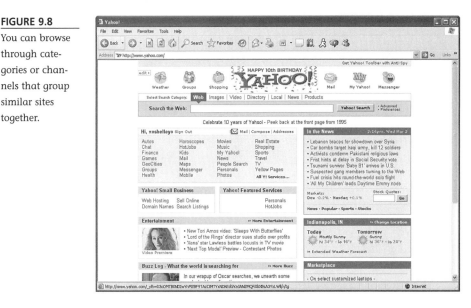

- **Current headlines.** The search site may also list headlines of current entertainment, financial, or other news.

- **Phone number and address information.** Sites may also include links to look up phone numbers, businesses, or residents in local or nationwide directories.

- **TV listings.** Many search sites enable you to view TV listings for your particular area and cable provider (if applicable) as well. Figure 9.9, for instance, shows the TV listings for my area; I entered my ZIP code and cable provider to get this listing.

tip

Many search sites enable you to customize the search page, selecting what features are included (horoscopes or stock quotes, for instance) and the area in which you reside (for local weather, news, sports, and so on). Use the links on the site to customize the site to include the information and features you use most often.

FIGURE 9.9

You can browse through TV listings for your area by entering your ZIP Code.

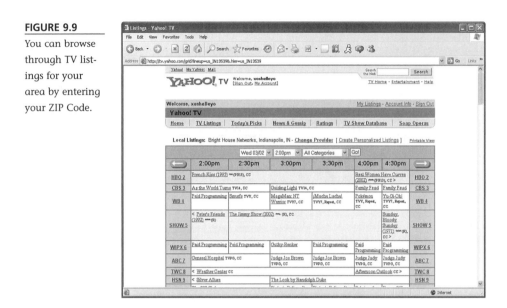

THE ABSOLUTE MINIMUM

When you don't know a Web site address or what content is available, the best way to find out is to search. You can search using MSN's search feature (which is built into Internet Explorer), or you can use any of the other search sites. Keep the following guidelines in mind:

- You can use Internet Explorer's Search button to open a search pane. When the results are displayed, you can go to any listed site by clicking its link.

- In addition to Internet Explorer's search tool, you can use any of the many Internet sites devoted to searching. Type the address to that site and then follow the specific instructions for searching from that site. Basically, you type the topic or question and click the search button.

- To fine-tune your search, look for a link to advanced or more search options. Then limit your search with these features.

- Many search sites include directories (or channels) through which you can browse to find sites related to that category. You can also find features for TV listings, weather, maps, and more at many search sites.

10

SENDING AND RECEIVING FAXES

In addition to communicating via email, you can also use Windows XP to send and receive faxes. Windows XP includes a program called Fax Console that organizes your incoming faxes and enables you to create new faxes.

To fax from Windows XP, you must have a fax modem. (Most dial-up modems also function as a fax.) If you have a broadband connection (such as a cable modem), you cannot use this modem to send a fax.

This chapter covers the basics of sending and receiving faxes.

Setting Up the Fax Console

Before you can use your fax modem to send and receive faxes, you must set it up in Windows, which involves entering information about the fax phone number and fax device. To help you with this process, Windows XP includes the Fax Configuration Wizard. This program starts the first time you open the Fax Console. To start Fax Console, click Start, All Programs, Accessories, Communications, Fax, and finally Fax Console. You'll see the welcome screen of the wizard.

To start the Fax Configuration Wizard manually (if it does not start when you open Fax Console), click Tools from within Fax Console and then click the Configure Fax command.

To set up your fax, complete each step in the wizard, entering information and clicking Next to move to the next step. You can expect to complete the following:

- Enter your contact information (name, fax number, email address, company, and other phone information). Figure 10.1 shows the first screen you see after the welcome wizard screen.

> **caution**
>
> If the fax component is not installed, you can install it through the Add/Remove Programs Control Panel (see Chapter 20, "Upgrading Windows"). You can also find information by searching for this topic at `support.microsoft.com`.

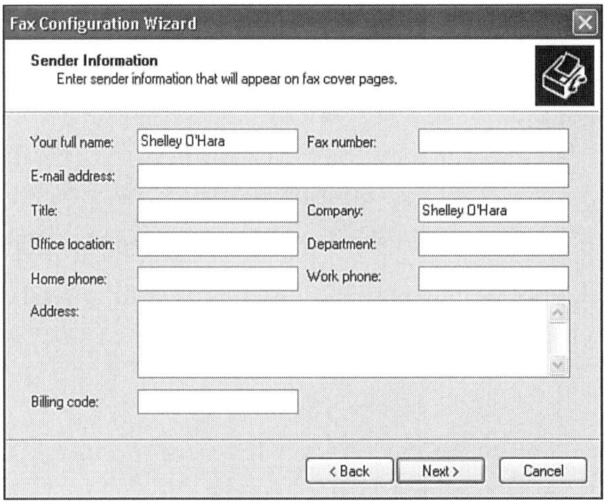

FIGURE 10.1

To use your fax, you need to set it up, which involves entering information about your setup.

■ Select the fax device for sending and receiving. To do so, select the fax device from the drop-down list. You can also enable Send and Receive by checking the respective check boxes. Finally, you can select to manually answer a fax call or to automatically answer the call after the number of rings you designate. Figure 10.2 shows this step of the Fax Configuration Wizard.

FIGURE 10.2

Set up your sending and receiving options in this step of the Fax Configuration Wizard.

Fax Configuration Wizard

Select Device for Sending or Receiving Faxes
Select the device that you want to use to send or receive faxes.

Please select the fax device
U.S. Robotics 56K Voice INT PnP

☑ Enable Send
☑ Enable Receive
　○ Manual answer
　⊙ Automatically answer after ⬚1⬚ rings

< Back　　Next >　　Cancel

■ Enter the TSID. A TSID is a text line that identifies your fax machine when it sends a fax. You can type your business name or fax number.

■ Enter the CSID. The CSID is a text line that identifies your fax machine when it receives a fax.

■ Select how received faxes are handled (either printed directly or stored in a folder). If you choose to print the faxes upon receipt, you can select the printer from the drop-down list. If you select to store the faxes in a folder (which you can then open and use to view the faxes), check this option and then select the folder to use. Figure 10.3 shows these options.

tip

Be sure to check Enable Receive in this wizard step. A common problem is being unable to receive faxes, and this occurs if this option is not checked. (You can make this change later if you forget to do so here.)

The fax is now set up and ready for use.

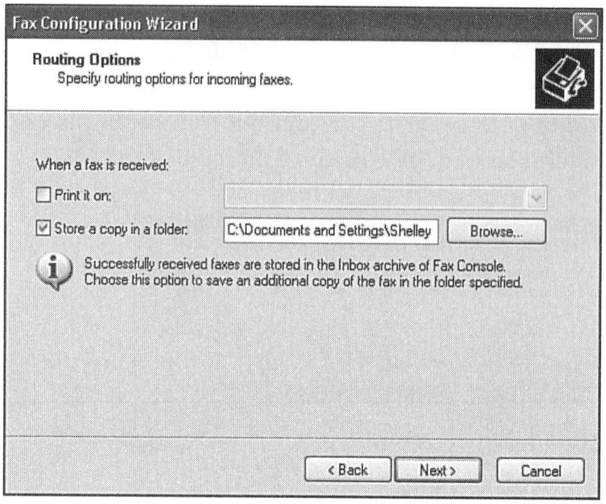

FIGURE 10.3

When you
receive a fax,
you can choose
to print it on a
printer or store it
within a folder.

Fax Configuration Wizard

Routing Options
Specify routing options for incoming faxes.

When a fax is received:

☐ Print it on:

☑ Store a copy in a folder: C:\Documents and Settings\Shelley [Browse...]

(i) Successfully received faxes are stored in the Inbox archive of Fax Console.
Choose this option to save an additional copy of the fax in the folder specified.

[< Back] [Next >] [Cancel]

Sending a Fax

After the Fax Console is set up, you can use it to send and receive faxes. To help you create and send a fax, Windows XP provides a Send Fax Wizard. This wizard leads you through the steps for creating and sending a fax cover page. You can also send a fax from within a program. For instance, you may want to fax a document you created in Word. To fax within another program, you "print" to the fax. This section covers both these methods for sending a fax.

Sending a Fax with the Send Fax Wizard

To send a fax using the wizard, follow these steps:

1. If the Fax Console is not open, click Start, All Programs, Accessories, Communications, Fax, and finally Send Fax Wizard.

   If the Fax Console is open, click File and then click the Send a Fax command. Both start the Send Fax Wizard.

2. Click Next to move from the welcome screen to the first step.

3. Enter the name and fax number of the recipient (see Figure 10.4). Click Next.

4. If you want to use a different cover page template, display the template drop-down list and select the template you want. You'll see a thumbnail sample of the cover sheet to help you decide which is most appropriate.

5. Type a subject and the note for the fax cover sheet (see Figure 10.5). Click Next.

6. Select when to send the fax, as well as the fax priority (see Figure 10.6). Click Next.

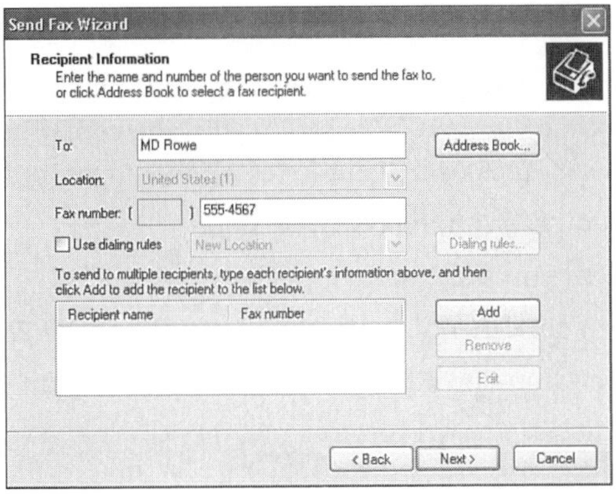

FIGURE 10.4

Enter the recipient's name and fax number.

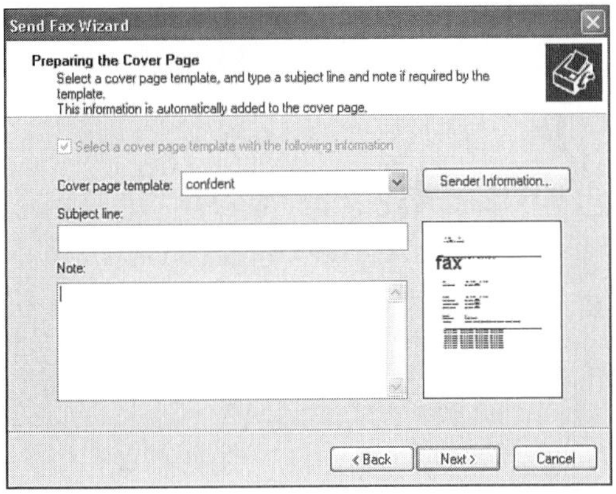

FIGURE 10.5

Type the contents for the fax cover page in this dialog box, including the subject and note.

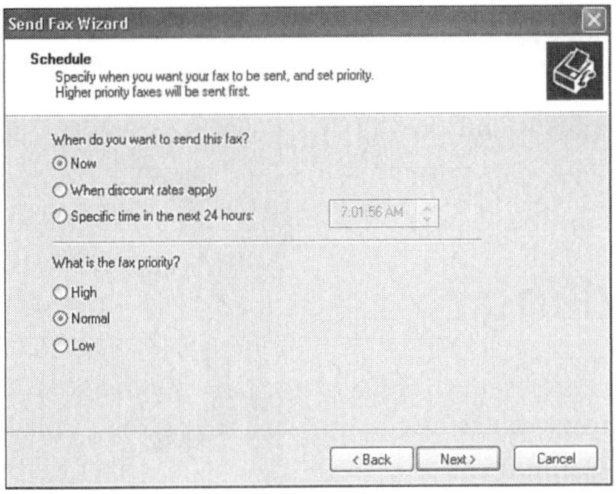

FIGURE 10.6

You can send the fax immediately or schedule it for delivery at another time.

7. Click Finish. After completing these steps, the fax is sent at the time you selected in step 6.

Faxing from a Program

You can also fax documents created in Windows programs by "printing" to the fax; the program uses the fax modem you have set up with the configuration wizard. This method starts the Send Fax Wizard, but faxes all the pages in the document.

To fax a document from a program, follow these steps:

1. Open the document you want to fax.

2. Click File and then click the Print command. You'll see the Print dialog box.

3. Display the printer drop-down list and select Fax (see Figure 10.7).

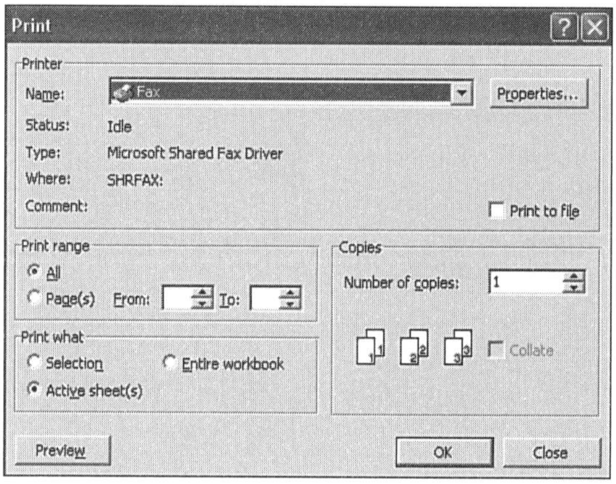

FIGURE 10.7

To fax a document from within a program, print it, selecting Fax as the printer.

4. Click the OK button. This starts the Send Fax Wizard. Follow the same steps as covered in the preceding section. That is, complete the recipient and other information for the fax, clicking Next to complete each step in the fax wizard. The document is then faxed to that recipient.

Receiving and Handling Faxes

Depending on what options you selected when you used the Fax Configuration Wizard to set up your fax modem, receiving faxes can vary. For instance, if you set up your fax to automatically answer a fax call, all fax calls are answered. If you set up your

tip

You can also access and send a fax using the Send Fax Wizard from the Printers and Faxes Control Panel. Click Start, Control Panel. Then, click Printers and Other Hardware. Under Pick a Task, click View Installed Printers or Fax Printers. Then, under Printer Tasks, click Send a Fax and follow the steps to complete and send the fax.

fax to manually answer the call, you are notified when a fax is being sent. You can then choose to answer the call.

If you set up your fax to automatically answer calls, the modem receives any incoming faxes and handles them according to the options you selected. If you selected to print the faxes upon receipt, they are printed on the printer you selected. If you selected to store them in a folder, they are placed in that folder. You can open that folder and then view the faxes. You can also view faxes from the Fax Console by selecting Inbox in the Fax list.

Opening Faxes

To open the Fax Console and view any stored faxes (either new faxes or faxes you have received previously), follow these steps:

1. Click Start, All Programs, Accessories, Communications, Fax, and finally Fax Console. You'll see the Fax Console window (see Figure 10.8). Notice that Fax Console is similar to Outlook Express. Both include a list of folders on the left side of the program window. In Outlook Express, you see mail folders. In Fax Console, you see fax folders. You can click any of the folders to view the faxes in that particular folder.

2. To open a fax you have received, click Inbox in the Fax folder list. You'll see a list of the faxes you have received. The fax list also contains identifying information about each fax, including when the fax was received, the number of pages, and so on.

3. To open a fax, double-click it (see Figure 10.9).

> **tip**
>
> You can customize the fax configurations, including setting notification options. To do so, click Start, Control Panel, and then Printers and Other Hardware. From these options, click Printers and Faxes. You should see your fax listed. Right-click the fax printer and then select Properties. You can then use the tabs in this dialog box to set options, such as notification options, for your particular fax.

> **caution**
>
> If you have problems receiving faxes, your fax device might not be set up to receive faxes. You can, however, enable it to both send and receive them. To do so, click Start, Control Panel, Printers and Other Hardware, and finally, Printers and Faxes. Right-click the fax device, right-click Receive, and then click Auto.

FIGURE 10.8

Use Fax Console to open and view faxes.

Save As button

Print button

Mail To button

Delete button

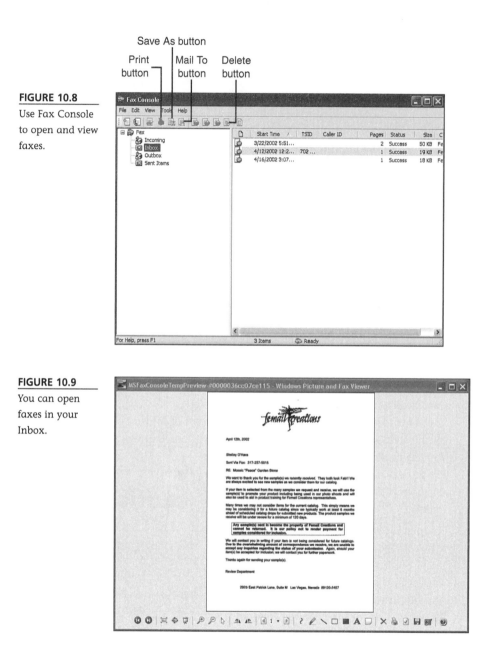

FIGURE 10.9

You can open faxes in your Inbox.

Handling Faxes

You also have other options besides simply viewing faxes. You can't do much from the preview window, but from the Fax Console, you can print, delete, or email any of the received faxes.

To do so, follow these steps:

1. Click the fax in the fax list.

2. Do any of the following:

   To print the fax, click the Print button or click File and then click the Print command. Select print options in the Print dialog box and then click OK.

   To save a fax to another folder, click the Save As button. Select a folder, type a name, and choose a file type. The default is .tif (a popular graphic file format). Click Save.

   To email a fax, click the Mail To button. You'll see a New Message window with the fax attached. Complete the recipient, subject, and message and click Send. For more information on sending email messages, see Chapter 7, "Sending and Receiving Email."

   To delete a fax, click the Delete button. Then confirm the deletion by clicking Yes.

THE ABSOLUTE MINIMUM

This chapter covers the basics of using your computer to both send and receive faxes. Windows XP includes the Fax Console for these tasks. The important fax points to keep in mind include the following:

- Before you can use your computer to fax, you must set up the Fax Console. You do so by using the Fax Configuration Wizard. This starts automatically the first time you open the Fax Console.

- You can send simple faxes by typing a subject line and a note using the Send Fax Wizard. You also can fax a document from within a program.

- You can set up Fax Console to handle faxes the way you want. For example, you can choose to answer a fax call manually or automatically. You also can choose to print any received faxes or to store them in a fax folder.

- To view and work with received faxes, open the Fax Console. There, you can view, print, save, or delete any of the faxes.

PART

ENTERTAINMENT

11

PLAYING MUSIC

Windows XP includes a wealth of entertainment features, including turning your PC into a boom box, music mixer, radio, or video player. This chapter covers the basics of each of these entertainment elements.

Playing Audio CDs with Windows Media Player

If you like to listen to music while you work or if you simply want to play some music, you can play audio CDs using Windows Media Player. In addition to playing music, you have many more options. You can adjust the volume, view visualizations, download track information for the CD, and more.

The first time you start Windows Media Player, you are prompted to select its playback options. You can select how music files are handled (see Figure 11.1) and whether Media Player is the default player for certain music file types (see Figure 11.2). Make your choices and click Next to move from screen to screen. When you have completed all of your selections, click Finish.

FIGURE 11.1

You can control how music files are handled by selecting options here.

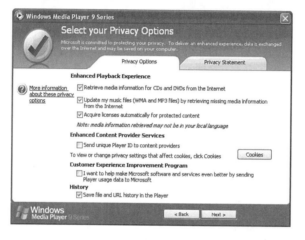

FIGURE 11.2

Select whether Windows Media Player is the default player for each of these file types.

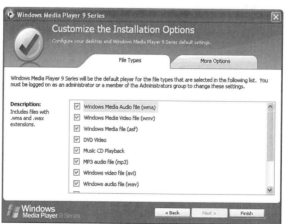

Playing a CD

To play an audio CD, simply insert it into your CD drive. Doing so starts Windows Media Player automatically, and the CD begins to play. If the CD does not play (which indicates that your drive may not be set up for Autoplay), click Start, All Programs, and Windows Media Player. Then, click the Play button. The music plays, and you'll see the default visualization.

If the CD has the title information on it or if you have downloaded the CD information from the Internet, you see the name of the album and each of the tracks (see Figure 11.3). You also see the time of each track, as well as the total CD play time. The current song is highlighted in the playlist.

> **tip**
>
> You can use other programs to play music, and your computer may be set up to use another media player as the default. Popular media players include RealPlayer, MusicMatch Jukebox, and iTunes. If you use one of these programs, you can accomplish the same tasks covered in this chapter. For the exact steps to follow, consult your particular program's online help.

FIGURE 11.3

When you play a CD, you see track information in the playlist. You also see a visual representation of each song.

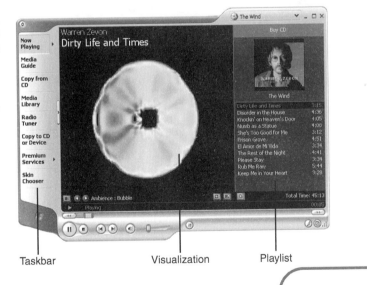

Taskbar   Visualization   Playlist

If you see generic names (Track 1, Track 2, and so on), you can often download the track information from the Internet. To do so, connect to the Internet while the CD is playing. A quick way to connect is by using the Media Guide. See "Playing Music and Videos from the Internet" later in this chapter.

> **caution**
>
> Note that the quality of the playback is determined by the quality of your speakers. Don't expect stereo quality!

The taskbar appears to the left of the Media Player window and includes buttons for performing other music-related tasks. You learn more about these options later in this chapter.

Working with Windows Media Player Controls

The Media Player window provides several buttons for controlling the playback of the CD. These controls let you adjust the volume, play another track, and start and stop the playback. Figure 11.4 identifies the basic controls. With these controls, you can do any of the following:

tip

To hide the taskbar, click the little red arrow on the bar that divides the taskbar from the media play area.

FIGURE 11.4

You can use the controls in the Windows Media Player window to play a different track, change the volume, and more.

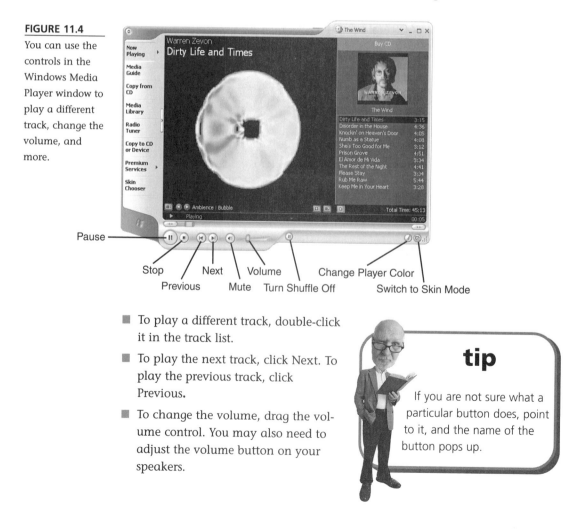

- To play a different track, double-click it in the track list.
- To play the next track, click Next. To play the previous track, click Previous.
- To change the volume, drag the volume control. You may also need to adjust the volume button on your speakers.

tip

If you are not sure what a particular button does, point to it, and the name of the button pops up.

- To mute the music (say, when you get a phone call), click the Mute button.
- To stop the playback, click Stop. If you stop and want to restart, click the Play button again.
- To pause the playback, click Pause. To restart, click the Play button. (The Pause button becomes the Play button when the playback is paused.)
- If you want to shuffle the order in which the tracks are played, click the Turn Shuffle On button. (This button is a toggle; click it again to turn shuffle off.)
- To keep the music playing but hide the Media Player window, click its Minimize button.
- To stop the music and close Media Player, click the Close button.

tip

See the next two sections for help on changing the Player colors and switching the Player skin.

Changing the Appearance of the Window

You can change the appearance of the Media Player window using one of two methods: changing the Player color or changing the skin.

To change the Player color, click the Change Player Color button. Each time you click the button, the Player changes color. Click the button until you see a color that you like.

In addition to the color, you can choose a different skin. A *skin* is a layer over an application that changes how it looks. You can also make both changes: change the skin and color. These are purely personal choices. You can experiment and pick the style you like.

To change the skin, follow these steps:

1. Click the Skin Chooser button in the taskbar. You'll see the different skin choices.

2. Click any of the listed skins. You'll see a preview of the selected skin. Figure 11.5, for instance, shows the Heart skin selected.

3. Click Apply Skin, and your newly designed player appears, playing the CD.

tip

You can click More Skins to go online and select from other Windows Media Player skins.

FIGURE 11.5
FIGURE 11.5

You can change
the look of the
Windows Media
Player window.

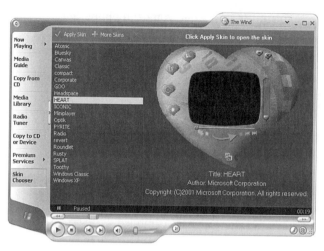

To return to the main playback window, click the Now Playing
button in the taskbar.

Changing the Visualization

In addition to changing the appearance of
the player, you can choose from several visualizations. A *visualization* is a moving graphic
image displayed during a song, making the
music more of a multimedia experience.
Again, pick the one you like best. You may
want to vary the visualizations according to
your mood. You can use the buttons for
changing the visualizations that appear in
the Now Playing window (see Figure 11.6).

To select a visualization, do any of the
following:

caution

With some of the skins,
the control buttons are
not easy to figure out. If
you use a new skin, you
may need to experiment
to figure out which button does
what. Also, remember that you can
display a button's name by placing
the mouse pointer on the edge of
the button.

■ Click Next Visualization to display the next visualization, or click Previous
  Visualization to display the previous visualization. When you use these but-
  tons, you select different options within the visualization. For instance, if
  Ambience is selected (usually the default), you can select Warp, Falloff,
  Water, and others.

■ To display another category of visualizations, click the Change Now Playing
  button and then click Visualizations. From the list of the different categories,
  select the one you want. You can select from Album Art, Bars and Waves,
  Battery, Particle, Spikes, and several others. Then from that category's submenu, select the visualization you want.

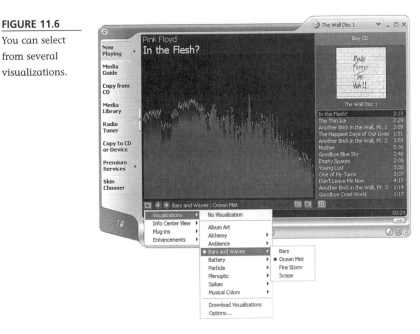

Playing Music and Videos from the Internet

In addition to playing audio CDs, you can go online and play music tracks. You can find many sites devoted to music. You can also listen to the radio or play videos using Windows Media Player. This section discusses these Windows Media Player features.

Finding Music Online

Windows Media Player conveniently provides access to its music site. Click Media Guide in the taskbar to access WindowsMedia.com. From here, you can find not only music, but also videos and other links (see Figure 11.7).

You can choose to sample music from this site. For instance, you may listen to the samples of the tracks of a new CD to see if you want to purchase it. Use the links to navigate to the page that contains the links. (You'll find new CDs highlighted on the opening page of WindowsMedia. You can also click Music at the top of the page to view specific music information.) To play a track, simply click the appropriate link.

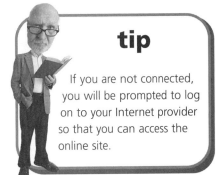

tip

If you are not connected, you will be prompted to log on to your Internet provider so that you can access the online site.

FIGURE 11.7

Use the Media Guide to get sample tracks, view movie clips, and get entertainment news.

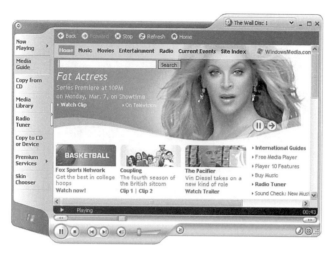

You can also download free or purchased music from this site. To do so, click the link for the song you want to download. New songs are often listed on the start page, but you can also use other links to view current songs. Figure 11.8, for instance, shows some songs that are available for downloading.

FIGURE 11.8

You can view songs available for downloading.

Viewing Videos

The Windows Media Player is not just for playing music—you can also view video clips and animation. These might be files sent to you (such as a video clip of a friend's wedding) or files you have created. To playback a video, double-click the video file.

You can also access online sites and view clips from those sites. To playback an online clip, click the link for that particular video.

tip

In addition to being able to play video clips within Media Player, you can play video clips from Internet Explorer.

For instance, WindowsMedia.com provides links to video clips of current movies. Click the link to see the movie clip.

Tuning the Radio

In addition to listening to music, playing music online, and viewing videos, you can also tune into your favorite radio station and listen to taped or live radio broadcasts right from your computer. You can select from several preset radio stations, including NPR (National Public Radio), MSNBC, and others. (To use this feature, you must be connected to the Internet.) Click the Radio Tuner button in the Media Player window's taskbar to find and listen to radio stations (see Figure 11.9).

FIGURE 11.9

Tune into the radio from the Radio Tuner tab in Windows Media Player.

Using Other Media Players

In addition to WindowsMedia.com, you can find many other sites devoted to music where you can get information about CDs and artists, hear sound clips of tracks, purchase albums, and download music to your computer. Popular sites include iTunes.com, MusicMatch.com, and Realplayer.com.

You can sometimes download free music, such as promotional songs. You can also purchase and download specific songs or entire albums. At iTunes, for instance, you pay 99 cents for each song. If you use another player, follow the specific instructions for using that player to purchase, download, play, and handle music files.

caution

One hassle is that sites usually require you to use their player to play their music files. For instance, you must download and use the iTunes Player to play (and copy to a CD) music files from that site. Expect this to change as users demand more compatibility among different players.

Creating Your Own Music CDs

With Windows Media Player (and other players as well), you can create your own custom CDs. For instance, you might create a CD with party tunes for an upcoming event, or you might create a CD for a friend, sharing your latest favorite songs. You can create a CD from any songs on your computer. In addition to creating a CD, you can also download music to a portable music player. This section covers the basics of creating your own music CDs.

Copying Music Files

To create a CD, you first must make sure that the tracks are stored on your computer or network. If you use Windows Media Player, all of your music (and video) files are stored in the Media Library. This includes music you have downloaded using Windows Media Player, any music already on your computer (such as sample songs that may be included with Windows Media Player), and songs you have copied to the Media Library.

You can copy music from existing music CDs to the library. To do so, follow these steps:

1. Insert the music CD into the CD drive and stop its playback.

2. Click the Copy from CD button to display and select the tracks you want to copy. To select a track, make sure its checkbox is checked. If you don't want to include a track, uncheck its checkbox (see Figure 11.10).

FIGURE 11.10

Select the songs you want to copy from the CD.

3. When all the tracks are selected, click the Copy Music button. The files are then copied from the music CD to the Media Library. You can then select from these tracks to create your own custom CD.

Note that the first time you copy music files, you are prompted to select how to handle them. Follow these steps:

1. Review the copyright information, select the option, and click Next.

2. Review the information on new music file formats, select a format, and click Finish. You'll see the Options dialog box (see Figure 11.11).

tip

You can also view and change these options by clicking Tools and then Options. Click the Copy Music tab in the Options dialog box.

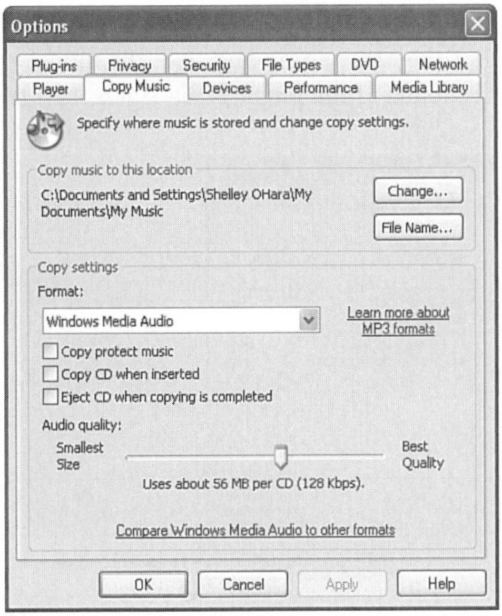

FIGURE 11.11

Use this dialog box to set copy options, such as the location for the music files.

Options

| Plug-ins | Privacy | Security | File Types | DVD | Network |
| Player | Copy Music | Devices | Performance | Media Library |

Specify where music is stored and change copy settings.

Copy music to this location

C:\Documents and Settings\Shelley OHara\My Documents\My Music

Change...

File Name...

Copy settings

Format:

Windows Media Audio

Learn more about MP3 formats

☐ Copy protect music
☐ Copy CD when inserted
☐ Eject CD when copying is completed

Audio quality:

Smallest Size — Best Quality

Uses about 56 MB per CD (128 Kbps).

Compare Windows Media Audio to other formats

OK   Cancel   Apply   Help

3. Make any changes to the Copy Music options. For instance, you can select a different folder for the music files, select what happens after the files are copied (such as whether the disk is ejected), and you can make other changes.

4. Click OK.

caution

When copying audio files, be sure that you understand the legal ramifications of copyright protection.

Creating a Playlist

The next step in creating your own CD is to create a playlist that includes the songs you want. To do so, follow these steps:

1. Click the Media Library button to view all of the various music files on your computer. (The first time you view the library, you are asked whether you want Windows Media Player to search for and include all of the media files on your computer. Follow the prompts to complete the search.)

2. Click the Playlists button and then click New Playlist. You'll be prompted to type a name, and you'll see the songs in your library listed.

3. Type a name for the playlist.

4. In the list of available songs, select each song to add by clicking on its name. (You may have to expand the list to display the song name. For instance, you may have to click the artist name and then the album name.) When you click a song, it is added to the playlist (see Figure 11.12).

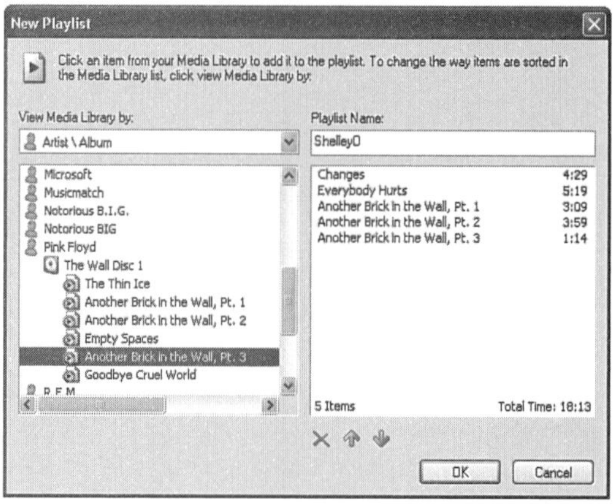

FIGURE 11.12

Type a name for this new playlist and then add the songs.

5. When all the songs are added, click OK. You can then use this playlist to copy the songs to a CD, which is the topic of the next section.

Burning a CD

After you've set up a playlist, you can copy the songs in that list to a CD. Follow these steps:

1. Click Copy to CD or Device.

2. In the Items to Copy pane, click the down arrow and then select the playlist or category of tracks that you want to copy (see Figure 11.13).

FIGURE 11.13
Select the playlist
to copy from this
drop-down list.

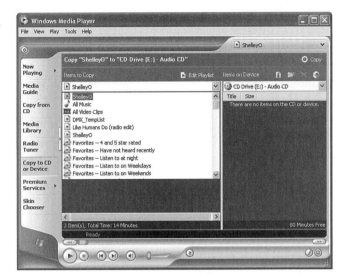

3. All of the songs are selected. If you want to exclude some songs, uncheck the check boxes for those particular songs. The number of selected items and total time are displayed at the bottom of the Items to Copy pane.

4. Insert a blank CD into the CD drive. Then click Copy, and the songs are copied to the CD.

You can also copy the songs and playlists from your computer to a portable music player, such as an MP3 player. To do so, connect your player and then select the device from the drop-down list in the Items on Device pane.

Playing and Recording Sounds with Sound Recorder

For simple audio needs, you can use the Sound Recorder accessory program to play back and record sounds. You can record your own sounds and insert the sound files into your documents or attach them to an email. To use Sound Recorder, you need a sound card and speakers, which are standard on most computers.

note

MP3 is a popular format for music files, and you can purchase these players to store and play back music (much like a Sony Walkman, but without a CD disc). MP4 players are starting to hit the market at the time of this book's writing. Expect that newer file format (and player) to become the standard as time goes on.

Playing Sounds

Follow these steps to play a sound file:

1. Click Start, All Programs, Accessories, Entertainment, and select Sound Recorder. You'll see the Sound Recorder window.

2. Click File and then click the Open command.

3. Change to the drive and folder containing the sound file you want to play.

4. Double-click the sound file to open it in Sound Recorder (see Figure 11.14). Then click the Play button to hear the file.

tip

To sample one of the Windows sounds, select the Windows\Media folder.

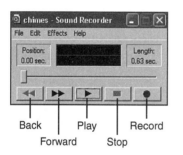

FIGURE 11.14

You can play sound files in Sound Recorder.

Back   Play   Record
Forward   Stop

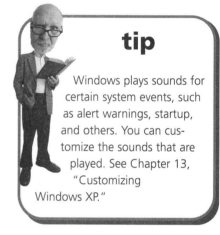

tip

Windows plays sounds for certain system events, such as alert warnings, startup, and others. You can customize the sounds that are played. See Chapter 13, "Customizing Windows XP."

5. Click the Close button to close the Sound Recorder window.

Recording Sounds

You can also record sounds using Sound Recorder. For instance, you might want to attach a recording of you signing happy birthday to an email message, or you might record notes about a particular project to send along to a co-worker.

To record sounds, follow these steps:

1. Start Sound Recorder.

2. Click File and then click the New command.

note

To record sounds, you must have a microphone or other sound input device connected. Check with your particular sound system for instructions on connecting and testing this device.

3. Click the Record button.

4. Speak into the microphone to record your sound. When you are finished recording, click the Stop button.

5. To save your sound, click File and then click the Save As command. Select a folder, type a filename, and click Save. See Chapter 2 for more information on saving files.

6. Click the Close button to close the Sound Recorder window.

THE ABSOLUTE MINIMUM

This chapter explores some of the ways you can use Windows XP as an entertainment system. You can play audio CDs, go online to view video clips or play music tracks, and more. When working with entertainment media, keep these key points in mind:

- To use the media features, you must have the proper hardware, and you must have the hardware set up. To play back music, you need speakers and a sound card (which are standard on most computers).

- You can play any audio CDs. The quality of the playback is determined by your speaker quality. When playing a CD, you can select a different track, adjust the volume, view visualizations, and stop the music.

- If you want to personalize your Media Player, you can do so by selecting a skin. A skin is like an "outfit" that the program puts on to change how it looks. The program works the same and has the same features; it simply looks different.

- One place that's convenient to access for online music and videos is WindowsMedia.com. You can access this from the Windows Media Player window.

- You can use Windows Media Player to copy music from audio CDs to your music library. You can create playlists from all of your various tracks. You can then play back these lists or use them to create your own custom CDs.

- For simple sounds, you can use Sound Recorder to play them. You can also record sounds and include them in email messages or documents.

12

WORKING WITH PHOTOGRAPHS AND MOVIES

One of the newest additions to a computer is a digital camera. Digital cameras are affordable and provide some additional benefits over traditional cameras. This chapter covers the basics of setting up a digital camera and then working with the picture files. You can print or email the pictures, or you can order prints of the pictures from online photo services.

In addition to using a digital camera, you can scan images from a book or an existing photograph and use those pictures. For instance, you might scan in old family photographs so that you have safe digital copies of important pictures. You can edit, print, and share these photos, just as you can with digital photos captured with a camera. This chapter also covers using a scanner.

You also learn a little about Windows XP's movie program. If you have a digital video camera, you can use it to record movies. You can then download the movies to your computer and edit them using Windows MovieMaker.

Using a Digital Camera

A digital camera works basically the same way as a regular camera, and the features available on a digital camera are similar. That is, to take a picture with a digital camera, you point and shoot. Instead of film, however, the digital camera saves the image in its internal memory or on a special memory card. You can then copy the pictures from the camera's memory or the memory card to your computer for editing, printing, emailing, and so on.

You can find a wide range of cameras. High-end cameras provide higher-quality pictures and have extra features, such as additional lenses, zoom features, and so on. With some cameras, you can even shoot and store a short video.

The exact steps for using your particular camera vary depending on the model you have. Consult the documentation that came with the hardware to learn how to take pictures. Taking pictures isn't difficult, but you need to learn about the special features of your camera, including the following:

> **note**
>
> Digital cameras range in price from a couple hundred dollars all the way up to several hundred. You can find reviews of digital cameras in several computer publications and Web sites, including www.pcworld.com. Before shopping, read the reviews so that you know what key features you need and what the price range is for those features.

- Some cameras let you shoot pictures at different resolutions (quality or sharpness of the image). You usually select the resolution from the camera's menu system or with a dial on the camera. Quality affects not only how well the pictures look, but also how big the file is (how much memory is used to store the image). The higher the quality, the more memory it takes and the fewer pictures you can store at one time on your camera.

- Most cameras enable you to preview the picture immediately after you take it. Don't like it? Delete it, and reshoot the picture. This is one of the great benefits of a digital camera. You no longer waste film on "bad" pictures. Your camera will have some method for scrolling through the pictures stored in memory, as well as deleting any images you choose not to keep.

- Digital cameras don't use film. As mentioned, the images are stored in the camera's internal memory or on a memory card (called a SmartMedia or CompactFlash card). When the memory is full, you can download the pictures to your computer via a cable and then delete the images from the camera's memory. You can then take your next batch of pictures. Your camera most likely came with a cable used to attach the camera to your computer.

Also, you usually receive a photo program for transferring, viewing, and even editing the pictures with the camera. Again, these vary from camera to camera. With Kodak cameras, for instance, you use the Kodak Picture Transfer software (see Figure 12.1).

note

Some newer cameras can save pictures to a floppy disk or CD directly. For instance, Sony's Mavica line offers these capabilities.

FIGURE 12.1
You can transfer pictures from your camera to your computer.

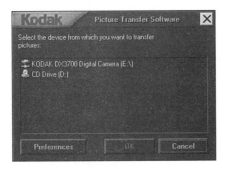

- You can print your pictures on a regular printer (from which the quality will be so-so) or on a special photo printer with special photo paper. Additionally, you can order prints online from printing services. Also, you can take your camera storage media (the memory card) to regular film service sites and have the prints developed. You learn more about this in the section "Printing Pictures" later in this chapter.

tip

If your camera did not come with a photo software transfer program, you can use Windows XP's Photo Wizard. See "Setting Up Your Digital Camera" later in this chapter for more information.

Setting Up Your Digital Camera

Windows XP recognizes common cameras and scanners, so often you need only attach the device to your computer and Windows XP will recognize the new hardware and set it up automatically. You'll know this is happening because Windows XP alerts you with messages that pop up in the system tray.

If you have a camera that Windows XP does not recognize, you can set it up manually using the Scanner and Camera Installation Wizard. Follow these steps:

1. Click Start and then click Control Panel.

2. Click Printers and Other Hardware.

3. Click the Scanners and Cameras Control Panel icon.

4. In the task pane, click the Add an imaging device link (see Figure 12.2) to start the Scanner and Camera Installation Wizard.

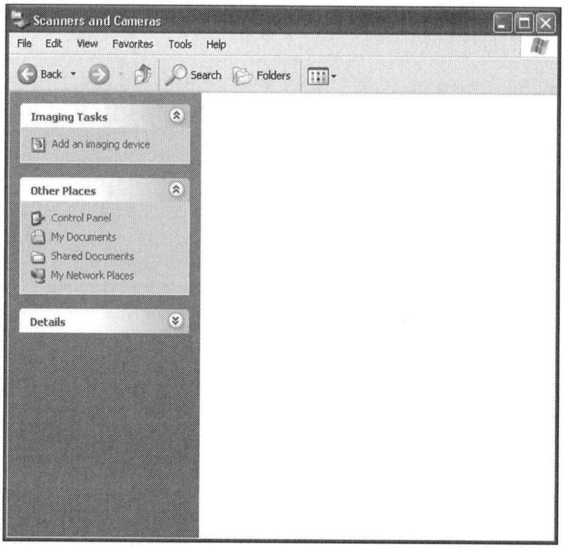

FIGURE 12.2

You can start Windows' Scanner and Camera Installation Wizard from the Control Panel.

5. Follow the steps in the wizard, entering or selecting the correct settings and clicking Next to move from one step to another. The basic steps ask you to select the manufacturer and model of your particular device (see Figure 12.3). You also select the port to which the device is attached, as well as type an identifying name for the device. When you've entered all the information, click Finish to complete the setup.

tip

Your camera most likely came with a disk with the appropriate driver (the file that tells Windows the technical details about the camera). You can use this disk to set up your camera. (This may be your only choice if your camera model is not listed in the Scanner and Camera Installation Wizard.) To do so, click Have Disk when prompted to select the manufacturer and model and then select the drive that contains your camera's disk. Follow the steps for that process, clicking Next to go from step to step.

FIGURE 12.3

You can select
your particular
camera from the
list.

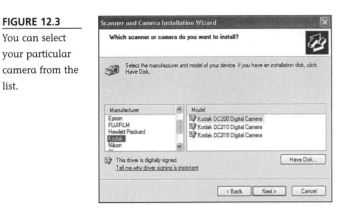

Transferring Pictures

The basic mechanics of using a digital camera are
that you take the pictures and then download
them to your computer. When downloaded, you
have several options for working with the pictures
as covered in this section.

The steps vary depending on your camera setup,
but the general process for transferring pictures is
as follows:

1. Connect the camera to your computer via a
   cable.

2. Using Windows XP's Transfer Wizard or
   your camera's Transfer Wizard, transfer the
   images from the camera's memory (or
   media card) to your hard disk.

3. Select any options for the download. For
   instance, you may choose to delete the pictures from the camera's memory after
   downloading. As another option, you may
   select to download only some of the images
   or all the images. Figure 12.4 shows the
   download options for Kodak's transfer
   program.

note

Windows XP prefers
that you store these images
in the My Pictures folder. Your particular camera software, however,
might automatically transfer the
images to another folder. For
instance, with my Kodak camera,
the transfer program places all the
images in the Kodak Picture folder
and names each folder by the date
the images were transferred. You
can always move and rename the
files. Chapter 3 covers how to
rename and move files.

FIGURE 12.4

You can down-
load pictures
from your
camera to
Windows XP.

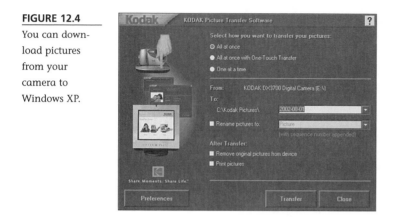

Check your particular camera and its transfer program for the specifics.

Working with Picture Files

After the images are transferred or scanned (scanning is covered later in this chapter), you have several options for working with the files. This section covers how to
organize, edit, and insert pictures into documents. The next section covers options
for printing photographs.

Managing Picture Files

Here are some of the common things you do with pictures to prepare them for
printing or emailing:

- To organize pictures, Windows XP includes a special folder named My
  Pictures. Consider placing all pictures within this folder. You can create subfolders within the main My Pictures folder to store similar pictures together.

- When you open a folder that contains pictures and then select picture files,
  the task pane displays picture-related tasks. For instance, Figure 12.5 shows
  some pictures from a digital camera.

- The default names used for the images are not descriptive. To effectively
  store your pictures, you should rename them. To do so, right-click the image,
  select Rename, type a new name, and press Enter. This process can be
  tedious, but you will be glad you went to the trouble when you are looking
  for a photo. The folder names are usually the dates of transfer (2005_12_09,
  for example). Again, rename these to something more descriptive (such as
  Michael's Birthday).

FIGURE 12.5

In the My
Pictures folder,
you see com-
mands for work-
ing with pictures.

■ Picture files can be large. You usually don't want to permanently store them on your hard disk. Instead, you can work with them and then print or email them. After those tasks are finished, you can consider a more efficient storage media. For instance, if you have a CD-R disk drive (the R indicates *recordable*), you can store pictures on a CD disk. To copy pictures to a CD-R disk, right-click the folder or picture(s) you want to copy and then select Send To. From the Send To menu, select CD drive and follow the instructions in the wizard.

■ You might also simply want to delete the picture files. (If you keep all your picture negatives from a traditional camera, you'll want to save them to another medium. If you throw out the negatives after receiving your prints, you might want to delete some, if not all, of the picture files.)

Editing Pictures

Most cameras come with software for working with the images. You can use this software to get rid of red eye, crop images, combine images, and make other changes. This is yet another benefit of digital cameras; you have many options for improving the shot.

For instance, Figure 12.6 shows a picture opened in JASC Paint Shop Pro. You can use the many features of this program to adjust the color, crop the image, add a frame, and even add special effects. For specific instructions on using your program, consult that program's manual or online help.

Inserting a Picture into a Document

You might want to insert some images into a document. For instance, you might include product pictures in a catalog, or you might include family photos in a Christmas letter. As another example, you might insert images into a Web document if you want to display them as part of your Web site.

To insert a picture into a document, look for the appropriate command in the Insert menu. In Word, for instance, you use the Insert, Picture, From File command or the From Scanner or Camera command to insert an image from a camera or scanner. Check with the specific program documentation or online help for the specifics on inserting images.

tip

If you don't have software or if you want more sophisticated program tools, you can purchase a picture-editing program. These range from simple—Adobe's $99 Photoshop Elements—to complex—the complete Adobe Photoshop. You can find other programs besides those created by Adobe, although Adobe is the most popular.

Printing Pictures

After your pictures are organized, renamed, and touched up (as needed), you can print them on a regular printer, on a special photo printer, or on a regular printer that has special photo printing features. You can also order prints online through a film service company. Windows XP includes wizards for both printing options; you can use these to guide you step by step through the process of printing pictures.

Printing Pictures on a Printer

Follow these steps to print pictures:

1. Open the folder that contains the pictures you want to print.

2. Click Print pictures in the task pane. This starts the Photo Printing Wizard.

3. Follow the steps in the wizard, clicking Next to move from step to step. You can select which pictures are printed (see Figure 12.7) by checking or unchecking individual pictures to make your selections. You can clear all selected pictures by clicking Clear All, or you can select all pictures by clicking Select All.

FIGURE 12.7

As one option in the Photo Printing Wizard, you can select which pictures are printed.

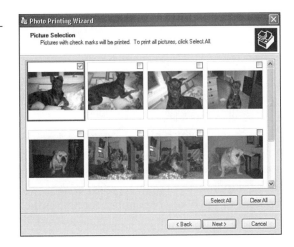

In the next steps, you select the printer to use and then the layout for the pictures (full page, 8×10, 5×7, and other common photo sizes). When the pictures are printed, You'll see the final step of the wizard, telling you the pictures have been printed. Click Finish to close the Photo Printing Wizard.

Ordering Photo Prints from the Internet

If you don't get the quality you want from your printer, you can select to order photo shop quality prints from the Internet. Windows XP includes a wizard that leads you step by step

tip

You can also include pictures within documents. The exact steps vary depending on the program. In Word, for instance, you use the Insert, Picture, From File command. Check your program documentation for the exact instructions on inserting pictures in your particular program(s).

through the process of ordering prints from popular print services. You can get pricing information when you order the prints. Also, expect to pay a small shipping charge. For payment, you must supply a credit card number and shipping information. Pictures usually arrive in a couple of days. Some services offer several free prints as a trial run.

To order copies from the Internet, you must be connected to it. If you are not connected, you are prompted to do so. When connected, follow these steps to order prints:

1. Open the folder containing the pictures you want to print.

2. Click Order prints online.

3. Complete the steps in the wizard to order your copies, clicking Next to move from step to step. The steps vary depending on the service you select, but you can expect to select which pictures you want to order (much like selecting which pictures to print), the size of the pictures (the costs for the print sizes are listed), and the shipping and payment information. Figure 12.8, for instance, shows some of the available options for Shutterfly.

4. For the final step, click Finish to submit your pictures.

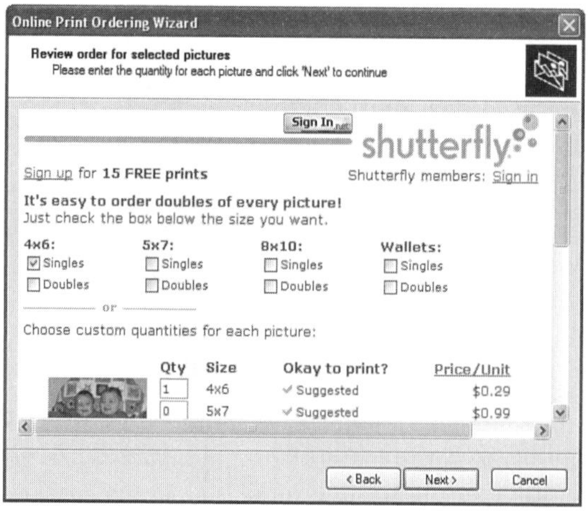

> **tip**
>
> You won't get photo-quality pictures with a regular computer printer. You can, however, purchase special photo printers and photo paper. Expect to pay from $100 to $800 or more for a special photo printer. Some new printers are good for both document, color, and photo printing. Visit computer retail stores to see the various options. The best way to pick a printer? Check the actual printouts from various printers to find one with an acceptable print quality.

FIGURE 12.8

You can select the size and other options for ordering prints online.

Emailing Pictures

It's fun to share pictures with friends and family. In addition to printing, you can email pictures using the E-mail Picture command in the task pane. You might, for instance, email a picture of your new puppy to your friends, or you might email pictures from a family reunion to your family members who live out of town. To email pictures, simply follow these steps:

1. Open the folder containing the pictures you want to email.

2. Select the picture(s) you want to send. Pictures are like regular files. You can change how they are displayed using the View menu, and you can select them just like you select regular files. (See Chapter 3, "Managing Files," and Chapter 16, "Viewing and Finding Files," for more information.)

3. In the File and Folder Tasks area of the task pane, click E-mail this file. You are then prompted to optimize the image (which speeds sending and opening the picture).

4. Make your selections and click OK. Windows opens an Outlook Express email window with the picture attached (see Figure 12.9).

> **tip**
>
> If your digital camera has a memory card, you can often take this card to a local print service and order prints from the card. Check with your favorite print shop to see what digital camera services it provides.

> **note**
>
> It is best to consider reducing the file size of the picture before emailing it, so it doesn't take as long to transfer on a slow connection. You can do this by reducing its size and image quality.

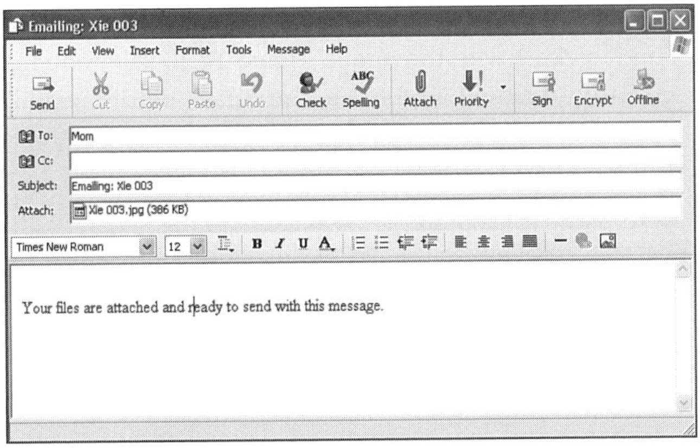

FIGURE 12.9

Enter the email address, type a message, and click Send to send the picture.

5. Complete the email address and any message you want to send with the picture attachment. Then click the Send button. See Chapter 7, "Sending and Receiving Email" for more information on sending messages.

Using a Scanner

Another way to work with not only photos, but also other illustrations, is with a scanner. With a scanner, you can take any image—a photograph, a drawing, a document, and so on—and scan the image, saving it as a file on your computer. Like with a picture, you can then modify, print, and email the image. You can even include the image within a document. For instance, you can scan a picture of your family and insert it into your annual Christmas letter.

The exact steps for using your particular camera and scanner vary depending on the model you have. Therefore, you'll need to consult the documentation that came with the hardware to learn how to scan images.

Setting Up a Scanner

As with a printer, Windows should recognize your scanner after it is hooked up, query it for information, and (if it's a Plug and Play device) install it automatically. If this doesn't happen, you can use the Camera and Scanner Wizard (see "Setting Up Your Digital Camera" earlier in this chapter). The steps are the same, except you select your scanner. You can use a Windows XP driver or the driver supplied with your scanner.

Scanning an Image

If you have a flatbed scanner, you insert the picture or document you want to scan and then use the buttons on the scanner or the commands in the scanner program window to start the scan. The available program options will vary, so you need to check your own particular program for specific instructions.

After the document is scanned into the scan program, you have options for modifying, saving, and working with the image. Figure 12.10 shows options in PaperPort. You can crop, rotate, add text, and more. You can also print, email, rename, and insert the image into a document. See the section "Working with Pictures" for more information.

FIGURE 12.10

This figure shows
the available
options for edit-
ing a scanned
image.

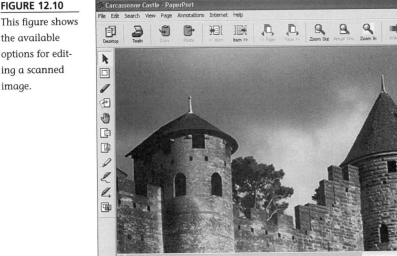

FIGURE 12.10

This figure shows the available options for editing a scanned image.

Creating Digital Movies

In addition to photos, you can create and edit digital movies using a digital camera and Windows XP. Moviemaking is beyond the scope of this book, but this section gives you a quick overview of how the process works. You start by recording the movie using your digital video recorder. (Depending on the type of digital recorder you have, the steps will vary.)

You can then connect your video recorder to your computer, which is much like hooking up a digital camera. The most difficult step is likely getting the hardware (the video recorder) set up to work with Windows XP. You can use the Add Hardware Wizard (covered in Chapter 20, "Upgrading Windows"). You can then transfer the digital movie file to your computer.

Once it is transferred as a file to your computer, you can open the movie file and make changes. You can rearrange the order, add transitions or narration, and make other changes. To do so, use a movie-editing program, such as Windows Movie Maker, the program that is included with Windows XP (see Figure 12.11). To start this program, click Start, All Programs, and then Windows Movie Maker.

Once the program is started, you can do any of the following:

■ Use the File, Open Project command to open the movie you want to view or edit.

■ To import a movie clip, click File, Import and select the media file you want to import. Click Open. Use this method if you have media files already on your computer.

■ To copy material from a video recorder to Windows Movie Maker, use the File, Record command. You can then use the Record dialog box to record the video from the player to Windows. Basically, Windows Movie Maker converts and then saves the video file into a format Movie Maker can work with.

■ The video source is divided into clips, and these are displayed in the pane along the bottom of the window. You also see the clips listed in the Collections bar along the left of the window. You can rearrange these clips into the order you prefer. You can also delete or trim clips if they are too long or are not appropriate. Finally, you can select transitions between clips.

note

Note that this list includes just a sampling of the many things you can do with Windows Movie Maker.

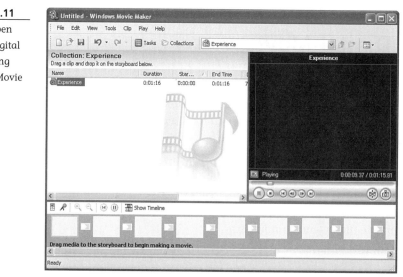

■ In addition to ordering the visual elements, you can record narration to go along with the clips.

■ As you edit the clips, you need to save your work. Windows Movie Maker stores a group of clips as a project. You can use the File, Save Project command to save the project.

■ As you work on your project, you can preview clips or play them back. You can also use the timeline along the bottom to play back certain segments of the project.

For more information on the varied features of this program, consult online help. Otherwise, if you use a different digital movie-editing program, consult the directions for that particular program.

THE ABSOLUTE MINIMUM

This chapter covers some of the fun and exciting things you can do with a digital camera. If you are thinking about buying a digital camera or already have one, keep these key points in mind:

- You can purchase a digital camera and use it with your computer. A digital camera offers many advantages. You can preview your images after you shoot them and delete or reshoot as needed. Also, you don't need to purchase film. You can edit the pictures before printing them, and you can print, email, or order prints online.

- When you attach your camera, Windows XP should query it and set it up automatically. If not, you can run the Scanner and Camera Installation Wizard to set up the camera manually.

- Cameras have different features and work in various ways, but the basics of taking a picture are the same: point and shoot. However, you need to look at your camera's documentation to find out how to change settings such as image quality, as well as how to preview and handle images.

- You can copy the images from your camera's memory to your computer, and you can then work with your pictures. You can make editing changes using a photo-editing program. You should also rename the files and folders because the default names are not very descriptive.

- You can print your pictures on a regular printer or a printer that supports photo printing. Usually, you get the best quality when you use a photo printer and special photo paper. You can also order prints online or take your camera's media card to a regular print service bureau and have copies made.

- In addition to cameras, another common imaging device is a scanner. You can use this hardware component to scan in photos, illustrations, documents, and other types of visual or textual information.

- If you have a digital video recorder, you can shoot movies and transfer them from the recorder to your computer. You can then edit the movie using movie programs such as Windows Movie Maker.

PART IV

YOUR OWN PERSONAL WINDOWS

13

CUSTOMIZING WINDOWS XP

Windows XP provides many customization options so that you can personalize your computer. Some of these changes are practical. For instance, if you are left-handed, you can change the mouse buttons so that the buttons work for the left hand. If you have trouble seeing the display, you can alter the size (the resolution) of the desktop. If you prefer the taskbar on another part of the desktop, you can move it.

Other changes are purely personal. For instance, you may want to display a wallpaper image on your desktop, or you may want to change the sounds that are played for system events (such as shutdown). This chapter covers the most common customization changes. The other chapters in this part of the book cover other customizing options, specifically for setting up programs and for customizing email and Internet Explorer.

Customizing the Taskbar

The taskbar, although small in size, actually tells you a lot. It lets you know which programs are running and which windows are open. It tells you the time and shows icons when other activities are going on. For example, if you see a printer icon, you know that your computer is sending data to the printer. If you see a connection icon, you know that you are connected to the Internet.

tip

If you share your computer with other users, make sure to create separate user accounts before making any dramatic changes to the interface.

Windows XP enables you to customize the taskbar and system tray. To make any changes, display the Taskbar and Start Menu Properties dialog box by following these steps:

1. Right-click a blank part of the taskbar and select the Properties command from the pop-up menu. You'll see the Taskbar and Start Menu Properties dialog box (see Figure 13.1).

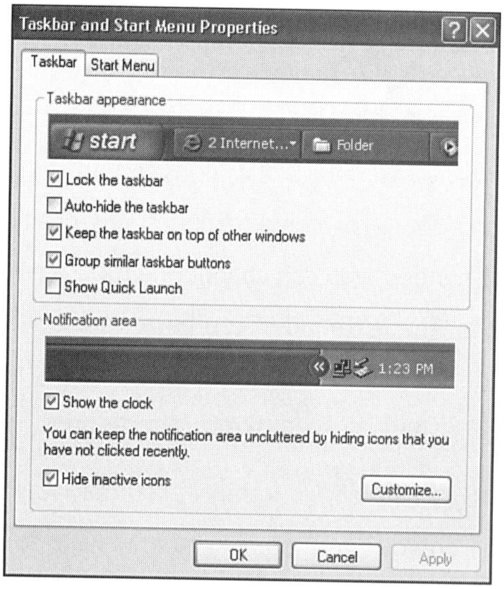

FIGURE 13.1

Use this dialog box to customize the taskbar and system tray.

Taskbar and Start Menu Properties

Taskbar | Start Menu

Taskbar appearance

🔳 start | 🌐 2 Internet...▾ | 📁 Folder | ◉

☑ Lock the taskbar
☐ Auto-hide the taskbar
☑ Keep the taskbar on top of other windows
☑ Group similar taskbar buttons
☐ Show Quick Launch

Notification area

《 🖳💬 1:23 PM

☑ Show the clock

You can keep the notification area uncluttered by hiding icons that you have not clicked recently.

☑ Hide inactive icons   Customize...

OK | Cancel | Apply

2. Make any changes.

You can lock the taskbar so that it can't be moved, or unlock it so that it can be moved. Check or uncheck Lock the taskbar.

You can hide the taskbar so that you have more room on the desktop. Check Auto-hide the taskbar. When the taskbar is hidden, you can always redisplay it by pointing to the bottom of the desktop.

You can also select to show the clock, hide inactive icons, keep the taskbar on top of all windows, group similar taskbar buttons into one stacked button, and show a Quick Launch toolbar with buttons for sending email and logging on to the Internet. Check any options to turn them on. Uncheck them to turn the options off.

3. When you are finished making changes, click OK.

The Taskbar and Start Menu Properties dialog box also enables you to customize the Start menu by selecting which items are displayed. For information on these changes, see Chapter 14, "Setting Up Programs."

Customizing the Desktop

You have a lot of choices for customizing the desktop. You can use a desktop theme, change the color scheme, use a screen saver, and more. You can also add the My Computer and My Documents icons to the desktop. All of these options are available in the Display Properties dialog box.

To get started making any of these changes, right-click an empty spot on your desktop and select Properties from the pop-up menu that appears. The Display Properties dialog box appears, with the Themes tab displayed. The following sections describe the most common changes. You can pick and choose which you'd like to try.

To make one change, select the options and click OK to close the dialog box. To make several changes, select the options and then click Apply, leaving the dialog box open to make additional changes. When you are done customizing the display, click OK.

tip

You can also move the taskbar to another location on the desktop and change its size. To move the taskbar, put the mouse pointer on a blank part of the taskbar and drag it to the location you want. To resize the taskbar, put the mouse pointer on the border and drag to resize it. To do this, the taskbar must be unlocked. (The Lock the Taskbar option should not be checked.)

tip

If the date and time are incorrect, you can correct them by right-clicking the time display in the taskbar and selecting Adjust Date/Time. Select the correct date and time. You can click on a date in the calendar or display other months or years from the drop-down list to change the date. You can type or edit the correct time in the text box or drag the hands on the clock. When the date and time are correct, click OK.

Using a Desktop Theme

Desktop themes consist of backgrounds, sounds, icons, and other elements. Windows XP offers numerous color-coordinated themes to choose from; alternatively, you can create your own.

To use a desktop theme, display the Theme drop-down list and select one of the options. If the theme you want to use does not appear in the Theme drop-down list, either select More Themes Online to download additional themes or click Browse and then, in the Open Theme dialog box, open the folder and select the theme you want to use. You can find Windows themes in the WINDOWS\RESOURCES\THEMES folder.

When you select a new theme, you'll see a preview in the Sample window. Figure 13.2 shows the Windows Classic theme.

FIGURE 13.2

You can apply a set of options called a theme.

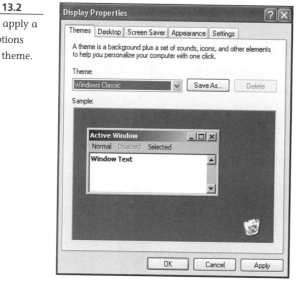

If you don't have the other Windows XP themes installed, you can do so by using the Add/Remove Windows Components Wizard. See Chapter 20, "Upgrading Windows."

Using a Background Image

If you want, you can use an image (such as a favorite picture or pattern) as your Windows desktop. To apply a background picture or pattern to your desktop, follow these steps:

> **note**
>
> If you make changes to any of the other settings discussed in this chapter (such as wallpaper), Windows creates a "modified theme" and lists it as the selected theme on the Themes tab. You can save it by clicking the Save As button and typing a name for this theme.

1. From the Display Properties dialog box, click the Desktop tab.

2. Select the background you want to use from the Background list. Figure 13.3 shows a picture of Stonehenge selected as the background image.

In addition to using one of Windows background images, you can use one of your own pictures. To do so, follow these steps:

1. Click the Browse button on the Desktop tab.

2. In the Browse dialog box, navigate to the folder that contains the picture and then select the picture you want to use. (For more information on navigating through folders, see Chapter 3, "Managing Files.")

3. Click Open. The image is added to the list of Background choices.

4. Select the picture to use it as your background.

5. If the picture doesn't fill the entire screen, you can select a placement for it. Display the Position drop-down list and select a placement.

tip

What's gone? Patterns are gone. Did anyone ever bother with patterns? I doubt it. And what about Active Desktop? It's not exactly called that, and you don't activate it via the desktop shortcut menu. Instead, it's buried a little within the Display Properties tab. See the next section, "Customizing Desktop Icons."

6. If you want to change the background color (for pictures that don't fill the entire screen), display the Color drop-down list and select a color.

7. Click OK to confirm the changes and use this image on your desktop.

Customizing Desktop Icons

By default, the Windows XP desktop does *not* contain the My Computer icon and the My Documents icon. If you are upgrading and prefer this setup, you can add these icons. Even if you are not upgrading, you may prefer fast access to these common folders from the desktop, rather than the Start menu.

To select which desktop icons are displayed, follow these steps:

1. From the Display Properties dialog box, click the Desktop tab.

2. Click the Customize Desktop button. You'll see the Desktop Items dialog box (see Figure 13.4).

3. Check any desktop icons that you want displayed. If an item is checked and you want to hide or remove it from the desktop, click the check box to remove the check.

4. Click OK.

> **tip**
>
> You can remove default desktop icons by unchecking their check boxes. But what about icons you have added yourself? You can delete them by dragging the icons to the Recycle Bin; by selecting the icons, pressing Delete, and clicking Yes to confirm the deletion; or by right-clicking the icons, selecting Delete, and confirming the deletion by clicking Yes.

FIGURE 13.4

You can add icons to the desktop using this dialog box.

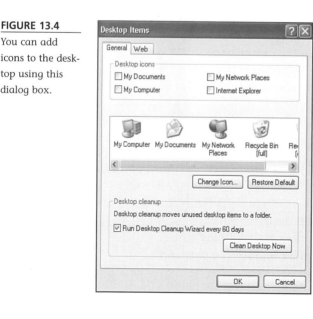

You'll also find these other options in the Desktop Items dialog box:

- You can also select a different icon style by using the Change Icon button. You can experiment by clicking the icon you want to change and then clicking the Change Icon button. Select the new icon and click OK.

- If you have made changes and want to go back to the original icons, click the Restore Default button.

- You can clean up the desktop by removing icons that you do not use. See Chapter 18 for help on using this feature.

- To add desktop content such as your home page, weather information, sports scores, or a stock ticker, click the Web tab (see Figure 13.5). Consult Windows XP's online help for the exact steps on how to add, modify, remove, and synchronize Web content on the desktop.

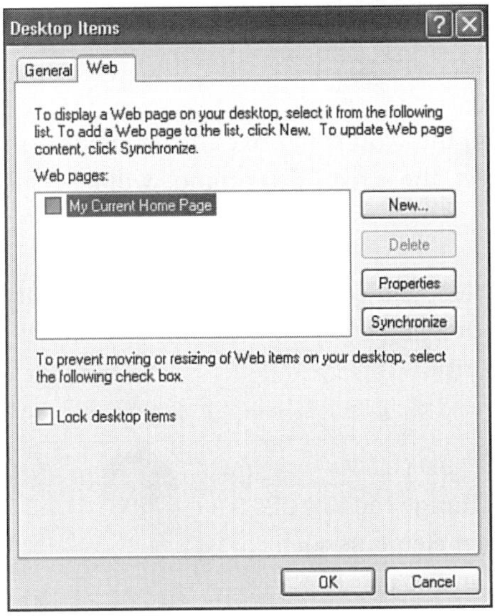

FIGURE 13.5

You can add Web content to your desktop using the options on this tab.

Using a Screen Saver

Screen savers are another desktop option. Are they necessary? Not really. On older monitors, an image could be burned into the monitor if the same text or image was displayed for long periods of time. This is not a problem with current monitors. Screen savers simply provide some pizzazz and a small bit of security for your computer when it is idle.

To use a screen saver, follow these steps:

1. From the Display Properties dialog box, click the Screen Saver tab.

2. Display the Screen Saver drop-down list and select the image you want to use. Figure 13.6, for instance, shows a preview of the Beziers screen saver.

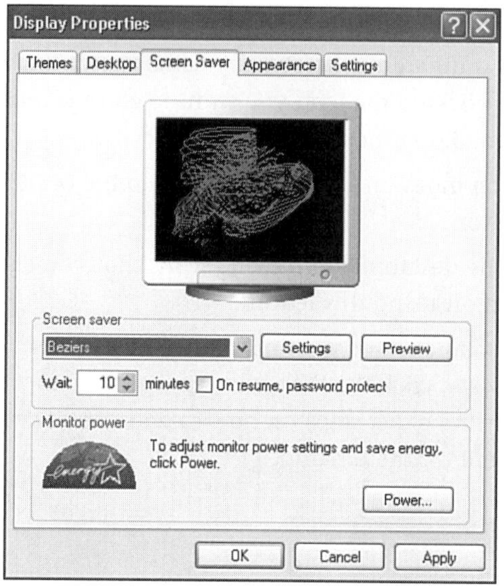

FIGURE 13.6

You can use a screen saver that will automatically turn on when your computer is idle.

Display Properties

Themes | Desktop | Screen Saver | Appearance | Settings

Screen saver

Beziers   [Settings] [Preview]

Wait: 10 minutes ☐ On resume, password protect

Monitor power

To adjust monitor power settings and save energy, click Power.

[Power...]

[OK] [Cancel] [Apply]

3. Set the time limit using the Wait spin boxes. When your computer is idle for the time limit you select, the screen saver image will be displayed.

4. Click OK.

When a screen saver is activated, you can stop its display and redisplay your desktop by moving the mouse or pressing a key. You can also password-protect your screensaver for increased security.

Changing the Color Scheme

Windows XP enables you to change the sets of colors used for certain onscreen elements such as the title bar, background, and so on. These sets of colors are called *schemes*, and you can select colors that work best for you and your monitor. Lighter colors might, for example, make working in some Windows applications easier on your eyes. On the other hand, you might prefer bright and lively colors. You can also select options for Windows and buttons, as well as font size.

To make a change to the desktop color scheme, follow these steps:

1. From the Display Properties dialog box, click the Appearance tab.

> **note**
>
> You can also create your own custom color scheme. To do so, select the scheme that is closest to the style you want. Then click the Advanced button and use the options in the Advanced Appearance dialog box to make changes.

2. Display the Windows and buttons drop-down list and select either Windows Classic style or Windows XP style. Windows Classic style has many more color scheme options; the color scheme options for Windows XP style are limited.

3. Display the Color Scheme drop-down list and select the scheme you want to apply. (The schemes that appear depend on the Windows and buttons style you have selected.)

4. Display the Font size drop-down list and select a font size. You may, for instance, use a larger font size if you find the onscreen text difficult to read. You'll see a preview of all your selections. Figure 13.7 shows Windows Classic style with the Lilac color scheme. The font size has also been changed to Large.

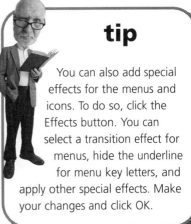

tip

You can also add special effects for the menus and icons. To do so, click the Effects button. You can select a transition effect for menus, hide the underline for menu key letters, and apply other special effects. Make your changes and click OK.

FIGURE 13.7

You can tinker with the colors and fonts used to display programs and windows on your desktop.

Setting Resolution and Color Settings

The term *resolution* refers to many different things that relate to computers and computer equipment. You might hear about resolution as a measure of the quality of a printer, scanner, or camera, for instance. Resolution, in terms of your display, means how big or small the images are, measured in pixels, such as 800 × 600. The larger the number, the smaller (and finer) the images. You can change the resolution as another desktop option.

In addition, you can change the number of colors displayed onscreen. To make these changes, follow these steps:

1. From the Display Properties dialog box, click the Settings tab. You'll see the options shown in Figure 13.8.

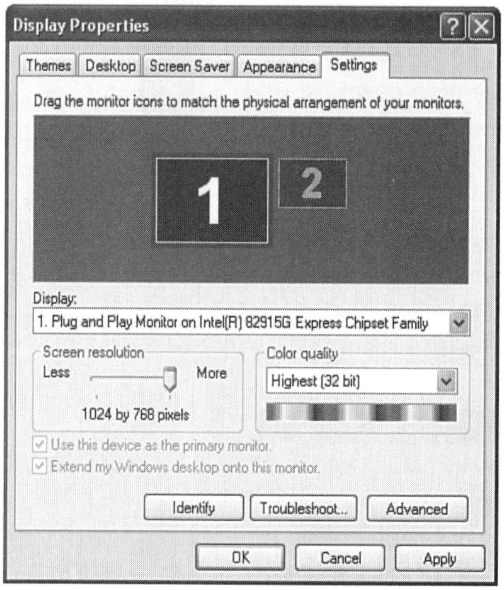

FIGURE 13.8

Yet another desktop option is to change the resolution and color settings.

2. To change the resolution, drag the lever in between Less (bigger) and More (smaller).

3. To change the number of colors that can be displayed, display the Color quality drop-down list and select the color quality. My options were Medium (16 bit) and Highest (32 bit). Depending on your video card (also called an adapter), your options will vary.

4. Click OK.

Customizing the Mouse

Most PC mouse devices have at least two buttons: a left button and a right button. These buttons are used for different purposes. The

caution

If you are having problems with your monitor, you can start the Troubleshooter from the Settings tab. To do so, click the Troubleshoot button, which starts the Video Display Troubleshooter. You can select from several different display problems, and Windows XP Troubleshooter will suggest possible remedies.

left mouse button is used for most tasks: clicking, dragging, opening menus, selecting commands, selecting text, and so on. The right
mouse button is used for less-common tasks. A
common use of the right mouse button is to display a shortcut menu.

If you are left-handed, you can change your
mouse so that the buttons are reversed: Right
does the main options, and left displays the
shortcut menu. You can also make other
changes to the mouse, including adjusting its
double-click speed or changing how the cursors
appear. Again, these changes are a mix of practical issues (such as the left-handed change) and
personal issues (such as the pointer schemes).

To customize your mouse, follow these steps:

1. Click Start and then Control Panel. You'll see
   the Control Panel options.

2. Click Printers and Other Hardware.

3. In the lower part of the window that lists
   Control Panel icons (see Figure 13.9), click
   Mouse. You'll see the Mouse Properties dia-
   log box.

4. Do any of the following:

   To change the button configuration (a common change for left-handed users), go to
   the Buttons tab and check Switch primary
   and secondary buttons (see Figure 13.10).

   You can also adjust the double-click speed.
   If you have trouble double-clicking, you
   might want to increase or decrease the
   speed to suit how you double-click. You can
   test the speed by double-clicking the folder
   in that area of the dialog box.

   To change the appearance (shape and size)
   of the various mouse pointers that appear,
   click the Pointers tab and then select a
   scheme from the Scheme drop-down list.
   The dialog box displays a preview of
   your selections.

tip

The following steps
assume that you are using
the Category View of the
Control Panel options. You
can also choose Classic View.
Use this if you have
upgraded and are more
comfortable with the Classic View.
Otherwise, you may select this
option if you are having trouble
finding the Control Panel icon you
want to use.

note

The Control Panel is the
main tool for all setup and
customization changes. Other
options are covered throughout
this book. For instance, setting up
printers and installing fonts are
covered in Chapter 19,
"Upgrading Your Computer." User
Accounts are covered in Chapter
22, "Setting Up Windows XP for
Multiple Users." For less common
options, either consult online help
or click a link and experiment.

FIGURE 13.9

Select the Mouse Control Panel icon to make changes to how the mouse works.

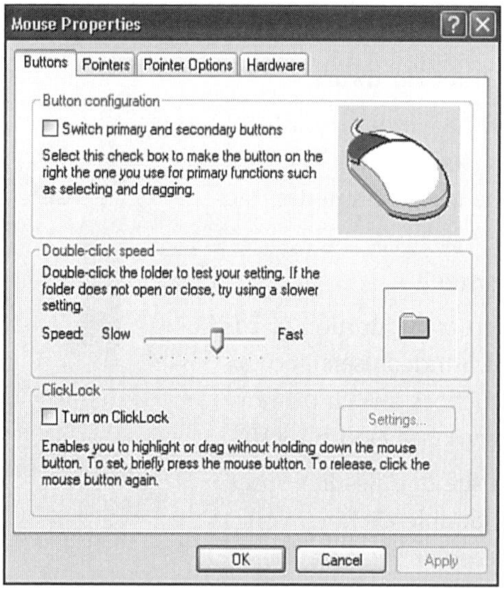

FIGURE 13.10

You can change the behavior of the mouse buttons and the double-click speed.

To add visual pointer clues (such as indicating motion, snapping to the default button in a dialog box, or displaying a trail), click the Pointer Options and make your selections.

For hardware changes, click the Hardware tab. You learn more about hardware changes in Chapter 19.

5. Click OK. Your changes are put into effect.

Customizing Sounds

Windows plays certain sounds for key system events, such as exiting windows, receiving new mail, logging on and logging off, and others. You can change these sounds, as well as adjust the volume, using the Sounds and Audio Devices Control Panel.

To select or adjust the speaker volume and/or use a different sound scheme, follow these steps:

1. Click Start and then Control Panel. You'll see the Control Panel options.

2. Click Sounds, Speech, and Audio Devices.

3. In the lower part of the window that lists Control Panel icons, click Sounds and Audio Devices. You'll see the Sounds and Audio Devices Properties dialog box.

4. Do any of the following:

   To adjust the volume of your speakers, use the Volume tab and drag the volume bar between low (quieter) and high (louder).

   To use a different sound scheme, click the Sounds tab. Display the Sound scheme drop-down list and select a scheme.

   You can also change the sound for individual events by selecting the program event from the list and then displaying the Sounds list and selecting the sound to play (see Figure 13.11).

tip

If an event does not have a sound icon next to it, a sound is not played. You can assign sounds to these items by selecting them and then choosing a sound.

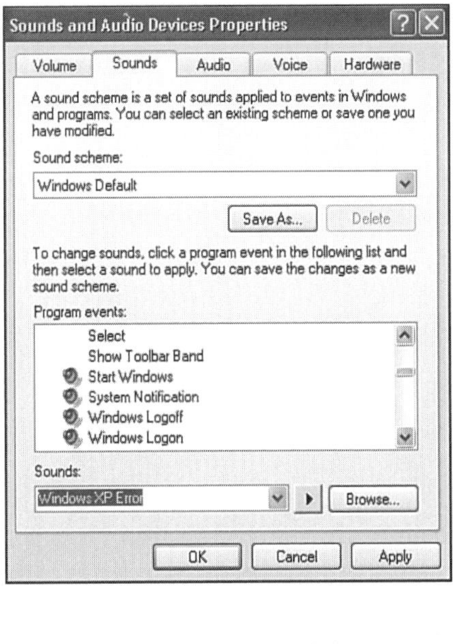

FIGURE 13.11

You can customize the sounds played for program events.

The other tabs help you troubleshoot and upgrade audio equipment as well as voice recognition features. These topics are not covered in this book, although you can find information about hardware settings in Chapter 19.

5. Click OK. Your changes are put into effect.

The Absolute Minimum

This chapter covers some of the many changes you can make to personalize Windows XP to suit your preferences. In particular, keep the following tips in mind:

- Making a change to the desktop is most often just for the appearance of it. You make all of these changes in the Display Properties dialog box. You can display this dialog box by right-clicking a blank part of the desktop and selecting Properties. You can select a theme for the display, choose a background image, use a screen saver, or change the appearance (color, font, and placement) of window elements.

- If you want to put the My Computer and My Documents icons back on the desktop, you can do so by clicking the Customize Desktop button on the Desktop tab. You then can check the desktop icons to display, change the appearance of icons, and have Windows get rid of desktop icons that haven't been used. To get rid of unused icons, use the Desktop Cleanup Wizard, which is covered in Chapter 18.

- On the Settings tab of the Display Properties dialog box, you can change the resolution and the color quality.

- You can change both how the mouse works and how the mouse pointers appear by using the Mouse Control Panel icon.

- Other common changes include using a different sound scheme or selecting different sounds for key system events, such as logging on or logging off. To implement such changes, you use the Sounds and Audio Devices Control Panel.

14

SETTING UP PROGRAMS

In Chapter 1, you learned the basics of how to start a program. In addition to using the Start menu to start programs, you can create shortcut icons to programs. You also can change the Start menu, for example, *pinning* commonly used programs to the main menu (the left side of the menu, with Internet and Email). Finally, you can install new programs and uninstall programs you do not use. This chapter covers all these methods for customizing and setting up programs on your computer.

Creating a Shortcut to a Program

You can create shortcuts and place them on the desktop to provide quick access to programs. You can then double-click a program shortcut to quickly start that program. Creating the shortcut is easy; finding the program file is the most difficult part. To do so, perform the following steps:

note

You can also update Windows and add Windows components. See Chapter 20, "Upgrading Windows."

1. Display the program file for which you want to create a shortcut. For help on navigating among your drives and folders, see Chapter 3, "Managing Files." Usually, most programs are stored within folders in the Program Files folder. Try looking there. For instance, to find Office files, look in Program Files and then Office.

2. Right-click the file and then click the Send To command. From the submenu, click the Desktop (Create Shortcut) command (see Figure 14.1).

FIGURE 14.1
Here, the Excel program file is selected and a shortcut to this program will be added to the desktop.

Windows adds the shortcut to your desktop (see Figure 14.2). Notice that it has a small arrow in the left corner. This indicates that the icon is a shortcut icon. The icon is not the program itself, but a link to the program.

After you add the shortcut icon, you can do any of the following:

- Windows XP uses "Shortcut to" plus the program file name for the shortcut name. For instance, a shortcut icon to Excel is named "Shortcut to Excel." You can change this name to a more descriptive one. To do so, right-click the shortcut, select Rename, type a new name, and press Enter.

- Remember that you can move icons around on the desktop. See Chapter 1, "Getting Started with Windows XP," for more information.

- You can delete a program shortcut icon: Right-click the icon and select Delete. Confirm the deletion by clicking the Delete Shortcut button. Keep in mind (as the confirmation message tells you) that when you delete the shortcut icon, you

tip

You can follow these same steps to create a shortcut to a file or folder. Open the drive and folder where the folder or file is stored. Then right-click and select Send To, Desktop (Create Shortcut). When you double-click a file shortcut, that file is opened in the associated program. For instance, if you double-click a shortcut to a Word file, the document is opened and Word is started. If you double-click a folder shortcut, the contents of that folder are displayed.

are not deleting the program itself, just the pointer to the program. If you want to get rid of the program (remove it from your computer), you must uninstall the program. See "Uninstalling Applications" later in this chapter.

■ Some programs add shortcut icons to your desktop automatically when you install them. You have the same options for working with these icons: You can rename them, move them, delete them, and double-click them.

■ The purpose of the desktop is to provide quick access to your most commonly used programs (files and folders also). If your desktop becomes too cluttered with icons, you defeat the purpose of having fast access. You can clean up your desktop by getting rid of program icons you don't use that often. You can find information on this process in Chapter 18, "Improving Your Computer's Performance."

Customizing the Start Menu

In addition to adding desktop icons, you can add programs to the Start menu and change how the Start menu looks. For instance, you may prefer the Classic Start menu (the one from previous Windows versions), or you may prefer to list more or fewer programs on the left pane. You can also select whether to list the Internet and E-mail programs, as well as which programs are used for these commands. This section covers these topics.

Pinning a Program to the Start Menu

When you install most programs, they are automatically added to the Start menu. You can then start programs by clicking Start, All Programs. Windows XP also enables you to *pin* a program to your Start menu. When you pin a program, it is always listed at the top left of the Start menu (with the Internet and E-mail programs).

To pin a program to the Start menu, follow these steps:

1. Display the program for which you want to create a shortcut. You don't have to find the actual program file. You can use the program name listed in the Start menu, either on the left side (for commonly used programs) or on the All Programs list.

tip

When you pin a program to your Start menu, it is placed in the left pane of the menu. You can drag the pinned program to the My Documents, My Pictures, or My Music folders, but nowhere else within the Start menu.

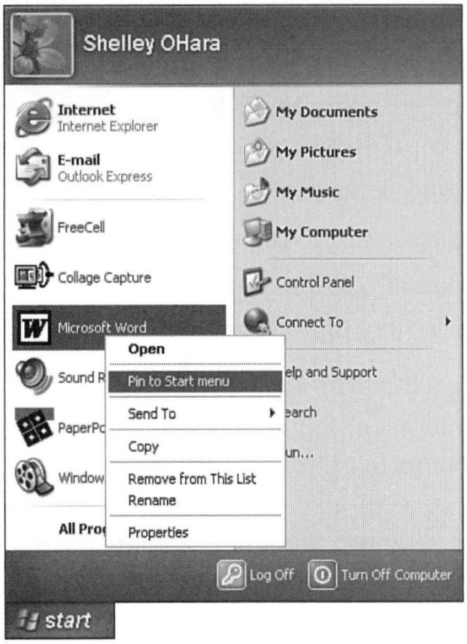

FIGURE 14.3

You can use the Start menu to list the program you want to pin.

2. Right-click the program name and click the Pin to Start menu command (see Figure 14.3). The program is then added to your Start menu. Figure 14.4, for instance, shows Word listed on the top left part of the Start menu. Word will always be listed there for fast access until you delete or unpin it.

FIGURE 14.4

You can pin commonly used programs to the Start menu so that the program is always listed.

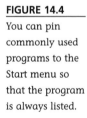

Unpinning a Program to the Start Menu

If you don't want the program listed anymore (at least not on the top part of the Start menu), you can remove it by unpinning it. To unpin a program, follow these steps:

1. Click Start to display the Start menu.

2. Right-click the program you want to unpin. You then see the shortcut menu.

3. Click Unpin from Start menu. The program is no longer listed on that part of the Start menu. (However, the program name still appears in the All Programs list.)

Note that you cannot unpin Internet or E-mail, but you can hide them by customizing the Start menu (a topic covered in "Changing the Appearance of the Start Menu," later in this section).

Rearranging Programs on the Start Menu

Another way to change the Start menu is to change the order of the programs listed. You can rearrange the order of the programs. To do so, click the item you want to move and then drag it to the new location in the Start menu.

Changing the Appearance of the Start Menu

You have more options on how the Start menu appears. For instance, if you have upgraded from a previous version of Windows, you may prefer the old style (called Classic). You may want to change the number of programs listed on the left pane. You may choose not to list the Internet or E-mail programs, or you may want to use programs for these tasks other than the defaults. (Internet Explorer is the default program for the Internet command. Outlook Express is usually the default program for the E-mail command.)

Follow these steps to make a change to the Start menu:

1. Right-click a blank part of the taskbar and select Properties from the shortcut menu.

2. Click the Start Menu tab (see Figure 14.5).

3. To use the Classic Start menu, click Classic Start menu. To use the regular, default menu, click Start menu.

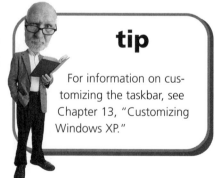

tip

For information on customizing the taskbar, see Chapter 13, "Customizing Windows XP."

FIGURE 14.5

Here you can select the Classic Start menu and access customizing features.

4. Click OK.

   Or

   If you want to make additional customizing changes, click the Customize button. You'll see the Customize Start Menu dialog box. This dialog box varies depending on what menu you selected for Step 3. Figure 14.6 and the following steps explain the options for customizing the regular Start menu.

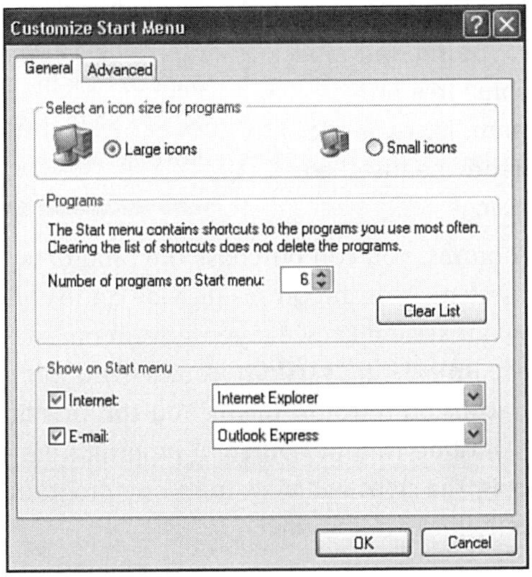

FIGURE 14.6

This figure shows the options for customizing the Windows XP style Start menu.

5. From this dialog box, you can do any of the following:

   Windows XP uses large icons. If you have several programs, making the Start menu long, you can choose to use small icons. Click Small Icons in the first part of the dialog box.

   Select the number of recently used programs to list on the left side of the Start menu.

   To turn off the commands for starting your Internet and/or email programs, uncheck the option(s). To use a different program for either, display the drop-down list next to the program type and then select the program to use.

6. Click OK to put your changes into effect.

Installing Programs

When you bought your computer, it most likely came with certain programs already installed. Depending on the brand and model, you might have received some free programs—an antivirus program, for example. These programs should already be installed and set up on your computer.

tip

To clear the list of programs on the Start menu, click Clear List.

tip

For more advanced options, click the Advanced tab in the Customize Start Menu dialog box and then make any changes. Here, you can add a list of recently opened Documents (as in past Windows versions). You can also select which items are listed. As a beginner, it's best to stick with the defaults, but you may want to click this tab and view the options so that you know what's available.

If you want to add new programs, you can purchase the programs you want and then install them on your system. Most programs provide an installation program that automatically checks your system (to see if you have room for the new program and whether you have an existing version), copies the appropriate files, and sets up its related program icons on the Start menu. You can just sit back and click, click, click through the installation routine. Different programs employ different installation processes. That is, the steps will vary from one program to another, but installing programs is usually fairly automated.

The first thing to do is to start the installation program. Depending on your particular program, this might happen automatically. If not, you can use the Windows Add or Remove Programs Control Panel icon to start the installation. Both methods are covered here.

Using the Automatic Install

To start the installation automatically, insert the program disc. Usually, the program has an autoplay feature that automatically starts the setup or installation process and displays your options. You should see a menu or dialog box with options for installing the program. Then, skip to the section "Completing the Installation."

Using the Add or Remove Programs Control Panel Icon

If the installation program is not automatically started, you can use the Windows XP's Add or Remove Programs feature. To do so, follow these steps:

1. Click the Start button and then Control Panel.

2. Click Add or Remove Programs. You'll see the Add or Remove Programs window (see Figure 14.7).

note

You learn how to uninstall programs later in this chapter. See Chapter 20 for information on adding Windows components.

FIGURE 14.7

Use this Control Panel feature to change or remove programs, install new programs, or add or remove Windows components.

Add or Remove Programs		
Currently installed programs:	Sort by:	Name
KODAK Camera Connection Software	Size	2.75MB
	Used	rarely
	Last Used On	7/30/2002
To change this program or remove it from your computer, click Change/Remove.		Change/Remove
KODAK Picture Software	Size	0.33MB
KODAK Picture Transfer Software	Size	2.75MB
Microsoft Office 2000 Premium	Size	212.00MB
OneTouch Version 2.2	Size	2.19MB
PaperPort 7.0		
QuickTime	Size	9.66MB
Windows XP Service Pack 1		

(Sidebar icons: Change or Remove Programs, Add New Programs, Add/Remove Windows Components, Set Program Access and Defaults)

3. Click the Add New Programs button in the taskbar. You'll see the choices for installing the program (see Figure 14.8).

FIGURE 14.8

When installing programs, select CD or Floppy. (Updating Windows, the other option, is covered in Chapter 20.)

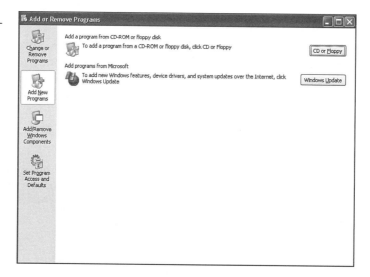

4. Click the CD or Floppy button. Doing so starts the installation wizard.

5. Insert the program's CD-ROM or floppy disk and click the Next button. Windows XP checks the floppy disk drive and the CD drive for installation programs. It then automatically selects the appropriate file, which is listed in the Run Installation Program dialog box (see Figure 14.9).

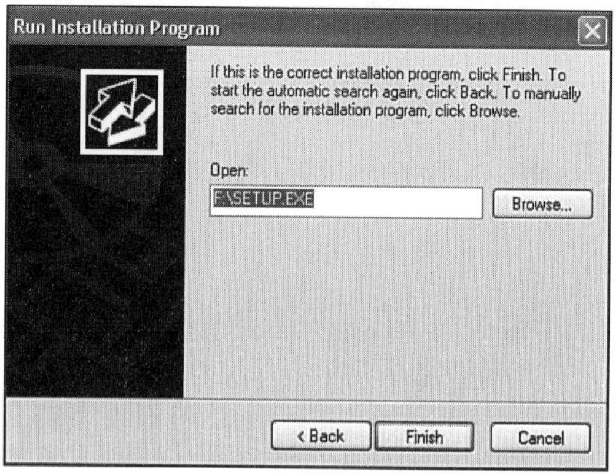

FIGURE 14.9

Click Finish to run the appropriate installation file, usually named Install or Setup.

6. Click Finish. What happens next depends on the software you are installing, so follow the onscreen directions. See "Completing the Installation" later in this section. The program is then installed, and the installation program usually adds program icons to the Start menu.

Completing the Installation

The installation program will prompt you to make selections, which vary from program to program. Here are some basic choices you can expect:

- You may be asked to accept a license agreement before proceeding with the installation. This is a legal document that says how you can use the program, under what circumstances, and so on. (Basically, you are agreeing to use the program on one PC and not to make illegal copies or to share it with others.) Accept the agreement by clicking the appropriate option.

- You may be prompted to select a type of installation. You can usually select a standard or customized installation. With a customized installation, you can select, for instance, which program components are installed. Most of the time, the standard installation is good enough. As you use it and learn more about it, you can always add other program components (that might not have been installed with the standard installation).

- You may be prompted to select the drive and folder used to store the program files. You may also be prompted to pick or create a new program folder for the program icons.

Each installation is different. Make your choices and click Next to go from one step to the next.

Configuring the Program Lineup

As another feature of the Add or Remove Programs Control Panel, you can set up a configuration that uses the programs you specify for browsing the Internet, sending email, and other common tasks. You can select to use your computer's manufacturer-set programs, Microsoft programs, non-Microsoft programs, or custom programs (where you individually select each program).

To make these changes, follow these steps:

1. Click Start and then Set Program Access and Defaults, or click the Set Program Access and Defaults button in the Add or Remove Control Panel window.

2. Click Custom and then click the down arrow next to this option to specify the programs (see Figure 14.10).

3. For each area, select the program you want to use. You can do so for Web browsing, email, Instant Messaging, and media player.

4. Click OK. Windows then uses the program you specified as the default for each action. For instance, if you select iTunes as your default media player, Windows will use this program to play music.

FIGURE 14.10

You can select
which programs
to use for each of
the areas listed.

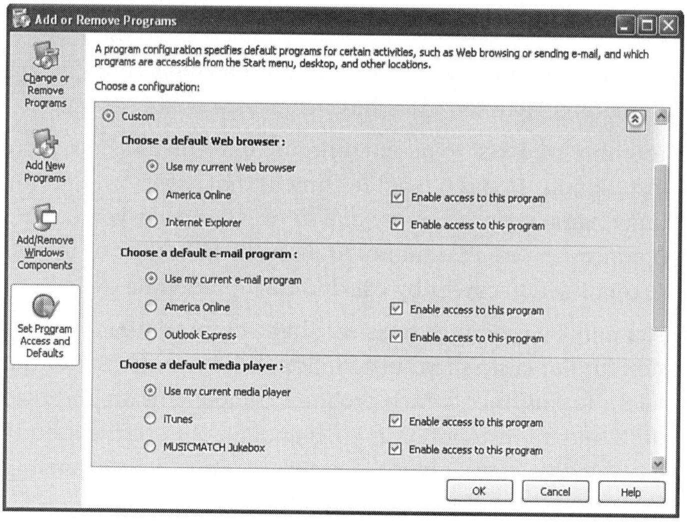

Uninstalling Applications

If you don't use a program, you can remove it
from your system. Doing so frees up disk
space. You could simply delete the program
files, but these files are not always stored in
one location. A program installation may
store files in other places on your hard drive—
for instance, in the Windows folder. Therefore,
uninstall the program using the Add or
Remove Programs Control Panel. This
removes the program and all its related files
and folders from your hard drive.

caution

If you have any folders
that contain your docu-
ments within the pro-
gram folders, be sure to
move them to other fold-
ers or drives so that they are not
deleted with the program.

Removing Programs

Follow these steps to uninstall or remove a program:

1. Click the Start button and then Control Panel.

2. Click Add or Remove Programs. You'll see the Add or Remove Programs window (refer to Figure 14.7).

3. Click the Change or Remove Programs button, if necessary. Usually, these
   options are displayed by default.

4. Select the program you want to remove (see Figure 14.11). Windows XP then provides you with some information to help you decide whether to uninstall. First, you'll see the size of the program (the amount of disk space you will gain by removing the program). Second, you'll see a rating of how often the program is used. If the rating is "rarely," you know you don't use that program often, so it's most likely safe to remove it. Third, you may see the date the program was last used.

> **tip**
>
> Some programs enable you to change their setup by adding optional items that may not have been installed. If you see both a Change button and a Remove button, you can click the Change button to change the program's setup.

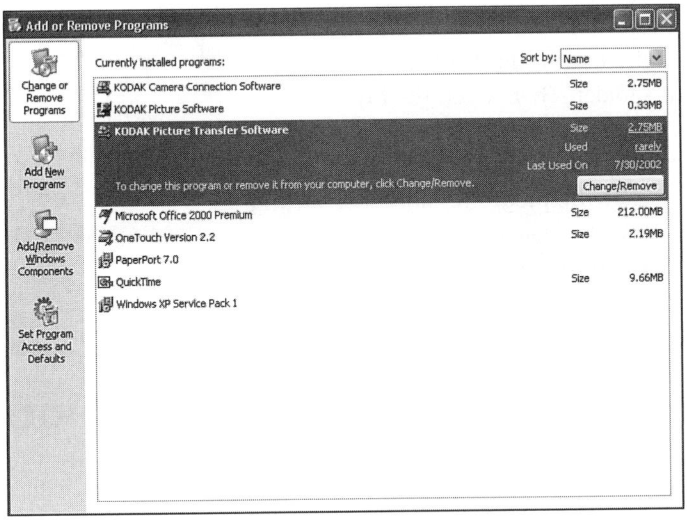

FIGURE 14.11

Use the information listed for each program to get an idea of how often you use the program.

5. Click the Remove button. (This button may be called Remove or Change/Remove.) Windows XP then removes the program. The steps will vary from program to program. Simply follow the onscreen instructions.

Removing Programs Manually

If your program is not listed in the Add or Remove Programs area of the Control Panel, you have to use a different method to remove it. You can try one of two methods: using the program disc or deleting the program folder.

You may be able to run an uninstall program from the program disc. Insert the disc and see whether options for uninstalling the program are displayed on the install menu. If so, use these. If the program disc doesn't automatically display your uninstall options, insert the disc, click Start, and then click My Computer. Double-click the icon for the drive that contains the program disc. Then look for a Setup, Install, or Uninstall icon. Double-click this icon and follow the steps for uninstalling. (Sometimes, the Install and Setup programs will display a menu, and one of the choices will be to uninstall the program.)

If the program doesn't have an uninstall program, you can delete its files manually. This method does not always remove all of the program files. It's common for programs to place certain program files within the Windows folder, for instance. But, you can get rid of the main files.

Click Start and then My Computer. Double-click the drive icon that contains your My Programs folder. Then, open the My Programs folder and look for the program folder (usually named the same as the program). Delete the program folder by selecting it and pressing Delete or by clicking Delete this folder. Confirm the deletion by clicking Yes.

> **tip**
>
> You can purchase programs to keep track of what programs you have installed, where they are, and what changes they have made to your system. You can use a program such as Uninstaller to uninstall programs not listed in the Windows Add or Remove Programs Control Panel.

More Tips on Starting Programs

In addition to these common methods for customizing programs, you have some other options for installing, running, and switching among programs. These options are the focus of this section.

Starting Programs When You Start Windows

If you shut down and restart each time you use the computer, you can have Windows start a program each time Windows starts by adding the program to your Startup Folder. Any program placed in this folder will be started each time you start Windows.

> **caution**
>
> If you *don't* start Windows each time—say you leave it running—you may wonder why the program didn't start when you sat down to work. Well, the program only starts automatically when you start Windows (that is, when you turn off and then turn on the PC). Don't fret. You can still start the program. You can do so with any of the other methods: the shortcut icon, the Start menu command, or the keyboard shortcut.

Follow these steps to start a program with Windows:

1. Right-click the Start button.

2. Select the Open command. You'll see the Start Menu folder.

3. Double-click the Programs folder. You'll see the Programs folder, which includes a folder called Startup (see Figure 14.12).

FIGURE 14.12

Put programs you want to start when you start Windows in the Startup folder.

4. Drag the program icon you want to start with Windows to the Startup folder. You may have to open another program window to display this program icon. Use the links under Other Places to find and display the program icon.

5. Click the Close button to close the Programs window.

The next time you start Windows, the program(s) you added to the Startup folder will be started also.

If you change your mind and want to remove a program from the Startup folder (thereby preventing it from starting all the time), you need to delete it from the Startup folder. To do so, open the Startup folder. You should then see icons for any programs you have added. Figure 14.13, for instance, shows Outlook Express added to the Startup folder. Select the icon, press the Delete key, and click Yes to confirm the deletion.

FIGURE 14.13

You can remove
any programs
you have added
to the Startup
folder.

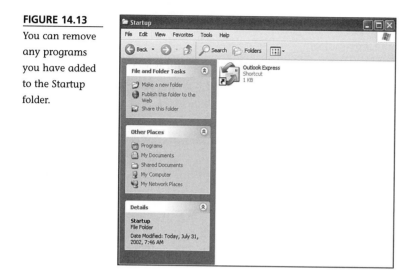

Tips for Switching Among Programs

After you have programs running, you can switch among them. Why switch programs? Well, you are talented and capable of multitasking, and so is Windows. Windows can run a word processor and a spreadsheet at the same time, for instance. As you've seen so far, you can use the mouse or the keyboard for most tasks. The same is true for switching programs.

To use the mouse method, click the taskbar button for the program you want. Remember that Windows displays a taskbar button for each program or window that is open on your system.

If you have multiple documents open in the same program and there's not enough room on the taskbar, Windows stacks the documents together into one button. You can tell if this has occurred by looking at the button. It should have a little arrow, plus the number of documents open in that program. You can click the button to display the various document windows and then click the window you want (see Figure 14.14).

To use the keyboard method to switch programs, press Alt+Tab to cycle through the programs running on your computer. When the one you want is selected, stop pressing Alt+Tab.

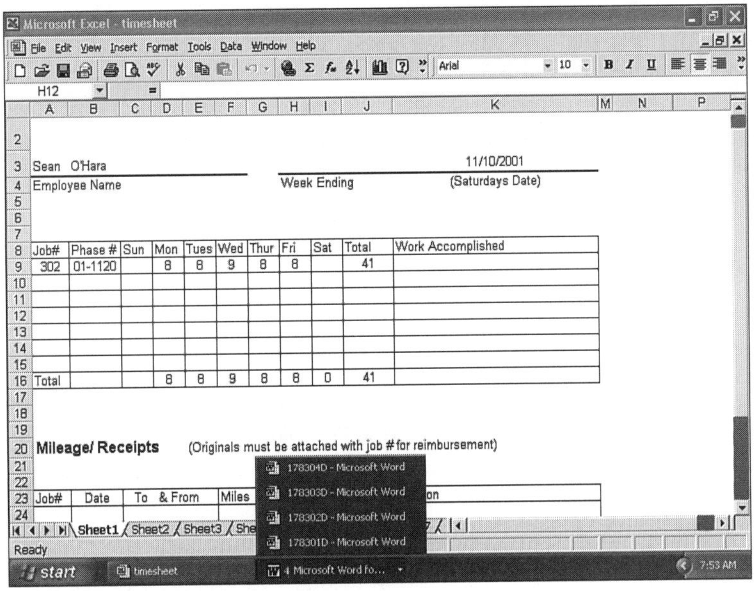

FIGURE 14.14

If the taskbar gets too crowded, Windows XP stacks similar windows together.

Using the Run Command

Another way to start a program is by using the Run command. You may have to do this to install older programs (DOS programs or programs without automated installations, for instance). How do you know when this is your only alternative? When you've tried the others or when the program's installation instructions specifically tell you to use this method.

In this case, follow these steps to use the Run command:

1. Click the Start button.
2. Click the Run command.
3. Type the name of the program you want to start (see Figure 14.15). To run the installation or setup program, type its name. If you don't know the program name, click the Browse button and browse through the drives and folders until you find the right file.
4. Click OK. The program then starts.

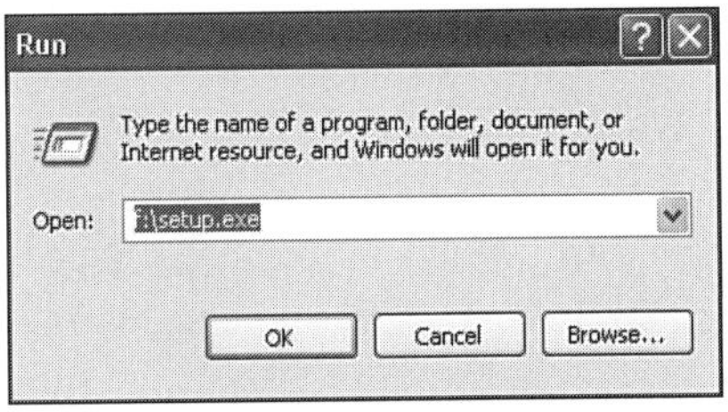

FIGURE 14.15

Use the Run command as a last resort to get finicky programs to start.

The Absolute Minimum

This chapter covers some of the ways you can customize the Start menu as well as how to install new programs and get rid of programs you no longer need. Here are the key points to remember from this chapter:

- For fast access to commonly used programs, files, or folders, add a shortcut icon to the desktop. When you double-click a program shortcut icon, you start the program. When you double-click a file shortcut icon, you open the associated program and that document. Double-clicking a folder shortcut icon displays its contents.

- You can change how the Start menu appears. You can pin commonly used programs to the top left pane. You can select whether the Internet and E-mail commands are listed, as well as which program is used for these commands.

- If you have upgraded to Windows XP and prefer the Classic Windows style, you can change the desktop to this style. Just right-click the taskbar, select Properties, and then click the Start Menu tab to view your customization options.

- When you purchase a new program, you can run the installation program to install the program onto your system. Most programs provide a step-by-step guide for installing the program, and this installation program copies the files to your computer, as well as adds the program to the Start menu.

- You can start the installation program manually by using the Add or Remove Programs Control Panel icon. You can use this same icon to delete or uninstall programs you no longer use.

15

CUSTOMIZING EMAIL AND INTERNET EXPLORER

Windows XP is versatile and provides many options for changing how it works. For instance, you can customize how your email is handled. As another example, you can make changes to how Internet Explorer works. Like other chapters in this part, this chapter covers customization. In this particular case, you learn how to customize Outlook Express as well as Internet Explorer.

Setting Mail Options

As mentioned in Chapter 7, "Sending and Receiving Email," you have several options for controlling how messages are sent, received, formatted, and so on. To access all these settings, follow these steps:

1. Start Outlook Express.

2. Click Tools and then click the Options command. You'll see the General tab of the Options dialog box (see Figure 15.1). From this tab, you can select to go directly to your Inbox, to play sounds when messages arrive, and other options. You can also select how often Outlook Express checks for new messages.

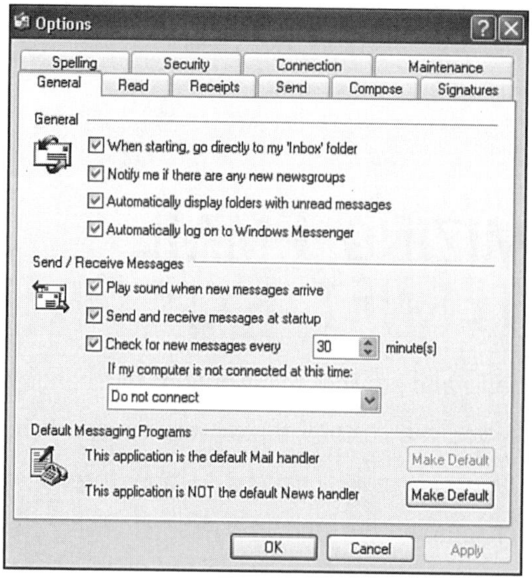

FIGURE 15.1

You have a wealth of options for handling email messages.

3. Make your selections.

4. Click any of the other tabs and then make additional selections. You can do any of the following:

   Click the Read tab and select read options, such as how long messages are displayed in the Preview pane before they are marked "read" and how messages are downloaded.

   You can request a receipt confirming that a recipient has received a message. Set receipt options from the Receipts tab. You can, for instance, request a receipt for all sent messages.

   Click the Send tab (see Figure 15.2) and specify whether a copy of all sent items are stored in the Sent Items folder, when messages are sent (for instance, immediately), the format for your messages (HTML or Plain Text), and other options.

Use the Compose tab to select formatting options for your email. You can select a particular font. You can also use stationery (basically, a pattern or style for the message).

To select whether messages are automatically spell checked, as well as to set your spell check options, use the Spelling tab.

Use the Security tab to set security options, such as message encryption.

On the Connection tab, you can, as just one example, have Outlook Express hang up or end your connection after messages are sent and received.

Use the Maintenance tab to control options, such as whether deleted messages are placed in the Deleted Items folder or are deleted for good, and to clean up old messages (see Figure 15.3).

5. When you are finished making changes, click OK to close the dialog box.

caution

You can only use fonts or stationeries if you use HTML mail, and some recipients may not prefer this email format. Therefore, use formatting with caution.

tip

You can also change what items are displayed in the Outlook Express window. Use the commands on the View menu to turn on or off the various program window features.

Working with the Address Book

One of the most useful things you can do to customize your email is to set up your Address Book. Rather than typing an address each time, you can display the Address Book and select a name from it. This method is not only easier and quicker, but also less error-prone.

You can also use the Address Book to set up a contact group so that you can easily send one message to several people without creating multiple messages or selecting several addresses.

Finally, if you want to put in the effort, you can store a lot more information for a contact with the Address Book. If you do so, you can then use the Address Book in mail merges in Word or Access.

The following sections cover these Address Book options.

tip

If you upgraded to Windows XP and have your old Address Book (either on another computer or stored as a file on your PC), you can import it to Windows XP.

Then you don't have to re-create the list you so painstakingly created before.

To import an Address Book, from the Address Book window, open the File menu and select Import. From the submenu, select Address Book (WAB). In the Select Address Book File to Import From dialog box, select the file to import and click Open. By doing this, your addresses are imported into the new Address Book from Outlook Express in Windows XP.

Adding Addresses

The easiest way to add an address to your Address Book is to pick up the address from an existing message. This saves you from having to type the information. To add an address from a mail message, follow these steps:

1. Display the message with the name you want to add to your Address Book.

2. Right-click the name and select Add to Address Book (see Figure 15.4). You'll see the Properties dialog box.

FIGURE 15.4

You can add names to your Address Book.

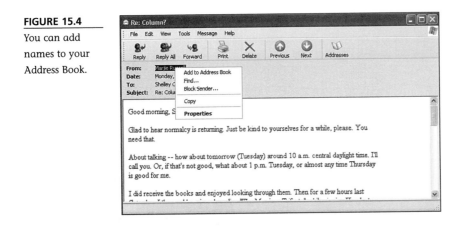

3. To simply add the name, click OK. You can also add other contact information. See "Using the Address Book as a Contact List" later in this section.

If you don't have an email message from the person you want to add, or if you prefer to type the address book entry, you can do so. Simply follow these steps:

1. From the Outlook Express main window, click Address Book. You'll see a list of entries you already have in your Address Book (see Figure 15.5).

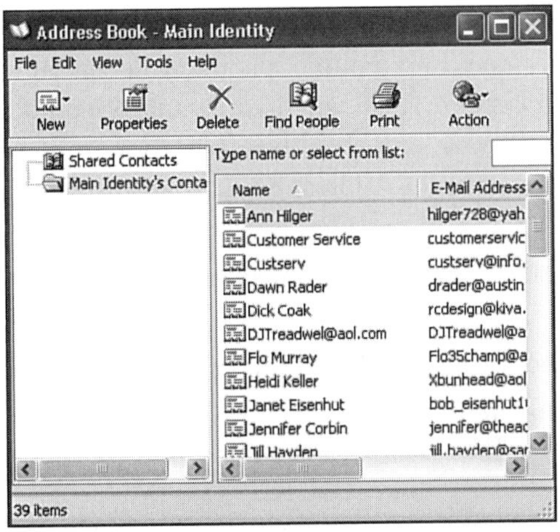

FIGURE 15.5

You can display the entries in your Address Book at any time.

2. Click the New button and select New Contact from the drop-down options. You'll see the Properties dialog box for a new contact (see Figure 15.6).

FIGURE 15.6

Complete the information for the contact you want to add.

3. The first tab contains the basic contact information. Complete the entries on this tab. At the minimum, type the first and last names, as well as the email address. You can also type any title or assign a nickname.

4. Complete any of the other information. (See the section "Using the Address Book as a Contact List" later in this chapter.)

5. Click OK to add the contact.

tip

A nickname is a shorthand reference to a contact. You can type this shorter name when creating a new mail message.

Setting Up Contact Groups

If you commonly send messages to a group of people, you can set up a group, rather than selecting each person. Then, when you want to send a message to that group, you select the group name, and each person in that group receives the message. You can create groups from the Address Book. Follow these steps:

1. Open the Address Book by clicking Start, All Programs, Accessories, and then Address Book. You'll see the list of contacts in the Address Book window (refer to Figure 15.5).

2. Click New and select Group. You'll see the Properties dialog box.

3. Type a name for the group.

4. Add members to the group. To add a member, click Select Members and then select any contacts already in your address book. Otherwise, type the name and email address for the person and click Add (see Figure 15.7).

5. When you have added all the members, click OK.

Now when you want to send a message to all members in this group, you can click the To button in the New Mail Message window and then select the group from the Address Book.

Using the Address Book as a Contact List

In addition to keeping track of email addresses, you can also add other information for each contact, including address, phone numbers (phone, fax, cell), business information (company, title, web page), personal information (spouse, children, birthday), and notes. To add other information, follow these steps:

1. Open the Address Book by clicking Start, All Programs, Accessories, and then Address Book. You'll see the list of contacts in the Address Book window.

2. Double-click the contact for whom you want to add more information. The Properties dialog box for that contact is displayed. The first tab includes summary information. The Name tab includes email information.

3. Click the Home tab. You'll see the various fields of information you can enter (see Figure 15.8). Complete any or all of the fields.

4. Click any of the other tabs and complete any or all of the fields for that category. For instance, click Business to enter company information.

5. Click OK when you are finished entering information.

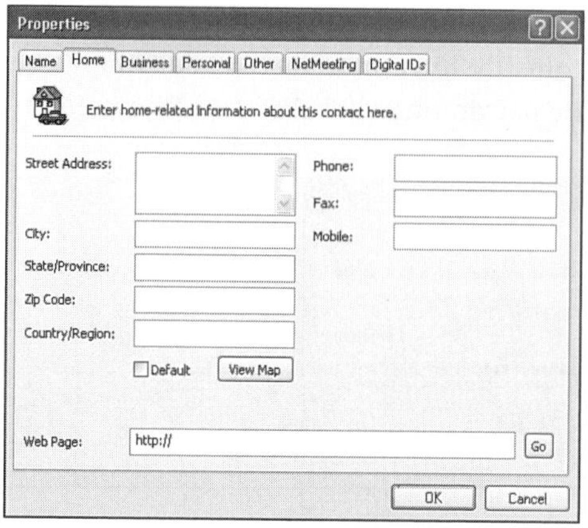

FIGURE 15.8

You can keep track of other information, such as mailing addresses, company information, and other data, in your Address Book.

Customizing Internet Explorer

In addition to customizing email settings, you have a variety of options for customizing Internet Explorer. As one common example, you can change your home page. You can also organize your list of favorite sites by breaking it into folders of related sites, rather than one long list. This section covers these common changes.

Setting Your Home Page

You are not stuck with the home page set up by your Internet provider or by Microsoft (MSN). You can use any page as your home page. For instance, you may prefer to use a search site so that you start with tools for finding information. If you have your own Web site, you might want to make it your home page. You can select any site for your home page by following these steps:

1. Start Internet Explorer.

2. Click Tools and select Internet Options. You'll see the Internet Options dialog box (see Figure 15.9).

3. Do any of the following:

   Type the address for the page you want as your home page in the Address text box.

   To use the current page as your home page, click Use Current.

   To use the default home page, click Use Default.

note

You'll find options for controlling security and privacy settings in the Internet Options dialog box. You can find key information about these features in Chapter 8, "Browsing the Internet."

FIGURE 15.9

You can cus-
tomize your
home page as
well as make
other changes
from this
dialog box.

4. Click OK. Now when you start Internet
   Explorer, the home page you selected is
   displayed. Also, when you click the
   Home button, this is the page that is displayed.

Organizing Your Favorites List

In Chapter 8, "Browsing the Internet," you
learned how to add sites to your Favorites list. If
you add several sites, the list can become too
long and unwieldy. To make it easier to find a
site when using this list, you can organize your
Favorites list into folders.

tip

You can also set the num-
ber of pages to keep in the
history folder. You can
increase or decrease the
number of days in the spin
box. To clear the history,
click the Clear History
button.

Start by clicking Favorites (the menu command, not the button) and then clicking the
Organize Favorites command. You'll see the Organize Favorites dialog box (see Figure
15.10).

From the Organize Favorites dialog box, you can do any of the following:

■ To create a new folder, click the Create Folder button and then type the folder
   name.

■ To move sites to a folder, select the site in the list and click Move to Folder. Then
   select the folder from the list and click OK. You can also drag the site in the list
   to the folder.

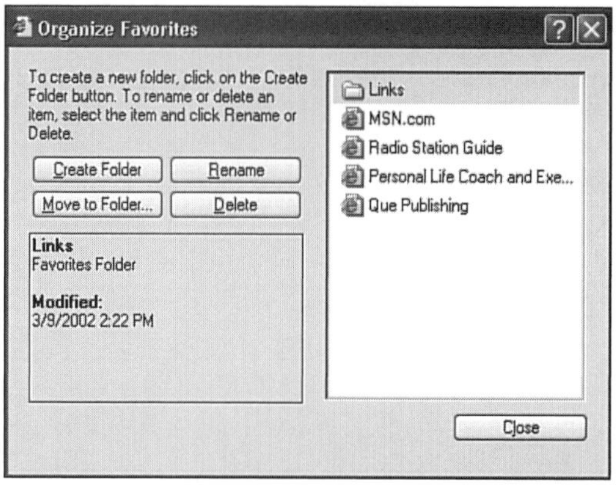

FIGURE 15.10

You can organize your list of favorite sites using this dialog box.

- To rename a site or folder, select it in the list and click Rename. Then type a new name and press Enter.

- To delete a site or folder, select it and click Delete. Click Yes to confirm the deletion.

caution

When you delete a folder, you delete the folder and all its contents. Make sure that this is what you want to do before clicking Yes to confirm the deletion.

THE ABSOLUTE MINIMUM

This chapter covers the many ways you can customize both email and Internet access to suit your preferences. In particular, keep these main points in mind:

- You can control how messages are sent, received, and handled using the Outlook Express mail options.

- To make addressing email messages easier, use the Address Book. Also, if you frequently send email messages to a set of people, create a contact group.

- You can select a different page for your home page using the Internet Options dialog box.

- To keep your Favorites list organized, create folders and then organize sites by category.

PART V

EVERYDAY PC MAINTENANCE

16

VIEWING AND FINDING FILES

Even if you are fairly organized with your files, you can still easily misplace a file or forget where a file is stored. Windows XP provides methods for viewing and sorting files to help you locate a particular file. In addition, you can search for a file based on name, creation date, or other file properties. This chapter covers these options for viewing, sorting, customizing, and finding files.

Viewing and Sorting Files

It is pretty common to save a file and then not be able to find it again. Either you didn't save it to the location you thought, or you cannot remember in which folder you saved it. Sometimes, you don't remember the exact filename. One way to find files is to change how they are displayed in the folder window. You can view the contents of a window in a variety of ways. You can also sort the contents so that files are listed in alphabetical order, by date, or by type. As another option, you can group similar files together (by name, type, and so on). All these viewing and sorting options are covered in this section.

Changing the View

You have several choices for how the contents of a window are viewed—thumbnails, tiles, icons, lists, and details. Changing the view can help you better locate the item you want. Each view has its advantages. For instance, if you want to see more of a window's contents at one time, you can change the view to List. Figure 16.1 shows files in List view.

tip

When you want to select a group of files, List view is the best view in which to work.

FIGURE 16.1

List view contains the bare bones—a simple, compact list of the filenames.

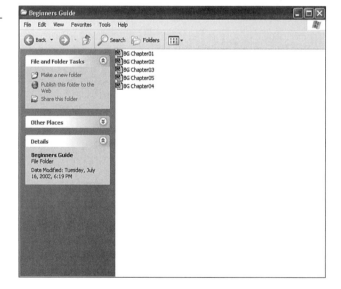

Another simple view is Icon view, which displays the filename and icon (see Figure 16.2).

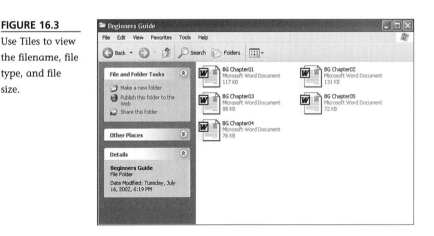

As another alternative, you can add a little more information by changing to Tiles. In this view, you see the file icon, plus the document type and size (see Figure 16.3).

Want even more information? Change to Details view to see the name, size, type, and modification date. Figure 16.4 shows Details view. Use this view if you want to find out, for instance, the date a file was last accessed.

FIGURE 16.4

If you want
detailed file
information,
change to Details
view.

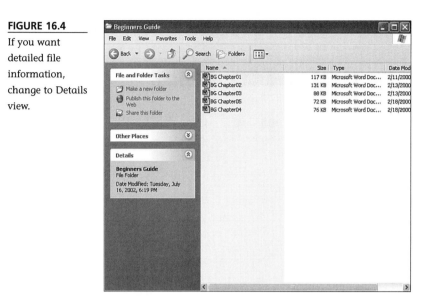

You can also select Thumbnails, which is useful for pictures, and you'll see a
thumbnail image of each picture. Also available for file windows with graphic files
is a view called Filmstrip view (see Figure
16.5). In this view, you can scroll through the
pictures, seeing both the selected image in
the main area as well as other picture files
along the bottom (or filmstrip).

To change to a different view, follow these
steps:

1. In the window you want to change,
   click the View menu. The current
   view is indicated with a dot (see
   Figure 16.6).

2. Select the view you want. The window
   displays the contents in that view.

tip

Another helpful way to
find a file is to view the file
properties. Right-click the file
and then select Properties.
Some files may have several
tabs with identifying information. When you are
done reviewing the file properties,
click OK.

Also, remember that when a file is
selected, you can view the Details
section in the task pane for information about the type and size of
the selected file.

FIGURE 16.5

For picture files, you can use Thumbnails or Filmstrip (shown here).

FIGURE 16.6

You can see the current view selection as well as select another view from the View menu.

Sorting Files

tip

If you see faint gray high-lighting in one of the columns, it means the con-tents have been sorted on that field. The field name also has an arrow next to it. You learn more about sorting in later sections of this chapter.

In addition to changing the view, you can sort the contents of a folder window so that you can more easily find the folders and files you want. Windows enables you to arrange the contents of a window by name, type, date, and size. Your sorting will be visible in all views, but the change is most apparent in Details view since this view includes columns for size, type, and date.

Follow these steps to sort files:

1. Open the window you want to sort.

2. Click View and then click the Arrange Icons By command. The current sort order is indicated with a dot. For instance, if you see a dot next to Name, you know the contents are sorted by filename.

tip

You can also use the View button in the file window toolbar. Click the down arrow next to the Views but-ton and then select the view you want.

3. Select the sort order you want. Windows XP then sorts the files in the selected order. For example, Figure 16.7 shows the files sorted by size (from smallest to largest). Note that the sort column is indicated with a very faint shading and an arrow in the heading.

To change the order (ascending to descending or vice versa), select the same command again. Doing so reverses the sort order.

> **tip**
>
> In Details view, you can also click the column heading as a shortcut for sorting. For instance, to sort by Date Modified, click this column header.

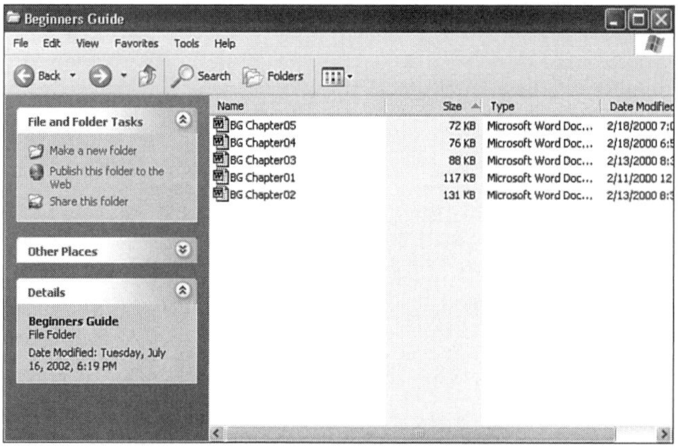

FIGURE 16.7

You can sort files to make it easier to find the file you need.

Grouping Files

Windows XP has added a new file view feature—the capability to group file icons. The grouping depends on how the items are sorted. If you sort by name, the contents are grouped alphabetically. If you sort by type, the contents are grouped by type. Grouping enables you to work with a select group of files or folders more easily.

To start, sort first and then group. You can group in any view. Follow these steps to group files:

1. Sort the contents by how you want them grouped. For instance, to group by type, sort by type.

2. Click View, Arrange Icons By, Show in Groups. Windows then groups the

> **caution**
>
> Grouping does not work in List view. Change to one of the other views (Thumbnails, Tiles, Icons, or Details) if you want to group a window's contents.

icons by the sort order. Figure 16.8 shows the files sorted and then grouped by type.

FIGURE 16.8

You can group files to keep similar file types together.

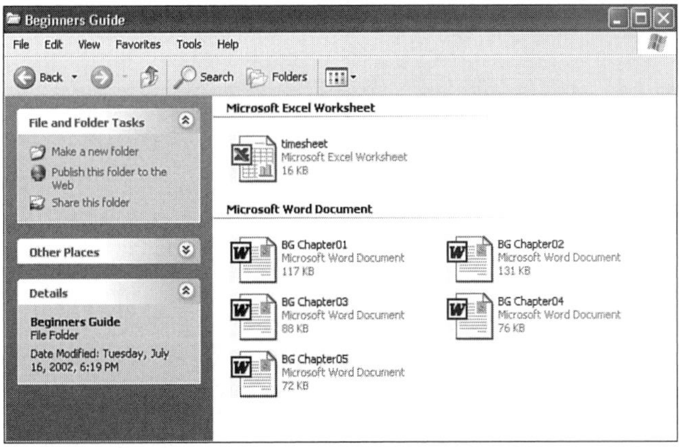

Choosing File Details

In addition to the file details in Details view, you can select to display other file information, such as author or the date the file was created. These details are especially helpful for picture and music files; you can display the date a picture was taken or the artist of a song. You can also hide other file details.

To choose the file details that are displayed, follow these steps:

1. Open the View menu and click Choose Details. You'll see the Choose Details dialog box (see Figure 16.9).

2. Check any details you want displayed. Uncheck any details you don't want included. You can scroll through the list to select from several different file detail options.

3. Click OK. The file list is then updated to include the details you selected.

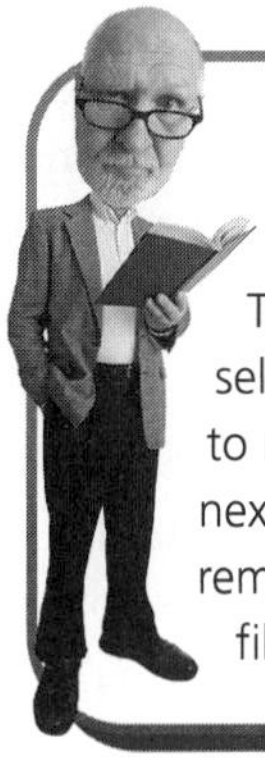

tip

To undo the grouping, select the command again to remove the checkmark next to Show in Groups and remove the grouping in the file window.

tip

These details are especially useful for viewing MP3 (music) files since most of the MP3 information does not show in the regular view.

FIGURE 16.9

You can select to display other file information.

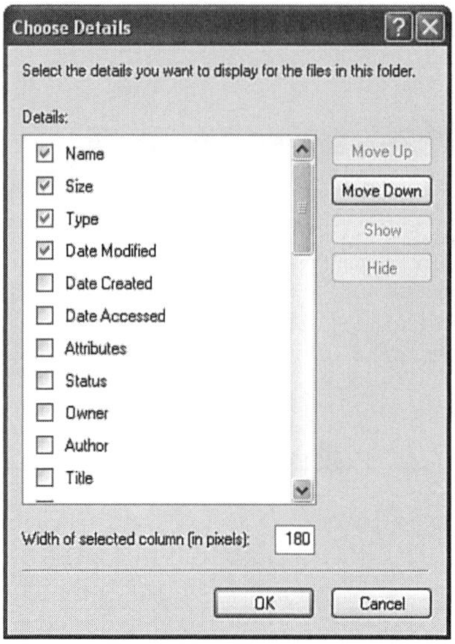

Setting Up Folder Options

In addition to viewing, sorting, and grouping, you can customize the appearance of your folders. Basically, you can change the way you open or display contents. Rather than double-clicking to open a folder, you can make the folder contents more "Web-like" and single-click. You can also hide the task pane. For instance, if you have upgraded to Windows XP, you may prefer the "classic" Windows style. You can change the folder options to more closely resemble previous versions of Windows.

To set folder options, follow these steps:

1. In the folder you want to change, open the Tools menu and select the Folder Options command.

   You'll see the General tab of the Folder Options dialog box (see Figure 16.10).

2. Make any changes to these options:

   To hide the task pane, select Use Windows classic folders. To display the task pane, select Show common tasks in folders (the default).

The General tab, as its name suggests, sets general options for how folders are displayed, browsed, and opened.

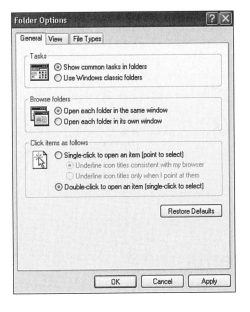

By default, when you open a folder, the contents are displayed within one window (the new contents replace the existing contents), not separate windows. If you prefer to open each folder in its own window, select this option: Open each folder in its own window.

By default, you double-click to open an item. If you want to single-click, select Single-click to open an item (point to select) and then select how the underlining appears for icon titles (either consistent with your Internet browser settings or underlined only when you point at them). Figure 16.11, for instance, shows the single-click option selected, with underlining consistent with the browser.

3. Click OK. Your changes are then put into effect.

note

This book assumes that you have your system set up to double-click, and all steps are written accordingly. Keep in mind that if you change this option, you'll single-click to open a file or folder.

FIGURE 16.11
You can single-click, rather than double-click, to open a file or folder.

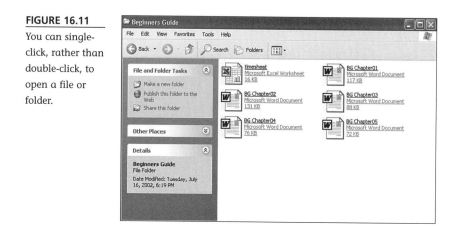

Searching for Documents

If you cannot find a particular file by browsing, even after changing the view or sorting, you have another option: You can search for it. You can search for several different file types. From the search results, you can then open, print, copy, or move the file.

Follow these steps to search for a file:

1. Click the Start button and then click the Search command, or click the Search button in a file window. You'll see the various search options (see Figure 16.12).

tip

The other tabs are more useful for reviewing information and making advanced changes. For example, you can click the View tab to select advanced settings for file view (such as displaying the full path for files or folders in the address or title bar, or selecting whether hidden or system files are displayed). Use the File Types tab to review the various file types with the associated program. This information is important because if you double-click a file icon, Windows uses the associated program to open that file. You can view the extensions, file types, and details from the File Types tab.

FIGURE 16.12

Help Windows
XP narrow your
search by select-
ing the type of
file you want to
find.

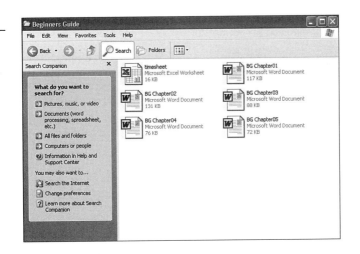

2. Select the type of file you want to find. You can search for pictures, music, or video files; documents (word processing, spreadsheet, and so on); or all files and folders.

3. Enter the search criteria. The available options vary depending on what you selected to search for. Figure 16.13 shows searching for all files or folders. You can type all or part of a word or phrase in the filename, select the disk to look in, as well as set other search options, including the last time the file was modified, the approximate size of the file, and other advanced options.

tip

To use additional search criteria, click the link for More Advanced Options. You can then limit the search to particular folders, choose whether subfolders (folders within the current folder or drive) are searched, select whether the search is case sensitive (whether capitalization has to match the word or phrase exactly as you've typed it), and more.

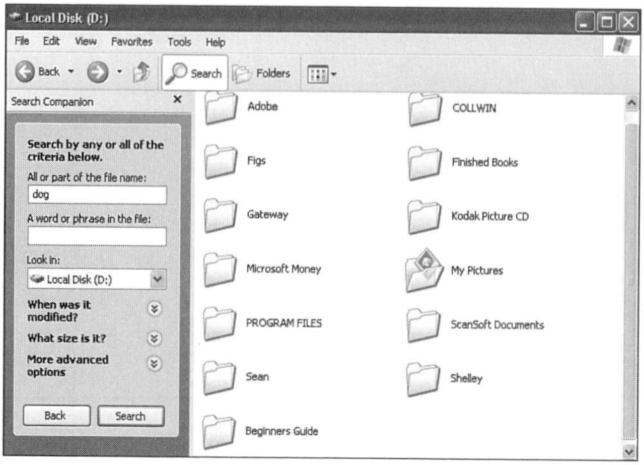

FIGURE 16.13

To search, enter the search criteria that you think will best help Windows XP find a match.

4. Click the Search button. Windows searches and displays a list of found files in the right pane of the window (see Figure 16.14). You can open, move, copy, or delete any of the listed files. For instance, you can double-click any of the listed files or folders to open that file or folder.

5. To close the search results window, click its Close button.

tip

The Search bar lists the number of files found as well as options for refining the search. If the results did not turn up the file you want, search again. Some options for refining the search include changing the file-name or keywords, looking in more locations, and changing which files and folders are searched.

FIGURE 16.14
The results of the search are displayed in the right pane of the Search Results window.

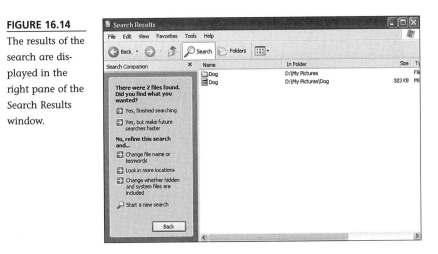

THE ABSOLUTE MINIMUM

It's easy to misplace a file. Luckily, Windows XP has several ways to help you locate a file, including changing how the contents are displayed, sorting files, grouping files, and finally searching for files. For finding lost files, use the following guidelines:

- The view of a file window can help you find a particular file. For instance, if you are looking for a picture, use Thumbnails view to see a small image of the picture. If you are looking for a particular type of file, use Details view. You can even select which file details are included in the view.

- To change the view, display the View menu and select the view, or use the Views button in the file window's toolbar.

- You can sort files by name, type, size, or modification date. To do so, use the Arrange Icons by command in the View menu.

- Another handy feature for working with files of the same type (or other grouping) is to sort and then group the files. For instance, you can group all worksheet files together, all word processing documents together, and so on.

- To further fine-tune how you work with a file window's contents (whether you single- or double-click, for instance), change the folder options.

- You can also search for a file, and Windows XP provides many search options. You can search for a file by type, modification date, name, or contents. You can also limit the search to a particular drive or folder.

17

SECURING YOUR PC

Many beginning computer users are skittish about using the computer. They think they are going to "break" it. Really, there's not much you can do to ruin your computer, but you should take some precautions to guard your data—that is, the document files stored on your computer. Another safety issue is checking a disk for problems or viruses. This chapter covers checking a disk for errors and defines what a virus is, as well as gives advice on how to handle this security issue.

You also learn about using System Restore, which is useful for going "back in time" on your computer. You can use this to troubleshoot any problems that might pop up when you make changes to your computer.

Finally, if you have trouble remembering to perform system maintenance tasks, you can set up Windows so that these tasks are performed automatically at the interval you specify.

Backing Up Your Work

The most important thing you can do to safeguard your data is to back it up! Yes, it can be time-consuming. Yes, it is a hassle. But the most valuable thing isn't the computer itself, but the data on it. Re-creating data is not easy, and in some cases is not possible. Say, for instance, that you store all your chapters for your next great book. Can you re-create them? Say, as another example, that you store all your contact information about your company on your computer. Can you re-create that data from a hodge-podge of business cards you might be able to round up?

tip

Another important security issue is protecting your computer while using the Internet. Internet security issues are covered in Chapter 8, "Browsing the Internet."

You take for granted the accessibility of your data. Take your Address Book. With it, you can easily send email to all your friends, colleagues, and relatives. Without it, do you really know all the email addresses in that simple file by heart?

That's why backing up your data is so critical. You should get in the habit of backing up your entire system at regular intervals and backing up your documents (data files) even more frequently.

Selecting Backup Programs and Equipment

To back up your files, you need backup media and a backup program. *Media* refers to the types of items you use to store your backup files. Before the hard drives on computers got so big, you commonly backed up your data to floppy disks. Now, backing up your system to floppy disks would be ludicrous (although you can use floppy disks as a quick method to back up important data files). Instead, you most commonly back up to a CD-R, CD-RW, or DVD drive. You also may purchase a special backup medium called a tape drive. You can then back up files using the tape drive.

To perform the backup, you need a backup program. The program not only performs the backup, but also provides options for selecting which files are backed up. Windows XP includes a backup program, but this program is not installed and is not easily accessed. (The program is stored on a folder on your Windows XP CD. See the following tip for information on finding this program.)

You can also purchase backup programs. If you purchase a tape backup system, for instance, it usually comes with software for backing up. Also, some utility programs (sets of programs handy for maintaining and troubleshooting your computer) include backup programs.

You can find many—sometimes even free—backup programs by visiting any of the freeware or shareware sites on the Internet. Some popular programs include Back it Up, Monday Backup, Winbacker, Sysback (for backing up system files), and Backup Pro.

Tips for Backing Up

Here are some tips to make backing up more efficient:

- If you don't perform routine backups, you should at least make manual copies of all your data files. You can make backups of important data files by copying them to floppy disks or to a CD drive (if you have a CD drive that can read and write data). See Chapter 3, "Managing Files," for information on copying data. You may want to compress the files first; compressing files is covered in Chapter 18.

- Consider doing a complete backup at least once a year and before any major system change (such as upgrading to a new operating system).

- You should do a complete backup, including your program files. Although you may have the disks to reinstall some programs, you may not have all your programs (programs you have downloaded, for instance). Also, you'll lose all your customized settings without a complete backup.

- Back up your data files more than once a year. You might consider daily or weekly intervals. I guarantee you that the minute you think you don't need a backup will become the minute you do.

- To facilitate backing up data files, create and store files in a solid organizational structure. You might store all data files within subfolders in the My Documents folder. You can then concentrate on this folder when creating data file backups.

tip

Finding the Windows XP backup program isn't easy because it is not listed as an optional component to install on the installation program. (Chapter 20, "Upgrading Windows," explains how to install additional Windows components.) However, you can find it by browsing your Windows XP CD. To do so, insert your Windows XP disc into the drive. You should then see the installation options. Click Perform additional tasks. Then click Browse This CD. Double-click the VALUEADD folder to open it. Double-click the MSFT folder to open it. Double-click the NTBACKUP folder to open it. Finally, double-click the NTBACKUP setup icon to install the Windows Backup program.

Checking a Disk for Errors

In addition to backing up your data, you should periodically check your disk for errors. It's not uncommon for parts of your hard disk get damaged. When this happens, you might see an error message when you try to open or save a file.

To scan the disk for damage and fix any problems, you can use a handy system tool called Check Disk that is included with Windows XP. Follow these steps to use this program:

1. Open My Computer. You can do so by clicking Start, My Computer, or if you have added a desktop icon for My Computer, double-click this icon to open the drive window. You should then see each of your drives listed.

2. Right-click the drive you want to back up and select Properties. If you have just one hard drive, it is named drive C. Some computers have more than one hard drive. If so, right-click the drive to select it.

   You'll see the General tab, which gives you useful information about the status of the drive (see Figure 17.1).

FIGURE 17.1

You can display the Properties dialog box for the hard drive(s) on your computer.

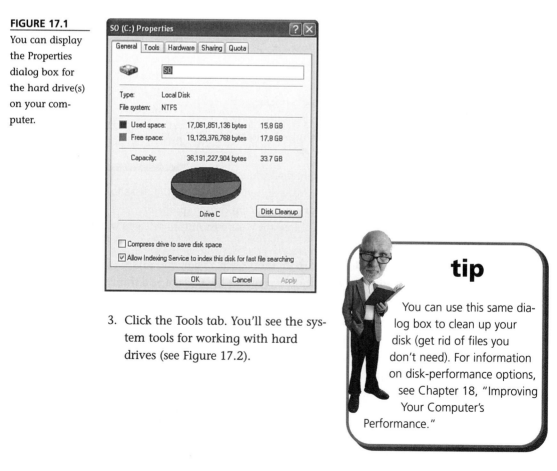

3. Click the Tools tab. You'll see the system tools for working with hard drives (see Figure 17.2).

tip

You can use this same dialog box to clean up your disk (get rid of files you don't need). For information on disk-performance options, see Chapter 18, "Improving Your Computer's Performance."

FIGURE 17.2

You can access
the Check Disk
program from
the Tools tab.

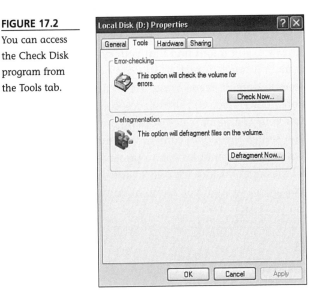

4. Click the Check Now button on the Tools tab. You'll see the available options
   for running the scan (see Figure 17.3). You can select whether errors are automatically fixed and whether the scan checks
   for and repairs bad sectors.

5. Click Start to start the check.

6. If Check Disk finds an error, a dialog box
   appears explaining the error. Read the error
   message and choose the option you want to
   perform. For instance, the check might find
   errors in how data is stored (such as sector
   errors, invalid file dates, and bad sectors).
   Click OK to continue. Do this for each
   message.

7. When the Disk Check is complete, click OK.

FIGURE 17.3

Select how to
perform the disk
check.

note

To store data, your
computer divides your disk
into parts called sectors. It's not
uncommon for a hard drive to
have some bad sectors. You can
check and repair these sectors, but
note that this type of scan takes
much longer.

Using System Restore

If you add new programs or hardware, you might find that your system does not work properly. Trying to troubleshoot a problem such as this can be difficult. To help, Windows XP includes System Restore. If needed, you can go back to any point in time before any of these restore points were set. For instance, suppose that you added a digital camera, and now your computer is not working properly. You can go "back in time" to before you installed the digital camera to get your computer back in working order. Using System Restore enables you to preserve recent work, such as saved documents, email messages, history lists, or favorites lists. You can then step through the installation again to see if you can pinpoint and fix the problem.

Understanding Restore Points

System Restore monitors changes to your system and creates *restore points* each day by default. There are several types of restore points:

- The *initial system checkpoint* is created the first time you start your computer after Windows XP is installed. Don't select this restore point unless you want to wipe your computer clean of everything you've done on it since installing XP.

- *System checkpoints* are created by Windows every 24 hours and every 10 hours your computer is turned on.

- *Program name installation restore points* are created automatically when you install a program using one of the latest installers. Select this restore point to remove installed programs and other settings.

- *Manually-created restore points* are those restore points you create yourself (and are covered later in this section).

- *Restore operation restore points* track restoration operations themselves, enabling you to undo them.

- *Unsigned driver restore points* are created any time System Restore determines that you are installing an unsigned or uncertified driver. (A driver is a system file that tells Windows XP the details of a hardware device, such as a camera. You learn more about device drivers in Chapter 19, "Upgrading Your Computer.")

Setting a System Restore Point

In addition to the restore points set by the system automatically, you can manually set a restore point. Then you are guaranteed a go-back-in-time point to when you know things were working. To set a system restore point, follow these steps:

1. Click Start, All Programs, Accessories, System Tools, System Restore. You'll see the Welcome to System Restore window. You have the option of restoring your computer or creating a restore point (see Figure 17.4).

FIGURE 17.4

Start System Restore to set a restore point or go back to a restore point.

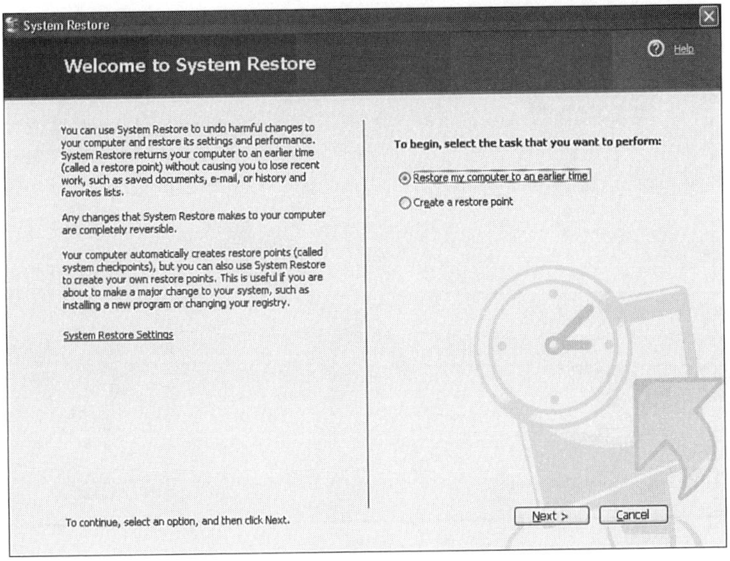

2. Select Create a restore point and click Next. You are then prompted to type a name or description for the restore point (see Figure 17.5).

FIGURE 17.5

To keep track of the different restore points, type a descriptive name.

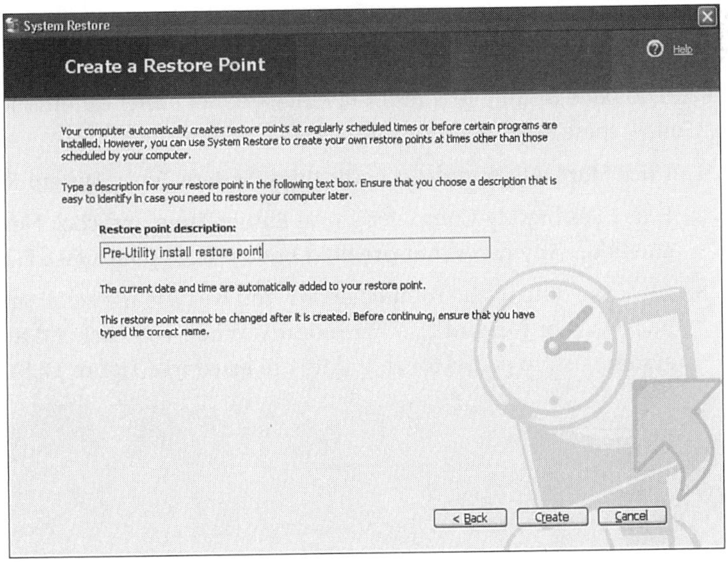

3. Type a description for the restore point and click Create. The point is created with the date and time you set the restore point (see Figure 17.6).

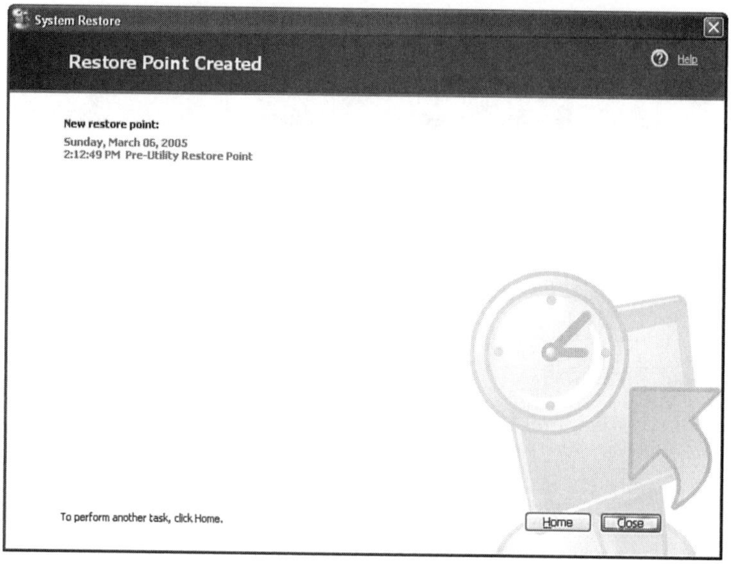

FIGURE 17.6

When you click Create, you see your new system restore point added.

4. Click Close to close the System Restore window.

Restoring Your System

When something does go wrong and you wish you could get in a time machine and go back to happy times when you could check your email and use your printer, you can go back in time to a restore point—one set either automatically or manually. Follow these steps to do so:

1. Click Start, All Programs, Accessories, System Tools, System Restore.

2. Select Restore My Computer To An Earlier Time and click Next. You'll see a calendar. Any dates that are bold have restore points (see Figure 17.7).

3. Click the date in the mini-calendar. You can use the scroll arrows to scroll backward or forward to other months. When you click a date, the available system restore points for that date are listed (see Figure 17.8).

FIGURE 17.7

You can go back days or months using System Restore.

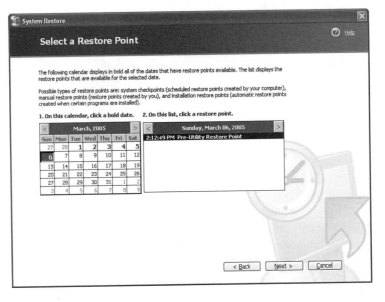

FIGURE 17.8

Select the restore point by first selecting the date and then selecting the restore point on that particular date.

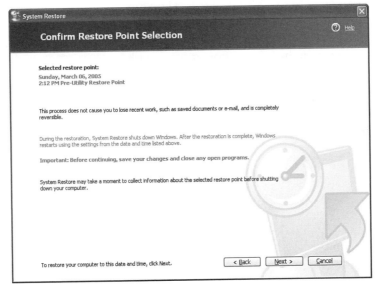

4. Select the restore point in the list and then click Next. You'll see a description of what happens. Note that saved documents and email are not affected, and you can reverse the actions of a system restore. As described in the dialog box, Windows is shut down, restored, and then restarted using the settings from the date and time of the system restore point.

5. Click Next. As described, the system is shut down and restored. You are then returned to the System Restore window with a message saying the restoration is complete.

6. Click OK to close the System Restore window.

Checking Your Computer for Viruses

Just like you can get a virus, so can your computer. Computer viruses range from simple, mischievous programs that might display stupid messages to really dangerous ones that can wipe out all the data on a drive. How does your PC get infected? Well, you can get a virus from any number of sources, including the Internet, email attachments, and opening a file that happens to be infected from a floppy disk or other removable type of media (like a CD drive).

To protect yourself, you should get and use a virus scan program.

tip

If you want to undo the restore, you can do so. Follow the same steps to open the System Restore window (Start, All Programs, Accessories, System Tools, System Restore). You now have the option of undoing the restore. Select this option and then follow the onscreen prompts, clicking Next to go from step to step.

caution

Another nuisance that you need to protect your computer from is spyware. This is a program that installs itself, usually without your knowledge. It then tracks what sites you visit on the Internet and relays this information back to its owners. Checking for and removing spyware is covered in Chapter 8.

Checking System Security with Windows Security Center

New with Windows XP Service Pack 2 is the Windows Security Center. You can use this feature to get an overview of the security of your PC. You can also turn on any Windows features such as a firewall for Internet safety (covered in Chapter 8).

To view the status of security on your PC, follow these steps:

1. Click Start, All Programs, Accessories, System Tools, Security Center. You'll see the Windows Security Center (see Figure 17.9).

2. Click the down arrow next to Virus Protection to view the status of this security item on your system.

3. If Windows has recommendations, you see a button. Click Recommendations to review recommendations about better virus protection for your computer. Then click OK.

4. Close the Security Center window by clicking its Close box.

> **caution**
>
> You might think you are safe by scanning just program files. (Usually, these files have the extension .exe and are called .exe files.) It's a common myth that you can only get a virus from this type of file. Not true. You can get viruses from documents with macros, as in an outbreak of Word viruses that you could get simply from opening the infected document.
>
> Don't just scan program files; be careful with other documents also, especially if they contain executable modules such as macros.

FIGURE 17.9

Use the Windows Security Center to review key security features on your system.

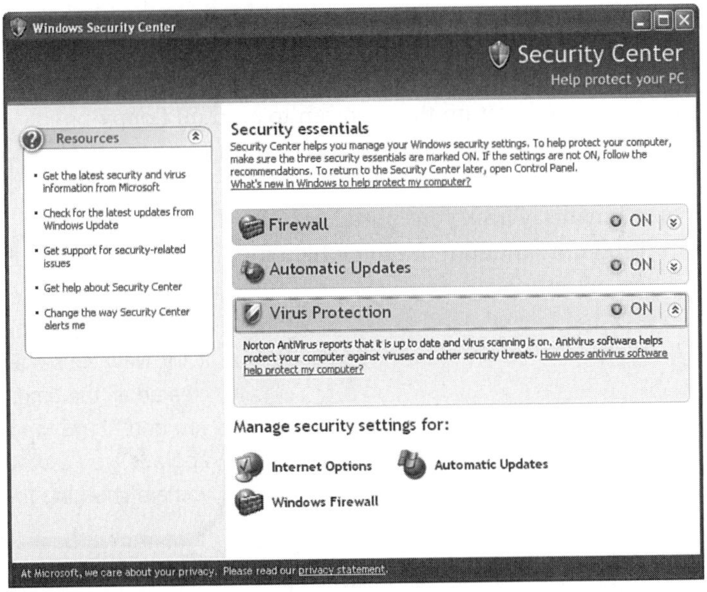

Using a Virus Protection Program

With a virus protection program, you can periodically check your system for known viruses, scan incoming files, and be warned before any infected files are copied to your system.

Popular antivirus programs include Norton's AntiVirus (visit www.symantec.com for more information) and McAfee VirusScan (visit www.mcafee.com for product information).

Antivirus programs each work differently. Most are started automatically when you start Windows and then scan your computer at a set interval. You can also set them up to scan every file you open. Finally, you can start and run them at any time by double-clicking the program icon for the antivirus program or by selecting it from the Start menu. Figure 17.10 shows the disk and file virus-checking options for Norton's Anti-Virus program.

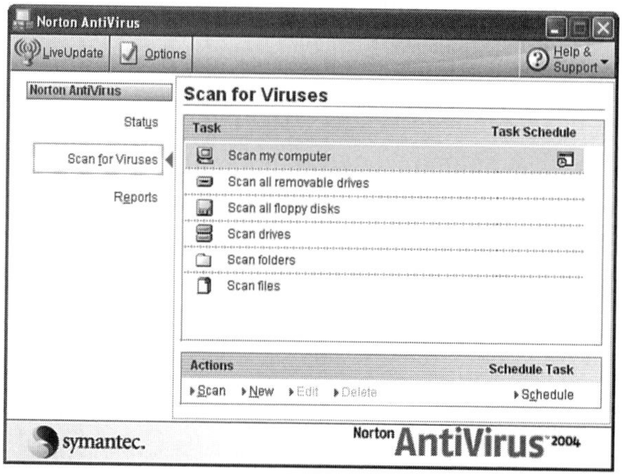

FIGURE 17.10

Use a virus program to periodically check your entire system for viruses.

For instance, you can set up the program to scan all floppy disks inserted into your system and all files that are downloaded to your system, including email attachments. Check your particular antivirus program's manual or online help for information on setting virus options.

caution

You need to update your antivirus program periodically. New viruses are created all the time, so if you don't have the latest upgrade, you can get a virus even if you are checking for viruses.

Handling an Infected File

When you scan for viruses, the program identifies any files that have been infected by any viruses it recognizes and usually offers you the option to repair the file if it can. In some cases, infected files can be "cleaned" by your virus protection software; in others, the files will have to be discarded. For really lethal viruses, you may have to reformat your hard disk and start over from scratch. In this case, you will be glad if you backed up your data (covered earlier in this chapter).

caution

Your antivirus program has a database of problems, viruses, and fixes. To make sure your program is working from the most recent list of viruses and fixes, you need to periodically update it. Many programs offer free updates for a period of time after their purchase. You can then subscribe for additional upgrades, and you should!

Scheduling Maintenance Tasks

Maintenance tasks are easy to overlook. If you are not good at remembering to perform these things, you can set up Windows XP to perform scheduled tasks at a set interval. For instance, you can set up the backup program to run once a week (or once a month or daily). You can schedule maintenance tasks as well as other tasks including checking and downloading mail. You basically can run any program at the time and interval you select. This section covers how to add and modify scheduled tasks.

tip

It's embarrassing, but when you do find out you have a virus, you should notify anyone with whom you've had contact and you might have unintentionally infected. Send them the fix if possible. If not, at least alert them so that they can check their own systems.

Adding a New Task

To set up a scheduled task list, follow these steps:

1. Click Start, All Programs, Accessories, System Tools, Scheduled Tasks. You'll see the Scheduled Tasks window listing any tasks that you have set up (see Figure 17.11).

2. Double-click the Add Scheduled Task item to start the Scheduled Task Wizard. The first screen introduces this feature.

3. Click Next to move to the next step. You are then prompted to select the program you want to run (see Figure 17.12).

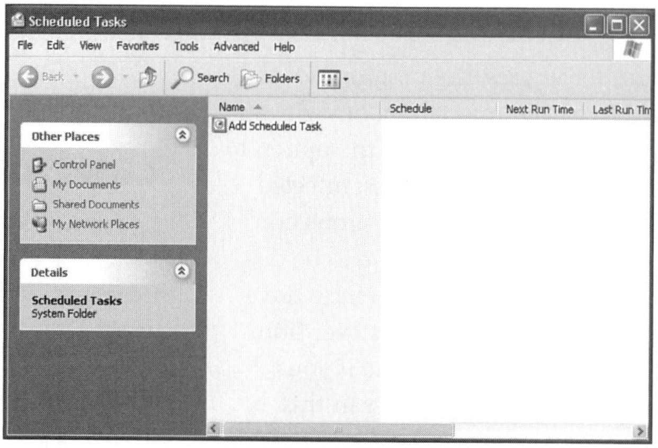

FIGURE 17.11

You can add and change scheduled tasks using the Scheduled Tasks window.

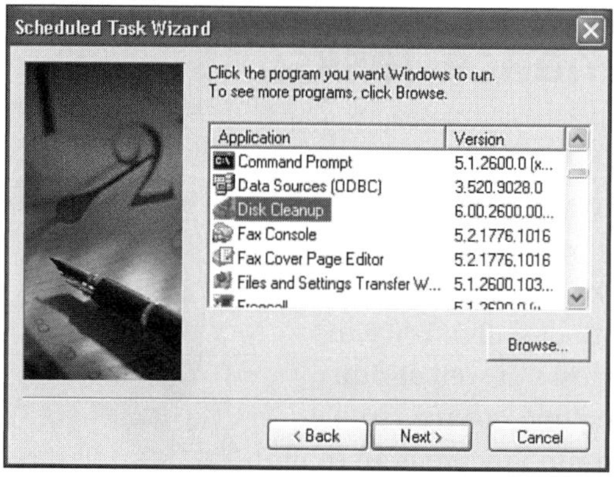

FIGURE 17.12

You can select to schedule and run any installed and registered programs on your computer.

4. Click the program to select it and click Next. You are then prompted to type a name for the task. This is the name that appears in the scheduled task list. You also select an interval for running this program. You can select daily, weekly, monthly, one time only, when my computer starts, or when I log on (see Figure 17.13).

FIGURE 17.13

Select how often you want to run this scheduled task.

5. Select the interval for running the selected program and click Next. You then set the schedule for the task (see Figure 17.14). The options for setting the schedule vary depending on the interval you select.

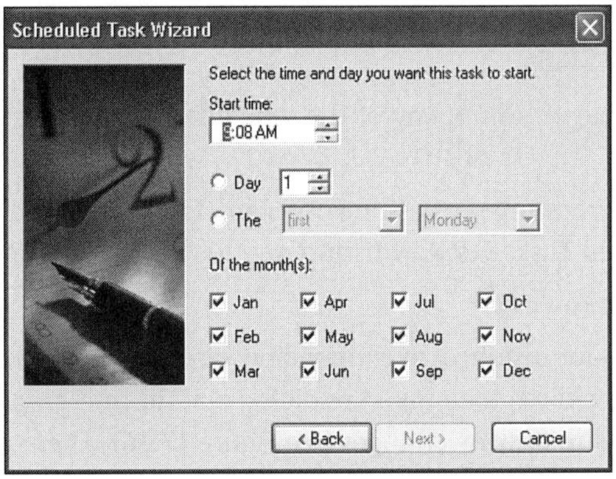

FIGURE 17.14

Here, you see the options for running the selected program monthly.

6. Select the start time and date(s) to run the program and click Next.

7. If required, type the username and password. You must type the password twice—once to enter it and again to confirm it. Then click Next.

The final screen displays all your entries—the selected program and when the program is scheduled to run (see Figure 17.15).

tip

If more than one person uses your computer, you can set up multiple users. Step 7 lets you select the user under which the task is run. See Chapter 22, "Setting Up Windows XP for Multiple Users."

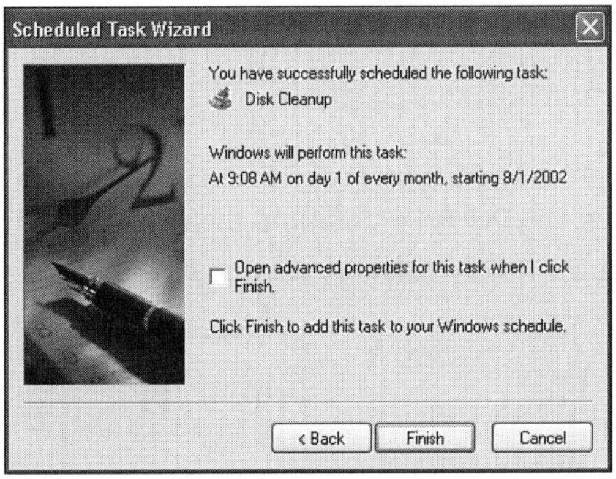

FIGURE 17.15

You see the details of the scheduled task.

8. Click Finish. The task is then added to the Scheduled Tasks list and will run at the interval you selected.

9. Click the Close button to close the Scheduled Tasks window.

Modifying Scheduled Tasks

If needed, you can delete or adjust any of the scheduled tasks. To do so, follow these steps:

1. Click Start, All Programs, Accessories, System Tools, Scheduled Tasks. You'll see the Scheduled Tasks window listing any tasks that you have set up.

2. Do any of the following:

   To edit an item—for instance, to change how often the program is run—double-click the item. You'll see the properties dialog box for that program. Click the Schedule tab and make any changes (see Figure 17.16). Then click OK.

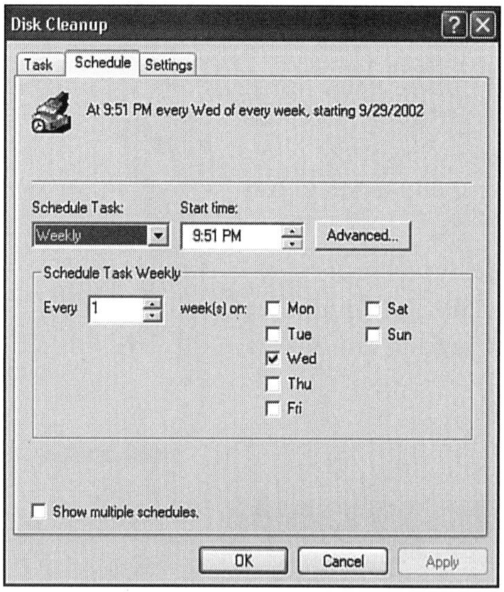

FIGURE 17.16

You can change when the scheduled item is run.

To delete a scheduled item, select it and then click Delete this item in the task pane or press the Delete key. Confirm the deletion by clicking Yes.

3. Close the Scheduled Tasks window by clicking its Close button.

The Absolute Minimum

This chapter focuses on how to keep your data and computer secure using a variety of Windows XP tools as well as other programs, including a backup program and a virus program. In particular, keep these main points in mind:

- Back up your data: It is the most important and valuable thing on your computer. A computer can be replaced; your data sometimes cannot.

- To back up, you need a backup program as well as backup media (a tape drive, or a CD-R or CD-RW drive). You can select how often to perform the backup as well as which files are backed up.

- You should periodically scan your computer for errors. You can use Windows XP's Check Disk to do so.

- Viruses are programs that can infect your computer and wreak havoc. Use a virus protection program to scan files and email attachments for viruses and to warn you of any viruses.

- To make sure that you perform key maintenance tasks, you can schedule and run them automatically.

18

IMPROVING YOUR COMPUTER'S PERFORMANCE

When you first start using your computer, it will seem pretty quick, especially if you have not used a computer before. However, as time passes, you might notice that the performance is a little sluggish. As another example, you may find that your desktop is cluttered with too many icons. To keep your computer working as efficiently as possible, every now and then you should use some tools to check and, if needed, optimize the computer's performance. This section covers how to display disk information; the rest of the chapter covers how to use Windows XP's tools to enhance your computer's performance.

Displaying Disk Information

To get an idea of the size of your hard disk and how much space is used, you can display disk information. This is handy if you think you are running out of room for your files. You also access several of Windows XP's disk tools from this dialog box.

To display disk information, follow these steps:

1. Open the My Computer window. You can click Start and then My Computer. Otherwise, if you added the My Computer icon to your desktop, you can double-click it.

2. In the My Computer window, right-click the disk for which you want information and click the Properties command. This displays the disk's Properties dialog box. On the General tab, shown in Figure 18.1, you can see the total disk space, the disk space used, and the free space.

3. Click OK to close the dialog box.

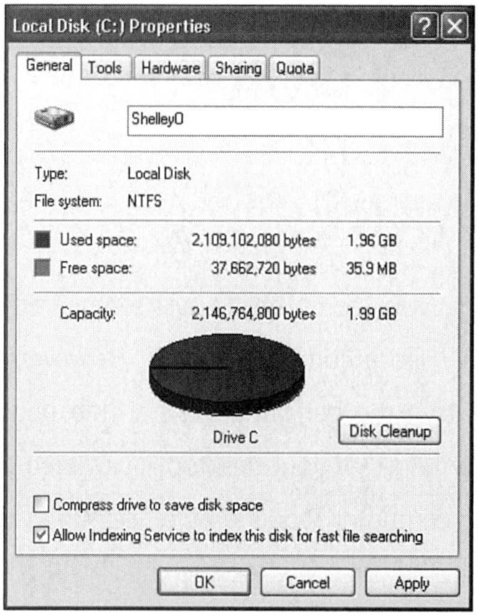

FIGURE 18.1

This hard disk is dangerously full. There is very little free space for storing files.

Other sections of this chapter cover how to use the tools in this dialog box to improve performance.

Cleaning Up Your Disk

Like any storage place (think closets, garages, and basements), eventually the clutter starts to overwhelm you, and you need to get rid of stuff you don't need. The same is true for your hard disk(s). You should periodically clean out files you don't need. To help with this task, you can clean up some temporary files, empty your Recycle Bin, and find some other hidden nooks and crannies of Windows that take up storage space.

Windows XP makes it easy to get rid of files you don't need with the Disk Cleanup Wizard. When you use this wizard, Windows XP recommends some files for deletion, as well as lists the disk space you'll gain. You can select from the list of items suggested for deletion and then have Windows XP remove these items to regain that disk space.

To clean up files using the Windows XP Disk Cleanup Wizard, follow these steps:

1. Open the My Computer window by double-clicking this icon on your desktop or by clicking Start and then clicking My Computer.

2. Right-click the disk you want to check and then select Properties. You'll see the General tab of the Properties dialog box for that disk (refer to Figure 18.1). From this tab, you can view the total capacity of the disk drive, the used space, and the free space.

3. To clean up files, click the Disk Cleanup button. The Disk Cleanup tab displays suggested files for deletion (see Figure 18.2). Any items that are checked will be deleted. For instance, notice that in Figure 18.2, temporary files take up quite a bit of space. You can regain this space by removing these files.

FIGURE 18.2

You can select which files are removed using Disk Cleanup.

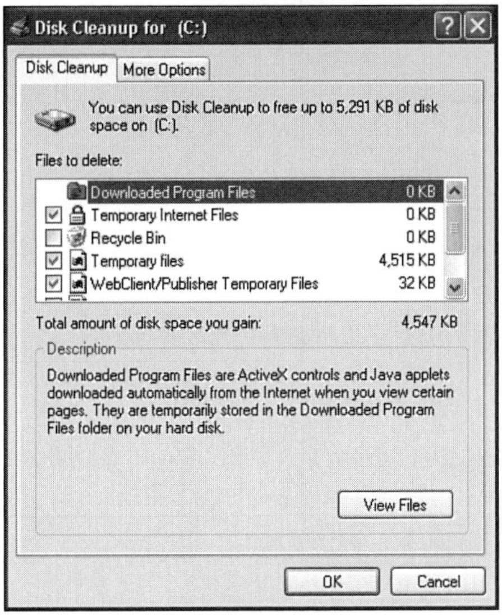

4. Check the items you want to delete. Uncheck items you do not want to delete.

5. Click OK.

6. Confirm the deletion by clicking Yes. The files are permanently deleted and that disk space regained.

For access to additional cleanup options, click the More Options tab in the Disk Cleanup dialog box. From here, you can select to remove optional Windows components, to remove programs you don't use, or to remove all but the last restore point (see Figure 18.3).

For instance, if you are running out of room, you can remove programs you do not need. For more information on adding and removing programs, see Chapter 14, "Setting Up Programs." You can also remove Windows components that you do not use. For information on this process, see Chapter 20, "Upgrading Windows." For information on what a system restore point is, see Chapter 17, "Securing Your PC."

caution

One of the first places Windows looks for space is in the Recycle Bin. Before you permanently delete those files, take a quick peek to make sure that the Recycle Bin doesn't contain any files you need. To view a particular file, select the item in the list and then click the View Files button. By doing so, you can confirm that the file can be deleted.

FIGURE 18.3

If you want to gain more space, use the More Options button to display other space-gaining options.

Saving Space by Compressing Files

As mentioned, you'll be surprised how quickly your computer fills up with files. You can delete unneeded files, but some files will fall into the category "I want to keep it, but I don't really use it." For these types of files, you can store them in a compressed folder, kind of like those magic shrink wrap storage devices they advertise on TV. In this case, the files are shrunk down in size and stored in a folder so that they don't take up so much space. These are often called zip files, and the folder icon includes a little zipper to indicate that the folder contains compressed files. When you need the files again, you can uncompress them.

Compressing Files

Follow these steps to compress files:

1. Select the file(s) or folder you want to compress.

2. Right-click any of the selected items and then select the Send To command. You'll see the Send To options (see Figure 18.4).

3. Select Compressed (zipped) folder. The files are then zipped up and stored in a folder with the default name of the first file you selected. However, the files still appear in the folder (see Figure 18.5).

4. To regain the disk space, delete the original files by right-clicking them, selecting Delete, and confirming the deletion by clicking Yes.

> **tip**
>
> If you are sending several files via email, compress them first. Doing so makes the file transfer quicker for both you and the recipient.

> **tip**
>
> You can add additional files to the compressed folder. To do so, drag the file icon to the folder icon. The file is added, but also appears in the list. You can delete the file because it is now stored in the compressed folder.

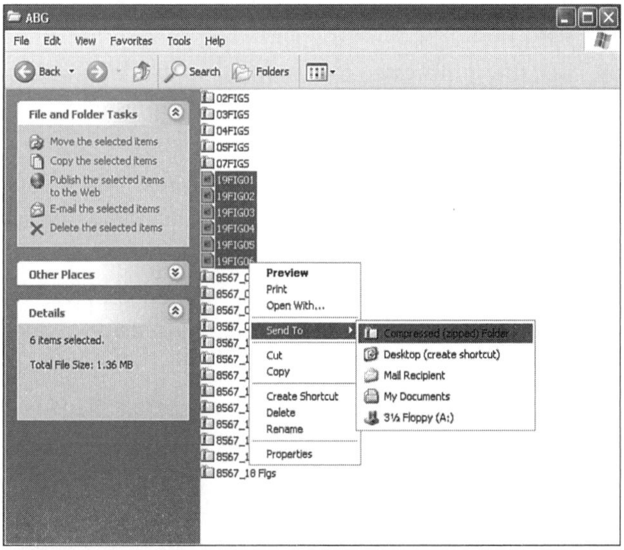

FIGURE 18.4

You can create a compressed folder from the Send To menu.

FIGURE 18.5

You see the compressed (or zipped) folder with the default name.

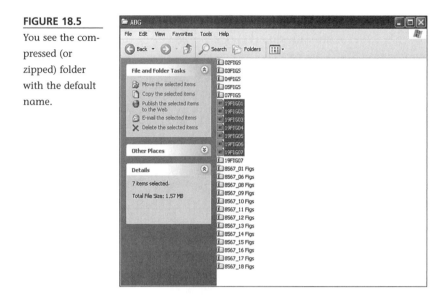

5. It's also a good idea to rename the compressed folder with a more descriptive name, rather than the default filename. To do so, right-click the folder, select Rename, type a new name, and press Enter.

Uncompressing Files

If you need to access these files again, you can uncompress or unzip them and then copy them back to your hard drive. To do so, follow these steps:

1. Open the drive and folder that contains the compressed folder. Note that the folder icon has a little zipper indicating that it is a compressed folder (see Figure 18.6).

2. Double-click the compressed folder. You'll see the files within the folder (see Figure 18.7). Note that the files are not uncompressed until you follow the next steps.

3. Select the file(s) you want to unzip and then select the Copy command. You can right-click and select Copy, or you can click Copy the selected items in the task pane.

4. Open the folder where you want to place the uncompressed files. Usually, you can click Back to go back to the original folder (the one that contained the compressed files).

5. Copy the files by right-clicking a blank area of the file window and selecting Paste.

Now the file(s) are uncompressed, and you can open and work with them as needed.

FIGURE 18.6

You can uncompress files stored in a compressed folder.

FIGURE 18.7

When you open a compressed folder, you see the contents of that folder.

Increasing Performance by Defragmenting Your Disk

Another way to improve performance is to *defragment* your disk. To understand how this process improves your disk performance, you first need to have a short introduction to how data is stored. Basically, when you defragment a disk, you rearrange how the files are stored so that Windows XP can open and display a file more efficiently.

Understanding The Basics of Disk Storage

When you store a document, the data in that document is written to your disk and saved as a file with a specific name in a specific location on your disk. To keep files organized, your disk is divided into sections called *sectors*, which are broken down into smaller sections called *clusters*. Each cluster can hold a certain amount of data.

When you give a command to save a file, Windows takes the file and stores it in a cluster. However, a file is often larger than one cluster. If the file is too big to fit in one cluster, Windows goes to the next available cluster, stores more of the file in that cluster, and so on until the entire file is stored on the disk.

Windows keeps a little cheat sheet that tells it where all the chunks of each file are stored.

When you want to open that file again, Windows checks its file system (its map of the disk) and collects all the pieces of the file. Basically, this involves putting all the pieces together again and displaying the file onscreen.

Initially, this storage does not cause performance problems because your disk is empty and files are usually stored sequentially. However, over time your disk files become fragmented and you might find that it takes a long time to open a file or start a program.

To speed access to files and to help prevent potential problems with fragmented files, you can use Disk Defragmenter to *defragment* your disk. Defragmenting basically reorders the files on the disk, putting file parts next to each other if possible and putting all the empty, available clusters together so that when new files are saved, they get a block of clusters together. Defragmenting your disk is a general maintenance job that you should perform every few months for best results.

> **note**
>
> Probably the biggest complaint and most noticeable performance issue is with online connections. Logging on to the Internet or displaying Web pages can take a long time, but this slowness is related to the type of Internet connection you have. For instance, dial-up accounts are limited to the speed of the modem, and modem speed is also limited because of phone lines.
>
> To get better Internet performance, you usually need to get a different type of connection, commonly called a *broadband connection*. The most common broadband connections for home users are cable connections (through your cable provider) and DSL connections (through a special type of phone line). You can learn more about connection types in Chapter 8, "Browsing the Internet."

Running Disk Defragmenter

You can run the defragmentation program on your hard disk by following these steps:

1. Open the My Computer window by double-clicking this icon on your desktop or by clicking Start and then clicking My Computer.

2. Right-click the disk you want to check and select Properties. You'll see the General tab of the Properties dialog box for that disk.

3. Click the Tools tab. You'll see the available system tools for disks (see Figure 18.8).

tip

Here's a little history note. Older Windows versions used a file allocation table (called FAT or FAT32) for file management as the "cheat sheet." Newer Windows versions, including Windows XP, use a more advanced file system called NTFS. This new file system lets you use huge storage media and long filenames. This file system also automatically replaces bad clusters.

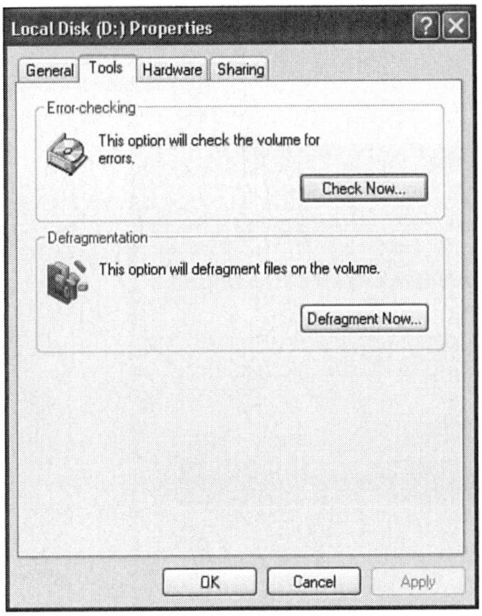

FIGURE 18.8
Use the Tools tab to access disk tools.

```
Local Disk (D:) Properties                    ? X

General   Tools   Hardware   Sharing

┌─ Error-checking ──────────────────────────┐
│        This option will check the volume for│
│        errors.                              │
│                            [ Check Now... ] │
└─────────────────────────────────────────────┘

┌─ Defragmentation ─────────────────────────┐
│        This option will defragment files on the volume.│
│                            [ Defragment Now... ]│
└─────────────────────────────────────────────┘

              [ OK ]   [ Cancel ]   [ Apply ]
```

4. Click the Defragment Now button. You'll see the Disk Defragment window.

5. To see whether the disk requires defragmenting, click the Analyze button. Windows analyzes the data on the drive and makes a recommendation on whether you should defragment the drive (see Figure 18.9). You can view the report, start defragmenting, or close the recommendation alert box.

tip

For information on checking a disk for errors, see Chapter 17.

FIGURE 18.9

Before you defragment, analyze your drive to see whether defragmenting is necessary.

Disk Defragmenter [?][X]

Analysis is complete for: (D:)

You should defragment this volume.

[View Report] [Defragment] [Close]

6. Click Close so that you can view a detailed map of the drive. You see this map in the Disk Defragmenter window (see Figure 18.10). The legend at the bottom of the Disk Defragmenter window helps you understand the map and identify the various file types (fragmented, contiguous, unmovable, and free space).

tip

You can also run this program from the Start menu. Click Start, All Programs, Accessories, and then System Tools. In the System Tools menu, click Disk Defragmenter.

FIGURE 18.10

In the analysis, you can see how the files are stored, which ones are contiguous (next to each other), and which ones are fragmented. You can also see where you have free space.

Disk Defragmenter [_][□][X]

File Action View Help

Volume	Session Status	File System	Capacity	Free Space	% Free Space
(C:)		NTFS	2.00 GB	35 MB	1 %
(D:)	Analyzed	FAT	2.00 GB	1.45 GB	72 %
(E:)		NTFS	2.00 GB	1.50 GB	75 %

Estimated disk usage before defragmentation:

Estimated disk usage after defragmentation:

[Analyze] [Defragment] [Pause] [Stop] [View Report]

■ Fragmented files ■ Contiguous files □ Unmovable files □ Free space

7. Click the Defragment button to defragment the drive. As the files are rearranged, you see the progress of the defragmentation (see Figure 18.11).

Disk Defragmenter may take a while to defragment your disk, depending on the size of the disk, the number and size of files on the volume, the extent of fragmentation in the disk, and the available system resources. Disk Defragmenter's progress is indicated by the progress bar in the Disk Defragmenter window.

FIGURE 18.11

You can view the progress of the defragmentation.

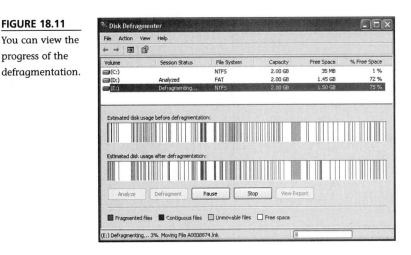

When the process is complete, Disk Defragmenter displays the results. You can also choose to display a report on the process; this report displays detailed information about the disk that was defragmented. Click the Close button to close the report and then the Disk Defragmenter window. Otherwise, you can click OK to close the Disk Defragmenter window without viewing the report.

Cleaning Up the Desktop

In addition to cleaning up files, you may also want to tidy up your desktop. Doing so won't necessarily improve the system performance, but it may help *your* performance—that is, it may help you find and access the icons on your desktop more efficiently. To help you determine which icons you really use and which ones can be deleted, you can use the Desktop Cleanup Wizard.

Follow these steps:

1. Right-click a blank part of the desktop. You'll see the Display Properties dialog box.

2. Click the Desktop tab.

3. Click the Customize Desktop button. You'll see the Desktop Items dialog box (see Figure 18.12).

tip

Performing back-to-back defrags can reclaim additional space. The first defrag is so busy cleaning up the mess that it doesn't do a perfect defrag, only a good defrag. If you've got time to defrag again, you'll have better results.

tip

For information on how to customize the desktop, see Chapter 13, "Customizing Windows XP."

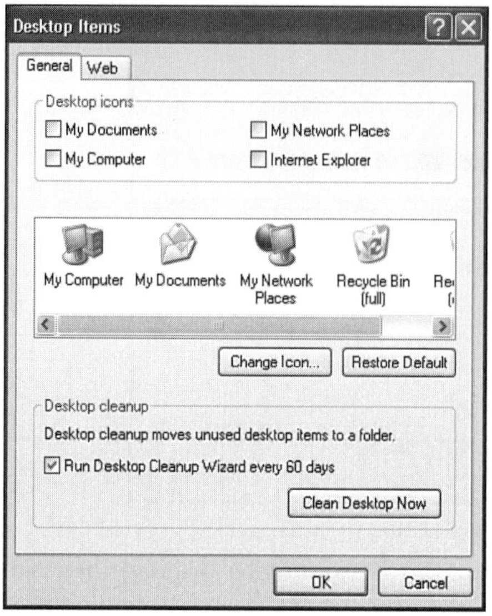

FIGURE 18.12

You can access the Desktop Cleanup Wizard from this dialog box.

4. Click Clean Desktop Now to start the wizard.

5. Follow the steps in the Desktop Cleanup Wizard, clicking Next to move from step to step. The first window displays a welcome that explains the purpose of the wizard. When you click Next, you see a list of desktop icons. You can also see the date the icon was last used (see Figure 18.13). If you do not use an icon, Windows XP checks its box and recommends it for deletion. Check any icons you want to remove; uncheck any icons you want to leave as they are. Click Next.

6. Click the Finish button to finish the cleanup.

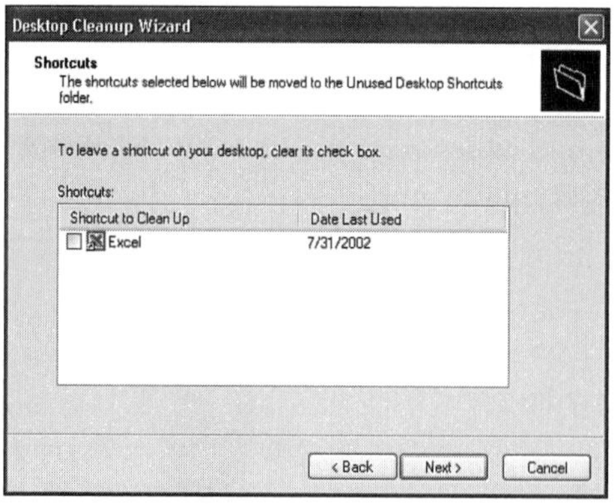

FIGURE 18.13

You can decide whether the icon is moved or left on the desktop.

If you select to remove an icon, it is not deleted, but moved to the Unused Desktop Shortcuts folder. You can always add back the icon if needed.

The Absolute Minimum

In this chapter you learn how to improve the performance of your computer by using some of the built-in tools in Windows XP. You may not need to use these tools if you have a new computer, but keep them in mind as you use the computer more and more. If you notice a drop in performance, take a look at some of the changes you can make to regain that initial performance. In particular, keep these main points in mind:

- You can view the disk properties of your hard disk to see how much total space you have, how much space is used, and how much space is free.

- If your drive is becoming too full and you want to remove files, you can help Windows select some commonly unneeded files for removal. To do so, use the Disk Cleanup Wizard. You can access this wizard from the Disk Properties dialog box.

- If there are files you want to keep (but don't need immediate access to), compress them.

- When performance is really slow, you may need to defragment the drive, which involves rearranging the data stored on the drive to optimize the performance. You can start the defragmentation process from the Tools tab of the Disk Properties dialog box.

- If your desktop becomes cluttered with too many icons, you can run the Desktop Cleanup Wizard to have Windows suggest icons to be removed.

19

UPGRADING YOUR COMPUTER

As you use your computer more and more, you may find that you want to add features to it. For instance, you may purchase a digital camera or music player such as an iPod. You may add a new printer for printing photographs. As another example, you may change how you connect to the Internet, such as by using a cable modem. When you want to add something to your computer, you first install that item, and then you set up Windows so that it recognizes and knows the features of that component. For the latter step, you install a *driver*, a special file that tells Windows the details of your particular component.

The most common addition to a computer is a printer, and Windows XP includes a wizard that leads you through the steps specific for installing a new printer. For other hardware additions, you can use the Add Hardware wizard. This chapter covers how to upgrade and improve your computer setup.

Adding a Printer

Even though you print from within a program, Windows XP manages the print job behind the scenes. Therefore, you set up a printer in Windows, and then all programs can access and use that printer. In many cases, Windows can automatically set up your printer after you attach it to your computer. Automatic setup is the easiest way to set up a printer. However, if that doesn't work, you have several other options.

If you have a newer printer that is not yet added to Windows XP's Plug and Play list (a feature that automatically recognizes and installs hardware) or an older printer, Windows XP might be unable to automatically install it. If this happens, you can add a new printer to your Windows setup using a step-by-step guide called a *wizard*. You can use one of Windows XP's drivers, or you can use a driver supplied with the printer. This section covers both automatic setup and using the wizard.

Automatic Setup

When you connect your printer, Windows XP queries the printer and then pulls key technical details about the printer, using that information to set up the printer. All you have to do is plug in the printer and wait.

Windows XP initiates the process and alerts you that the printer has been found and installed with messages that pop up from the system tray. If this happens, you are set. You can use your printer and skip the rest of this section!

Manual Setup Using Windows's Drivers

If the automatic setup doesn't work, you can add a printer using the Add Printer Wizard. You might need to do this if you have a printer that isn't on Windows's Plug and Play list. Cutting-edge printers, older printers, or budget printers,

note

A *driver* is a file that tells Windows the specific details of your hardware component, such as how it works and what features it has. The driver enables Windows to communicate with the hardware component and put the component to use. Printers, for instance, have drivers, as do other hardware components, such as modems.

note

The automatic setup feature is called *Plug and Play*, and it works with other components you add to your computer. The process of adding other components is covered later in this chapter.

for instance, may require a little push to get started on the installation.

You can see whether Windows XP has a driver that works with your printer, or you can use the disk that came with your printer. If you are upgrading to Windows XP and have had your printer for a while, you may not be able to find the printer disk. In that case, use this method.

Follow these steps to add a new printer:

1. Click Start and then click Control Panel.

2. In the Control Panel window, click the link for Printers and Other Hardware. You'll see a task for adding a printer, as well as Control Panel icons for printers and faxes, gaming options, the keyboard, scanners and cameras, and the mouse (see Figure 19.1).

3. Click the Add a printer link to start the Add Printer Wizard.

4. Click Next to move from the welcome screen to the first step of the wizard. For the first step, select to set up a local printer or network printer (see Figure 19.2).

tip

If you want to customize the printer—change the default settings that affect how the printer works—you can do so. This topic is covered later in this section.

note

If you are installing a printer that you want to share on a network, check out Chapter 24, "Setting Up Windows XP on a Home Network," to see what you need to do differently for printer setup.

FIGURE 19.1

You often use the Control Panel to add new hardware, including printers.

FIGURE 19.2

Select to install a local printer (one connected to the computer) or a printer connection (basically a network printer).

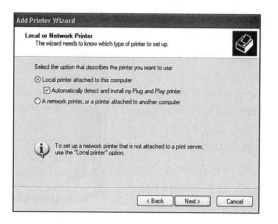

5. Select Local printer. If you want to install the printer manually, uncheck Automatically detect and install my Plug and Play printer. Click Next.

   If you selected to detect your printer and it is found and installed, you can skip the remaining steps. If the printer is not found or if you did not select automatic detection, you are prompted to select the printer port (see Figure 19.3). Printers are most often attached via USB or the LPT1 (parallel port).

FIGURE 19.3

The port is the plug that connects the printer cable to the computer.

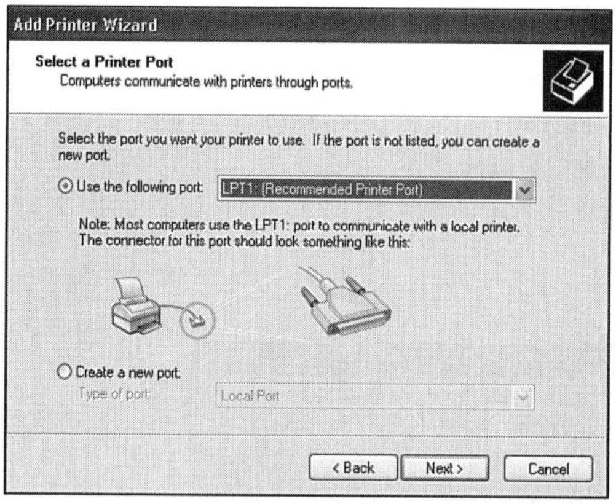

6. Select the port and click Next. You'll see a list of printer manufacturers and printers.

7. Select your printer manufacturer from the list on the left. Then select your particular printer from the list on the right (see Figure 19.4). Click Next.

   You are next prompted to type a name for the printer. This name is used to identify the printer icon for this printer.

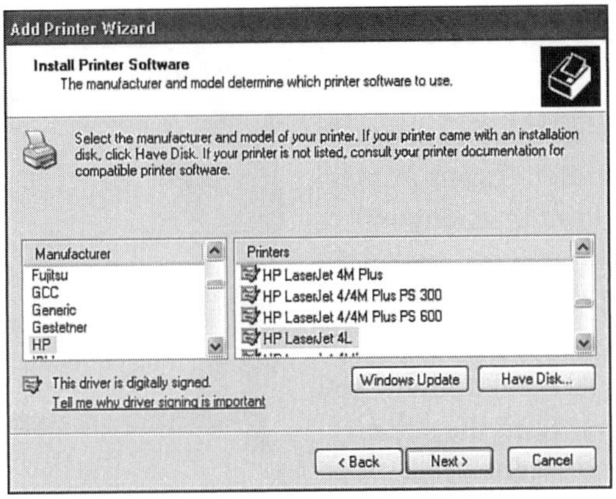

FIGURE 19.4
Windows XP lists the printer models for which it has drivers.

8. Type or accept the suggested name and also select whether you want to make this the default printer by clicking Yes or No. Click Next.

   You are asked whether you want to share this printer. Sharing a printer usually involves a home-networked PC. If you are connecting a network PC, see Chapter 24.

9. Select Do Not Share This Printer and then click Next. You are asked whether you want to print a test page.

10. Select Yes or No for the test page question and then click Next. The final step of the wizard lists all of your selections (see Figure 19.5).

11. Click Finish to install the printer driver.

note

When you select a printer and it is recognized by Windows, you see a note in the dialog box that says that the driver is digitally signed. This means that, according to the help information, "hardware products that display the Designed for Windows logo have been tested to verify compatibility with Windows." However, you can install printers even if they aren't digitally signed.

FIGURE 19.5
The final screen of the wizard lists all of your choices for confirmation. At this point, you can finish up or go back and make changes.

Manual Setup Using the Printer's Drivers

Most printers come with a disk that contains a driver for using the printer. If your printer is not listed in the Add Printer wizard and you have the printer disk, you can install the appropriate driver from the disk. You can also find drivers at different Internet sites (for instance, www.WinDrivers.com). Ultimately, you can find the printer driver from the site of the printer maker, from a Windows or Microsoft site, or from a general hardware help site, such as www.pcguide.com. Check your printer documentation to see what online resources you have. You can also try searching the Microsoft site at www.microsoft.com for printer drivers, or look for sites in computer articles for general help (www.pcworld.com).

If you have the disk, follow these steps to install the driver from the disk:

tip

Click the Back button in a wizard dialog box to return to the previous dialog box and review or modify your selections.

tip

See Chapter 8, "Browsing the Internet," for more help on visiting Web sites.

1. Follow the preceding steps to start the wizard.

2. When prompted to select the printer software, click Have Disk. You are then prompted to select the disk that contains the driver file (see Figure 19.6).

FIGURE 19.6

Select the drive that contains the printer disk.

Install From Disk

Insert the manufacturer's installation disk, and then make sure that the correct drive is selected below.

OK

Cancel

Copy manufacturer's files from:

A:\

Browse...

3. Insert the floppy or CD disk and then select the appropriate drive from the drop-down list.

4. Click OK to install the file from the disk. The driver is installed, and the printer is set up.

Customizing Your Printer

Chapter 2, "Saving and Printing your Work," covered the basics of setting up a printer and printing. As you use your printer more often, you may want to tinker with its setup. You might, for instance, change the way the page is printed (*portrait*, down the long side of the page, or *landscape*, across the long side of the page). Another common change is to add additional fonts to your computer so that you have more of a selection in changing how text and other data appear in your printed documents.

This chapter focuses on the common printer customization changes you can make.

Printing Preferences and Properties

After you have installed a printer, you can adjust the printer preferences and properties. Preferences are things such as the default orientation (portrait or landscape), page order, pages per sheet, and paper/quality options(including size, copy count, print quality, and other settings). Properties are things such as printer sharing, device settings, and other more techie printer-related features. You can make changes to either set of options. Look first at the preferences; these are things you are more likely to change. Look second at the properties; these are things you may change if you are a control freak or if you are having printer problems.

Changing Printing Preferences

Printing preferences are settings such as the order in which pages are printed (from beginning to end of a document, or from the end to beginning), orientation (portrait or landscape), and paper source. If you always print a certain way, you can change these settings.

Changing the printer's preferences changes them for all documents you print on this printer. If you want to change settings for just one document, change the settings in that document instead.

To change the printing preferences for all print jobs, follow these steps:

> **tip**
>
> The default printer is indicated with a checkmark. To select another printer as the default, right-click the icon for that printer and select Set as Default Printer.

1. Display the printer icon by clicking the Start button and then clicking Control Panel. Click the Printers and Other Hardware category. Click the Printers and Faxes Control Panel icon in the lower half of the Control Panel window. You'll see a list of all the installed printers and faxes (see Figure 19.7).

FIGURE 19.7

To customize
your printer, first
display the
Printers and
Faxes Control
Panel.

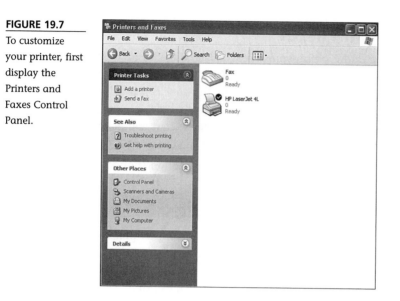

2. Select the printer you want to modify.

3. Click Select printing preferences in the Task pane. You'll see the Printing
   Preferences dialog box (see Figure 19.8).

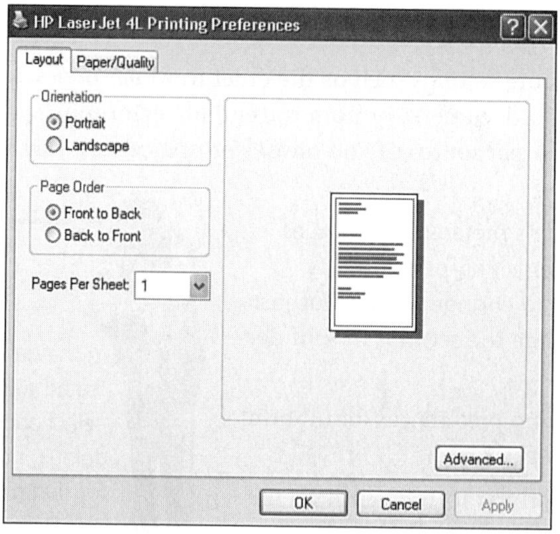

FIGURE 19.8

Use the options
in this dialog
box to control
the orientation,
page order, and
paper source for
all print jobs
printed with this
printer.

4. On the Layout tab, select a default orientation and a default page order.

5. Click the Paper/Quality tab. Select a default paper source.

6. Click OK.

Changing Printing Properties

In addition to printing preferences, you can view and change printer properties. These are more technical details of how your printer works—for instance, when the printer is available, the port to which the printer is attached, whether printer sharing is enabled, and other options. Follow these steps to modify printing properties:

1. Display the printer icon by clicking the Start button and then clicking Control Panel. Click the Printers and Other Hardware category. Then click the Printers and Faxes Control Panel icon. You'll see a list of all the installed printers and faxes (refer to Figure 19.7).

2. Click the printer you want to customize and then select Set printer properties. You'll see the Properties dialog box for your particular printer (see Figure 19.9).

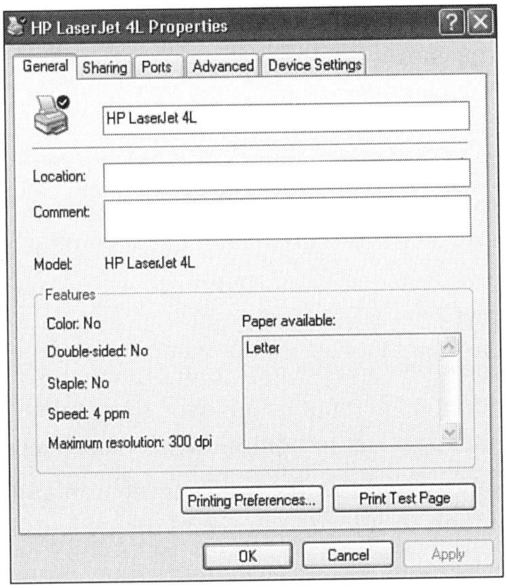

FIGURE 19.9

On the General tab, you can see which features your printer supports, as well as the printer speed.

3. On the General tab, change the printer name. If the printer is used on a network, you can also type a location and comment used to identify the printer.

4. To change the port to which the printer is connected, click the Ports tab and then select from the available ports listed.

5. To set printer-sharing options (more for network printers), use the Sharing tab.

tip

If you want help with an option, right-click the option and select What's This. Most instances refer you to your printer documentation since the various options are specific to the printer itself.

6. To change technical details, such as when the printer is available, the driver that is used, how spooling is handled, and other similar aspects of the printer, use the Advanced tab.

7. Click the Device Settings tab to make changes for the paper trays, printer memory, and font substitution.

8. Click OK to confirm your changes.

> **note**
>
> *Spooling* is when Windows XP takes the request for a print job and stores the document on your hard drive so that you can continue working. The spooler then sends the document that was temporarily stored on the hard drive to the printer.

Installing New Fonts

One of the most common formatting changes people make is changing appearance of the text by using a different font. You can select from business fonts to calligraphy fonts and from fancy fonts to silly fonts. The fonts that are listed within the program are the fonts you have installed in Windows XP. How do they get there, and what fonts do you have? This section answers these questions.

Where Do Fonts Come From?

Most people have no idea how they get the fonts that are listed within a program. They also don't realize that not all computers have the same fonts, and if they have used a font that the computer does not recognize, they'll most likely see gibberish.

Fonts come from several sources, and the first source is the printer itself. Every printer comes with built-in fonts that it can print, and these are usually indicated with a printer icon in font lists.

In addition to the fonts, Windows itself includes some built-in fonts; these fonts are actually TrueType files that tell the printer how to print particular fonts. Other TrueType fonts are installed when you install some programs. The programs themselves also include fonts, and when you install the program, you also install the fonts.

As another source, you can purchase fonts and install them within Windows. Once installed, they become available to all programs. Some sites, such as www.1001fonts.com, provide free fonts. You can download these fonts from the site and add them to your font list. This section covers how to view the fonts you already have on your system, as well as how to add new fonts.

Viewing Your Installed Fonts

Windows XP lets you view which fonts you have, as well as install new fonts. You complete these tasks by using the Fonts Control Panel. Follow these steps:

1. Click Start and then select Control Panel.

2. In the Control Panel window, select Appearance and Themes.

3. In the See Also area, click Fonts. You'll see the Fonts folder, which displays file icons for all the installed fonts (see Figure 19.10).

tip

You'll have to look pretty hard to find fonts in Windows XP. They aren't listed in the category view of the Control Panel. You find them in the See Also area of the task pane for other Control Panel options (as covered here). Alternatively, you can switch to Classic View and use the regular Font Control Panel icon.

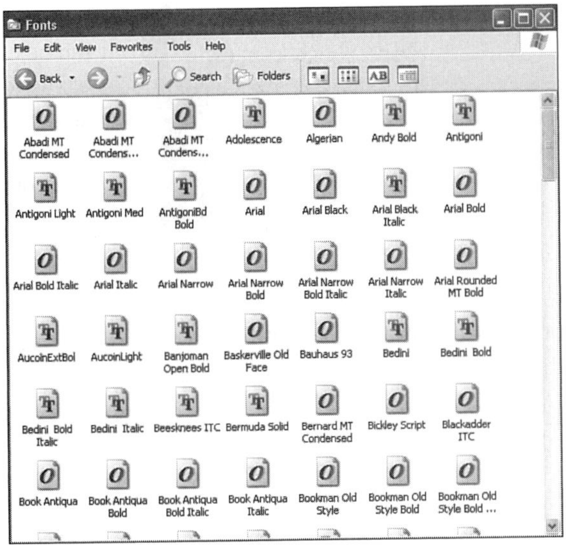

FIGURE 19.10

Fonts are stored as files on your computer and are indicated with a font icon.

4. To view a font, double-click the file. You'll see a sample of the font in various sizes, as well as information about the font (including its name, type, version, and file size). Figure 19.11, for instance, shows the information for Bauhaus 93. When you are finished viewing the font, click the Done button or the Close button for the font window.

5. Click the Close button to close the Font Control Panel.

FIGURE 19.11

You can see how each letter of the alphabet appears in the font, as well as a sample sentence in various sizes.

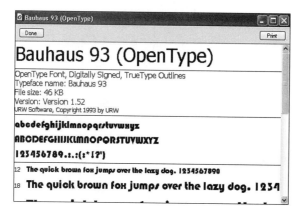

Installing New Fonts

If you purchase new fonts, you can install them in Windows. To do so, follow these steps:

1. Click Start and then select Control Panel.

2. In the Control Panel window, select Appearance and Themes.

3. In the See Also area, click Fonts.

4. Open the File menu and select Install New Font. You'll see the Add Fonts dialog box.

5. Select the drive that contains your font files from the Drives drop-down list.

6. If the files are stored within folders, select the folder from the Folders list. When you open the drive and the folder, all the available fonts are listed in the List of fonts (see Figure 19.12).

7. Select the font(s) to install. To select multiple fonts, Ctrl+click each font you want to select. To select all fonts, click the Select All button.

8. Click OK to install the selected fonts. The files are then copied to the Fonts folder and are available in all Windows programs.

9. Click the Close button to close the Fonts window.

> **tip**
>
> It can be overwhelming to see all the fonts and each variation (including bold, italic, and bold italic). You can select different views from the View menu. For instance, to group similar types of fonts together, click View and then click List Fonts by Similarity. To hide all variations of a font (bold, italic, and so on), click View and then click Hide Variations.

FIGURE 19.12

Many font collec-
tions include so
many fonts that
you probably
don't want to
install them all.
Instead, select
the fonts from
the collection
that you do want
to install from
this dialog box.

Add Fonts

List of fonts:

ABELARD Regular [TrueType]
ABRUPT Regular [TrueType]
ACCORD Regular [TrueType]
ACTION Regular [TrueType]
AIRCRAFT Regular [TrueType]
ALBRIGHT Regular [TrueType]
ALDUS Regular [TrueType]

OK

Close

Select All

Folders:

f:\2d

f:\
2d

Drives:

f: 4000

Network...

☑ Copy fonts to Fonts folder

Setting Up New Hardware

As you use your computer, you may find that
you want to add new components to your system. For example, you might purchase a digital
camera or scanner, or you might add a recordable DVD or CD drive. As another example,
you might add one of the many digital music
add-ons, such as an MP3 player or other
portable music devices.

In any case, setting up new hardware can be
straightforward. In the best-case scenario, you
simply attach or install the new device, and
Windows XP sets it up automatically. If that
doesn't happen, you can always install the device manually. Both methods are covered in this section.

tip

To add fonts you have
downloaded, you usually
copy the fonts from the
download location to the
Fonts folder. Don't add too
many, though, because it
can slow your system
down.

Setting Up New Hardware Automatically

To set up hardware automatically, simply follow the installation instructions for your
particular device. For some add-on components, you simply connect the device to an
available port. For example, most scanners plug into a USB port. (USB is short for *uni-
versal serial bus*, and it is a type of port found on most computers. You can connect
devices to these ports by plugging in the USB cable to the USB port on your computer.)

For other hardware, you may have to turn off your computer and remove the system
case. For instance, to install network or modem cards, you have to turn off the power,
remove the case, and then plug the cards into slots inside the system unit.

In either case, if Windows XP recognizes the new hardware, it automatically starts the
Add Hardware Wizard and queries the device for setup information. It then installs the

appropriate driver file and alerts you that the device has been found and installed. You should see alert messages in the system tray as this process is completed. You can then use your device.

Using the Manufacturer's Install Program

Usually, a hardware component comes with a disk with its own driver and installation routine. A *driver* is a special type of file that tells Windows XP the details about a particular hardware device.

If your component came with a disk, use this disk to install the new hardware. Usually, you connect the device and then insert the disk to start the installation process. Follow the specific instructions for your particular hardware component.

Installing New Hardware Manually

If Windows XP does not find and start your new hardware device automatically, or if you do not have a driver from the hardware maker, you can use the Add Hardware Wizard to manually set up the device. You can then have Windows search for and install the new device. Otherwise, you can select the device manufacturer and product from a list. Windows XP includes drivers for many popular hardware components.

Follow these steps to run the Add Hardware Wizard:

1. Click Start and then Control Panel.

2. Change to Classic view by clicking the Switch to Classic view link in the task pane. In the Control Panel window, double-click Add Hardware.

   Or

   In Category view, click Printers and Other Hardware. Then, in the See Also list in the task pane, click Add Hardware.

3. Click Next to move past the welcome screen. You are then asked whether the device is already connected.

4. You should have connected the device before starting the wizard, so click Yes, I Have Already Connected The Hardware. Click Next to move to the next step. You'll see a list of all the devices that are already installed (see Figure 19.13).

4. Select Add a new hardware device. (Scroll to the end of the list to find this option.) Click Next. You have the choice of letting Windows XP search for the new device and set it up automatically or setting up the device manually. Try searching first.

FIGURE 19.13

To add new hardware, select the last option in the list of hardware devices.

5. To have Windows XP search and install, select this option. Windows XP then searches for new devices. If the device is found, Windows XP installs the new device. Follow the onscreen prompts to install and set up the device. You can skip the remaining steps listed here.

   Or

   If the automatic method did not work or if you want to use the manual method, select this option. You'll see a list of common hardware categories (see Figure 19.14).

> **caution**
>
> If your device type is not listed, click Show All Devices.

FIGURE 19.14

Select the type of device you are adding.

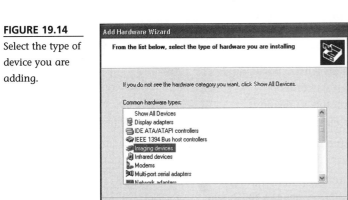

6. Select your device type and click Next. You are then prompted to select the manufacturer and model of the device you are installing (see Figure 19.15).

FIGURE 19.15

Select the manufacturer and model of the device from these lists.

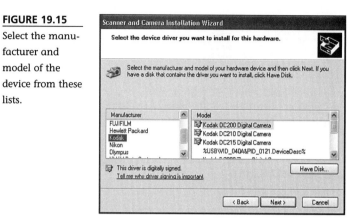

7. Scroll through the list of manufacturers until you see the manufacturer of your device and then click it. You'll see the available models from this manufacturer in the Model list. Click the model and then click Next.

8. Follow the onscreen instructions for completing the installation of your device. You can then use your new hardware device.

Troubleshooting Hardware Problems

Sometimes when you add a new device, your computer won't work properly. Perhaps the computer gets stuck or else the component doesn't work properly. For instance, if your printer driver isn't functioning, your printer might print random characters, or your monitor may not display text correctly.

If you are having problems with a particular hardware device, you can use one of Windows XP's troubleshooters to display common problems, as well as solutions.

Follow these steps to display help on a particular hardware device:

1. Right-click the My Computer icon and then select Properties to display the System Properties dialog box.

2. Click the Hardware tab (see Figure 19.16).

tip

If your computer gets stuck, you may have to undo the installation of the hardware component. To do so, you may use the System Restore points to restore the system to the settings *before* the installation. Chapter 17 covers using System Restore.

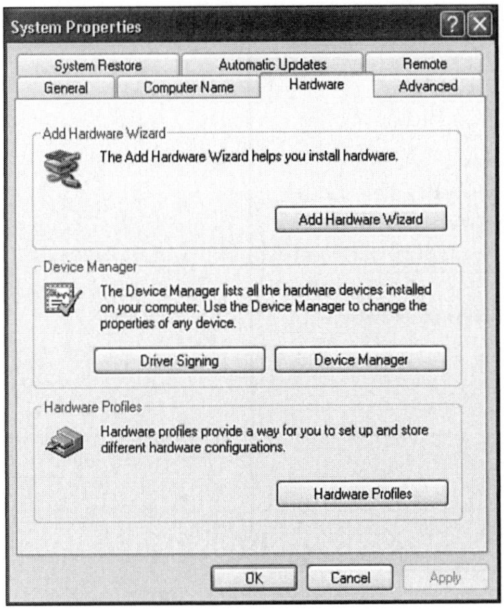

FIGURE 19.16

You can start the Add Hardware Wizard or display installed devices from this dialog box.

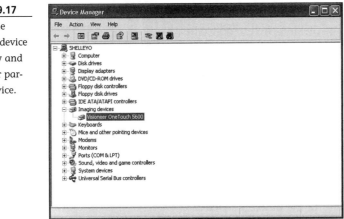

3. Click the Device Manager button. You'll see the Device Manager listing the categories of hardware devices. Each category has a plus sign next to it. You can click this plus sign to expand the list and see the device(s) installed for each category. Figure 19.17, for instance, shows the Imaging devices category expanded.

FIGURE 19.17

Expand the hardware device list to view and select your particular device.

4. When you see the device that's giving you problems, right-click the device name and then select the Properties command. You'll see the properties dialog box for this particular device (see Figure 19.18).

FIGURE 19.18

You can view device information from the properties dialog box.

5. Click the Troubleshoot button in the properties dialog box. Doing so launches the Windows XP help system and displays the initial troubleshooting help window.

6. Select your device (if needed). Windows XP displays queries to try to determine the problem. Answer the questions, clicking Next to go to the next step. For instance, if you are troubleshooting a scanner, Windows XP prompts you to select the type of scanner.

tip

If you need to update the driver or make more advanced changes, you start from the properties dialog box. However, that particular topic is beyond the scope of this book.

7. Review each screen, selecting the appropriate options and clicking Next. Windows then lists common problems. For instance, Figure 19.19 lists some common problems for scanners. When Windows identifies the problem, it recommends some ways to solve that problem. Try any of the recommended fixes. You may have to step through several pages of questions and help suggestions until the problem is fixed.

8. When you are finished troubleshooting the device, click the Help and Support Center window's Close button.

FIGURE 19.19

Windows displays several options for fixing the device.

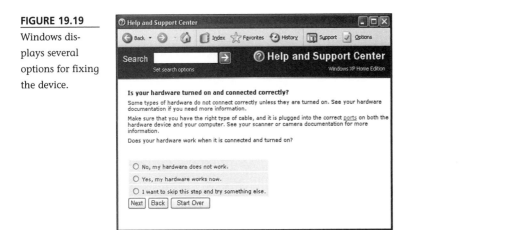

The Absolute Minimum

In this chapter you learn about some additional maintenance features available in Windows XP, particularly the following:

- You need to set up any printers you use with your computer. The easiest way is through automatic setup, which works for common printers. You can also set up the printer manually using a printer driver from Windows XP or from your printer manufacturer.

- Most of the time, you don't need to make that many adjustments to how your printer works. However, if necessary you can set certain options for a printer, including page layout options (the default orientation), as well as technical details.

- Fonts enable you to change the appearance of text within a document. The fonts available in your programs are the fonts you have installed through Windows or that were included with your printer. You can view these fonts, as well as add new fonts, by using the Font Control Panel icon.

- If you add new hardware, you can install it using one of several methods: automatically, by using the installation program and files provided with the hardware component, or by using the Add New Hardware Wizard.

- You can use the Device Manager to display information about installed hardware, as well as to troubleshoot a device if you are having problems.

UPGRADING WINDOWS

Windows XP is by no means perfect, so during its lifetime, Microsoft will fix problems (called *bugs*) with little programs (called *patches*). To keep your version updated, you can download updates to Windows XP. Periodically, Microsoft bundles several patches and bug fixes together into a service pack, and you can download and install this service pack. Currently, Windows Service Pack 2 is the most up-to-date version of Windows. You can check your current version and install updates as needed.

Also, depending on your Windows installation, certain components may not have been installed. You can review the list of components and add or remove them as needed. That's the focus of this chapter—upgrading Windows.

Checking Your Windows Version

If you are not sure what version of Windows your system is running, you can display the version number. You can then decide whether you need to upgrade. To check your version number, follow these steps:

1. Right-click the My Computer icon. If you have a desktop icon for My Computer, you can right-click the icon on the desktop. If not, click Start and then right-click My Computer from the Start menu.

2. Click Properties. Under System in the Properties dialog box, you should see the version number listed (see Figure 20.1).

If you don't see Service Pack 2 listed, you may want to upgrade. This service pack includes several key security features, including Windows Security Center. This book is based on Service Pack 2.

tip

If you are running Windows Millennium (ME) or Windows 98, you should consider upgrading to Windows XP (the most recent version and the version covered in this book). The previous versions of Windows and Windows XP are significantly different.

FIGURE 20.1

You can see which version of Windows you are running on your system.

Installing Windows Updates

To keep your system as up-to-date as possible, you should periodically check for and install Windows updates. These updates, as mentioned, fix bugs and provide software patches. A bug is a problem in the software code that causes problems. A patch is a small chunk of programming code that repairs the bug or provides some additional functions for Windows.

You have two ways to perform this task. This section covers both of these methods, as well as how to change the notification settings (specifically how and when you are notified about updates).

tip

To check for and install automatic updates, you must have an Internet connection. See Chapter 8, "Browsing the Internet," for more information on this topic.

Running Automatic Updates

As Windows XP is initially set up, critical updates are downloaded automatically, and you are prompted to install these updates when they are available. A little pop-up reminder will be displayed in the system tray reminding you to check for updates. From this reminder, you can choose to update Windows by clicking the reminder and then following the appropriate steps.

Checking for Updates

You can also check for updates at any time. For instance, in addition to critical updates, Microsoft provides driver updates and updates that add new features. To check for and install other updates, follow these steps:

1. Click Start and then click All Programs. In the top section of the Start menu, you should see Windows Update listed.

2. Click Windows Update. For dial-up Internet connections, you are prompted to get connected. For cable connections, Internet Explorer is started. You'll see the Windows Update page (see Figure 20.2).

3. If needed, click the option for scanning your system and checking for new links. Windows XP checks your system against the latest updates to see which updates are applicable (see Figure 20.3). This may take a while, depending on your Internet connection speed.

caution

Because the Microsoft Windows Update page is updated frequently, what you see when you choose to update will be different. Also, the process may vary some from these steps. Follow the onscreen steps or request help on the Web site if you have problems.

FIGURE 20.2

To check for and download updates, go to the Microsoft Windows Update page.

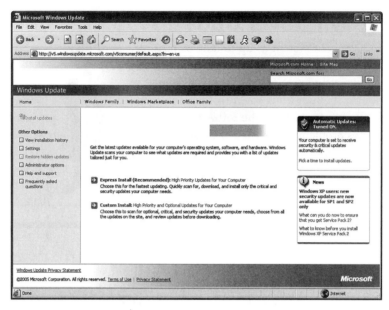

FIGURE 20.3

You can view the various updates that are available.

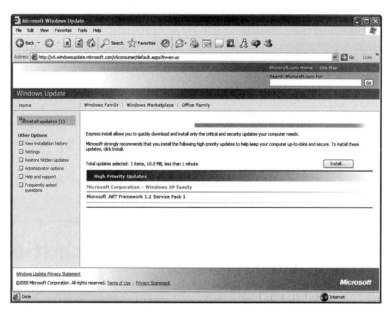

4. Click the update you want to install in the Windows Update pane and then follow the installation directions. The steps vary depending on the update type, so just read the screens carefully and make your selections based on the onscreen advice. Basically, you download (copy from this Web site to your computer) the upgrade files and then install them on your computer. Depending on the type of Internet connection and the size of the update

files, downloading the files can take a while. After the update is downloaded, you then install it, updating the Windows files on your system. Then you are sometimes prompted to restart Windows to put the new updates into effect. In some cases, you must restart your computer to activate the new features or updates.

Setting Automatic Update Options

If you want to review or change your update settings (when you are notified of updates, for instance), you can do so. For example, you may want to check more frequently for updates. You can make changes to how Automatic Updates are handled by using the Windows Security Center. Follow these steps:

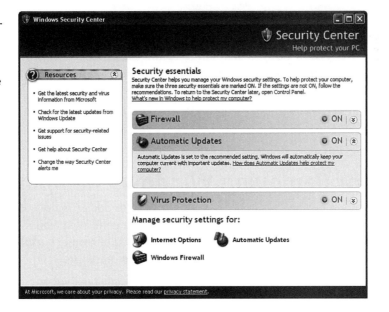

tip

From the Windows Update page, you can also review and select from a list of updates. Furthermore, you can view your installation history, change the settings for Windows updates, and get helpful information on these topics. To do any of these tasks, use the links in the Windows Update pane of the window or click any links in the main area of the Windows Update page.

1. Click Start, All Programs, Accessories, and then System Tools. Click Security Center to display the Windows Security Center (see Figure 20.4).

FIGURE 20.4

You can see the current settings for Automatic Updates from the Windows Security Center.

2. Note whether Automatic Updates is On. To display information about this feature, click the down arrow next to On (or Off if you have not turned this feature on).

3. To change the options, click the Automatic Updates link. You'll see the options for handling Windows updates (see Figure 20.5).

FIGURE 20.5

You can select when you are notified for updates.

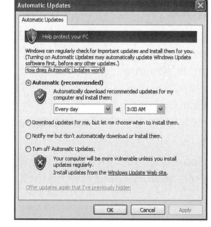

3. Select how updates are managed. You can choose to automatically download and install, to download but prompt before installing, to notify but not download, or to turn off this feature.

4. Click OK. Windows will handle any new updates in the manner you selected.

Installing or Removing Windows Components

In addition to Windows updates, you may need to add or remove Windows components. Depending on the type of installation you performed, you may not have installed certain features (such as fax features). On the other hand, to save disk space, you may want to remove components you don't use.

For instance, you may read in a book (including this book) about how to use your computer to play Solitaire. However, when you look at your Start menu, you don't see Solitaire listed. Perhaps the games included with Windows XP were not installed on your computer. If so, you can install them.

To make a change to Windows components, follow these steps:

1. Click the Start button and then click Control Panel.

2. Click Add or Remove Programs. You'll see the Add or Remove Programs window (see Figure 20.6).

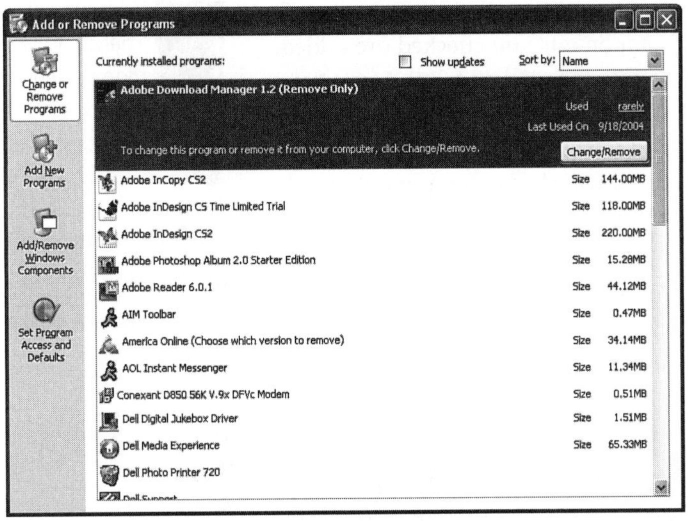

FIGURE 20.6

You can use this Control Panel item to add and remove programs, including Windows components.

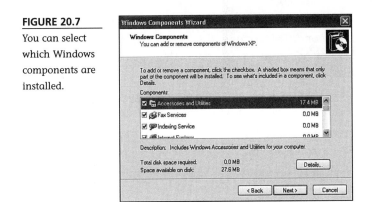

3. Click the Add/Remove Windows Components button. You'll see the Windows Components Wizard (see Figure 20.7). Items that are checked are installed. You can uncheck items to remove them from your setup. You can also check any items to add them to your setup.

FIGURE 20.7

You can select which Windows components are installed.

4. Check (to add) or uncheck (to remove) the components you want to change.

5. Click Next and then follow the onscreen instructions as Windows XP updates its installed components. The components you checked are added. You may be prompted to insert your Windows disk. Windows configures and sets up any new components. If you unchecked a component, it is removed.

6. Click Finish to complete the wizard. You may need to restart your computer to update Windows XP's configuration and put the update(s) into effect.

> **tip**
>
> Some listed components are actually several components. To view the various components within a group, select the item (such as Accessories and Utilities) and then click the Details button. You can then check or uncheck the components listed within this group.

THE ABSOLUTE MINIMUM

To keep your system up-to-date, you should periodically check for and install Windows updates. This chapter covers this topic, as well as installing or removing Windows components. Keep these main ideas in mind:

■ Usually, your computer is set up to automatically scan for and install updates. You'll know when an update is installed because Windows displays a notification icon.

■ To check for updates manually or to select from optional updates, use the Windows Updates command. This command starts Internet Explorer and takes you to the Microsoft Windows Update page. Here, you can review current updates and select to install those updates.

■ If you prefer to control when updates are installed, you can change the Automatic Updates settings. To do so, use the Windows Security Center.

■ To review, add, or remove installed Windows components, use the Add or Remove Programs Control Panel item.

PART VI

WINDOWS XP FOR SPECIAL SITUATIONS

21

USING WINDOWS ACCESSORY PROGRAMS

Windows XP includes more than just the necessary tools and programs to be your operating system. Windows XP also comes packed with several other programs, such as an email program (covered in Chapter 7, "Sending and Receiving Email"), an Internet browser (covered in Chapter 8, "Browsing the Internet"), a fax program (covered in Chapter 10, "Sending and Receiving Faxes"), a music player (covered in Chapter 11, "Playing Music"), and several others.

This chapter focuses on some of the other accessory programs included with Windows XP. Although they won't replace your need for full-fledged programs, they do serve some simple purposes. They are also great for tinkering around and experimenting. Many program skills—copying text, selecting a menu command, and undoing changes—work the same way in all programs. Use this chapter to explore some of Windows XP's accessory programs.

Checking Out the Accessories

You can get a good idea of the accessory programs included in Windows XP by displaying the Accessories folder. To do so, click Start, All Programs, and then Accessories. Some programs are grouped together into a folder (such as System Tools). Others are listed on the menu (see Figure 21.1). To open a folder and display the programs, click the folder name. To start any of these programs, click the program's name.

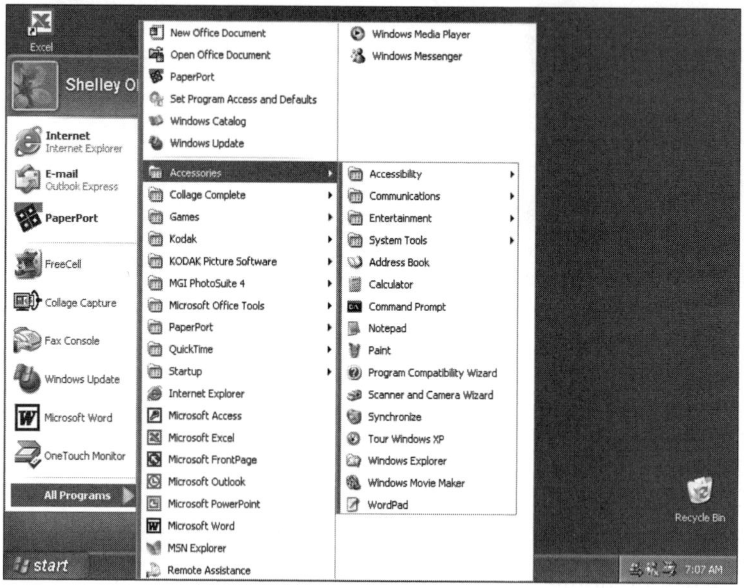

FIGURE 21.1

You can view the accessory programs included with Windows XP.

The following briefly lists the main uses of the Accessories program and provides references to other chapters where these features are covered.

- Accessibility accessories provide special features for those with special needs. For instance, you can display an onscreen keyboard and type from that. You can also magnify the screen. You can read more about these features in Chapter 23, "Using Accessibility Options."

- Communications features include the Home Networking Wizard and other networking features (covered in Chapter 24, "Setting Up Windows XP

caution

If you do not see a Windows program listed that is covered here or in other books, that component may not have been installed. To install additional Windows components, see Chapter 20, "Upgrading Windows."

on a Home Network"), the New Connection Wizard (covered in Chapter 8), and Fax (covered in Chapter 10).

- Entertainment programs include Sound Recorder, Windows Media Player, and Volume Control. Music is covered in Chapter 11. You can also use the new Windows Movie Maker (covered in Chapter 12, "Working with Photographs and Movies").

- System Tools include features for checking and optimizing your computer. These topics are covered in Part V of this book.

- Address Book helps you keep track of contacts. You can find out more about using Address Book in Chapter 15, "Customizing Email and Internet Explorer."

- Calculator is a basic calculator you can use to calculate mathematical equations. This program is covered later in this chapter.

- Command Prompt is a throw-back to those DOS days (before Windows). Even within the world of Windows, you might need access to a command prompt. For instance, you might use Command Prompt to run a DOS game or to execute a command for checking your system.

- Notepad is good for simple text files.

- Paint is fun for creating simple illustrations. This program is covered in this chapter.

- You can use WordPad to create simple text documents. Like Paint and Calculator, WordPad is described in this chapter.

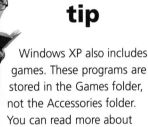

tip

Windows XP also includes games. These programs are stored in the Games folder, not the Accessories folder. You can read more about games later in this chapter.

- The Accessories folder also includes tools for checking program compatibility, setting up a camera or wizard, synchronizing data from a laptop with your desktop computer, viewing a tour of Windows XP, and managing files with Windows Explorer.

Using WordPad

WordPad is a simple word processing program with basic features for typing, editing, and formatting text. If you create simple documents, WordPad might suit you just fine. If you create a lot of documents, consider purchasing a word processing program with a more robust set of features. Popular word processing programs include Word for Windows and WordPerfect.

This section covers some basic features of WordPad. For more information, consult online help or experiment!

Taking a Look at the Program Window

You start WordPad as you do all other programs: Click Start, All Programs, Accessories, and then click WordPad to start the program and display the WordPad window (see Figure 21.2).

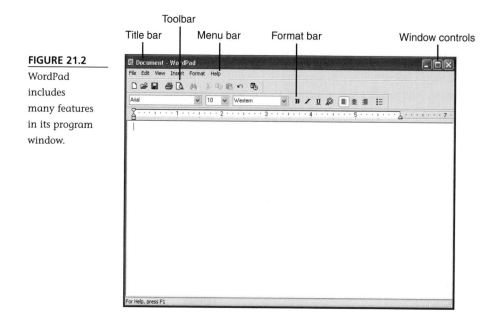

FIGURE 21.2

WordPad includes many features in its program window.

Toolbar

Title bar   Menu bar   Format bar   Window controls

Many onscreen features are included in WordPad. You'll find these same features in other programs. Table 21.1 describes common program elements found in WordPad and other programs.

Table 21.1 Common Program Elements

Item	Description
Title bar	Lists the name of the document and the program. If you have not saved the document, you see a generic name.
Menu bar	Lists the menu names. To select a menu command, click the menu name and then click the menu command.
Toolbar	As a shortcut to commonly used menu commands, most programs include a toolbar. In WordPad, for instance, you can use the toolbar buttons to open a document, create a new document, print your work, save your document, and more.
Format bar	Use this toolbar to make changes to the appearance of your document. For instance, you can use the Font drop-down list to change the font. Use the Bold button to make text bold.

Table 21.1 (continued)

Item	Description
Window controls	In addition to the program elements, the program window includes window controls for maximizing, minimizing, and closing the program window. See Chapter 1, "Getting Started with Windows XP," for more information on manipulating the window.

Typing and Editing Text

WordPad, as mentioned, is used to create text documents. If you want to create a simple document, WordPad has enough features and options to create it. If you are new to computing, WordPad is a great place to learn skills such as entering text, copying and moving text, deleting text, changing the appearance of text, and more. The skills you use in WordPad to perform these tasks will translate to other programs. That is, you follow the same basic steps to copy text in WordPad as in a full-featured word processing program such as Word for Windows. This section covers some common tasks.

tip

If you are not sure what a toolbar button does, display its ScreenTip name by putting the mouse pointer on the edge of the button. The button name should then pop up.

Typing Text

When you start WordPad, you see a blank document onscreen. You also see a flashing vertical pointer that indicates the current cursor location. Text you type is entered at this cursor location. (Later, when you edit a document, you can move this insertion point to any place in the document to add or select text. When you first open WordPad, because you have not typed any text, you cannot move the insertion point.)

To enter text, just start typing. You see the text onscreen and can make editing changes as you type. Notice also that the insertion point moves to the right as you type and that WordPad automatically wraps text to the next line. You do not have to press Enter at the end of the line.

caution

A common mistake is to press Enter at the end of each line, but you should, instead, let WordPad add the line breaks. That way, if you add or delete text, WordPad adjusts the line breaks as needed.

Do press Enter when you want to end one paragraph and start another or when you want to insert a blank line.

Editing Text

After you have entered text, you may need to go back and make some revisions. The following list covers the basic text-editing skills. Keep in mind that these skills also work in most other text programs.

Here are the basic editing tasks:

■ To make a change to text, you start by selecting it. For instance, if you want to move a section of text, you select it. If you want to format text (covered next), you select it. To select text, click at the start of the text, hold down the mouse pointer, and drag across the text you want to select. The text appears highlighted onscreen (see Figure 21.3).

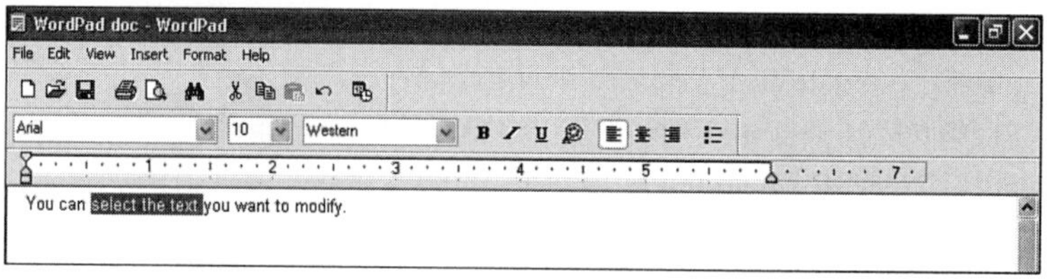

FIGURE 21.3

The first thing you do in most editing and formatting is select the text you want to modify.

■ To delete text, select the text and press the Delete key. Notice that WordPad adjusts the lines of text. Use this method when you want to delete more than a few characters. You can also delete characters one at a time using the Backspace key (which deletes characters to the left of the insertion point) or the Delete key (which deletes characters to the right of the insertion point).

■ Moving and copying text uses a cut/copy and paste metaphor. You start by selecting the text you want to move or copy. Then select the Edit, Cut command (to move text) or the Edit, Copy command (to copy text). Move to the location where you want to insert the text; this might be another location in the current document, in another document, or even in another program. Click the Edit, Paste command to paste the text in the new location. When you move text, the text is deleted from the original location and

tip

Most programs include multiple ways to perform the same task. Is one better? Not really. You can select the one most suited to your working style. In addition to using the menu commands (how most beginners learn), you can also use the Cut, Copy, or Paste toolbar buttons for moving and copying text. Furthermore, you can use the shortcut keys: Ctrl+X for Cut, Ctrl+C for Copy, or Ctrl+V for Paste.

appears only in the new location. When you copy text, the text appears in both locations: the original and the new.

■ If you make a mistake, you can undo it. Suppose, for instance, that you delete text by mistake. You can undo it by selecting the Edit, Undo command or by using the Undo toolbar button. (The shortcut key for Undo is Ctrl+Z.)

Formatting Text

When you want to make a change to how the text appears, you can use the Format commands or the Format bar. The fastest way to make a change is to use the Format bar, but if you have many changes or if you are unsure of what each button does, use the commands in the Format menu.

From the Format bar or menu, you can select another typeface; change the font size; apply emphasis (bold, italic, or underline); change the text color; change the alignment of paragraph(s) to left, right, or center; and make many other changes.

Select the text to change and then click the button or select the menu command. For instance, to make text bold, select the text and then click the Bold button. Figure 21.4 shows just a few of the changes you can make.

FIGURE 21.4

Use the Format bar to make formatting changes to the text.

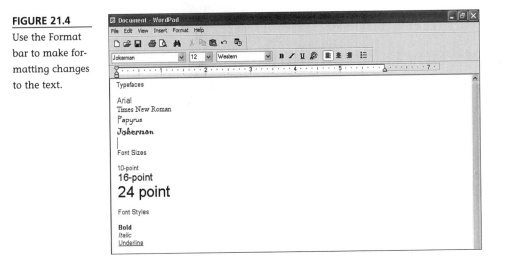

Saving Your Work

As you create documents (any documents, not just those in WordPad), you should save and save often. To save a document, use the File, Save As command. Select a folder for the document, type a name, and click the Save button. (You learn more about saving and naming documents in Chapter 2, "Saving and Printing Your Work.")

Once you've saved a document, you can open it again if you want to revise it. To open a document, use the File, Open command. If you don't see the document listed, change to the folder (or drive) you used to save the document. Then double-click the file name to open the document. Again, Chapter 2 provides step-by-step instructions on saving, opening, and printing documents.

Using Paint

In addition to a word processing program, Windows XP includes a drawing program called Paint. You can use Paint to create simple drawings. You can draw lines and shapes, add text, and change the colors. If you make a mistake, you can use the Eraser to erase part of the drawing.

To start Paint, click Start, All Programs, Accessories, and then click Paint (see Figure 21.5).

FIGURE 21.5

You can create simple diagrams and drawings using Paint.

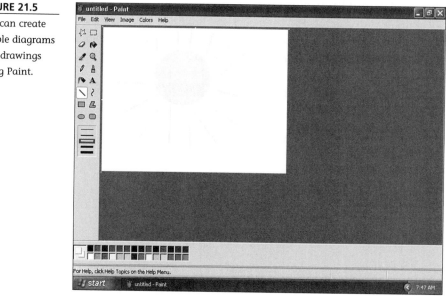

In Paint, you can do any of the following:

- To draw a shape, click the tool in the toolbar. Then click and drag within the drawing area to draw the shape.

- To add color, you can use the Fill With Color tool or the Airbrush tool.

- To draw a text box, use the Text tool. Then type the text to include. You can change the font, font size, and font style (bold, italic, or underline).

- If you make a mistake and want to get rid of something you have added, you can use the Eraser tool. Click the Eraser tool and determine the size you want the eraser to be. Then move the pointer to the drawing area, hold down the mouse button, and drag it across the part you want to erase.

- If you want to save your drawing, use the File, Save As command. To open a document you have previously saved, use the File, Open command. For more information on saving and opening a file, see Chapter 2.

- To change the colors of an object, use the color box (located at the bottom of the Paint window). Click the color you want to use for the lines used to draw the object. To change the color of the fill (for filled objects), right-click the color you want.

Using Calculator

One of my favorite accessory programs is Calculator. It's easy to pop it open and perform calculations. You can add, subtract, multiply, divide, figure percentages, and more with this handy tool shown in Figure 21.6.

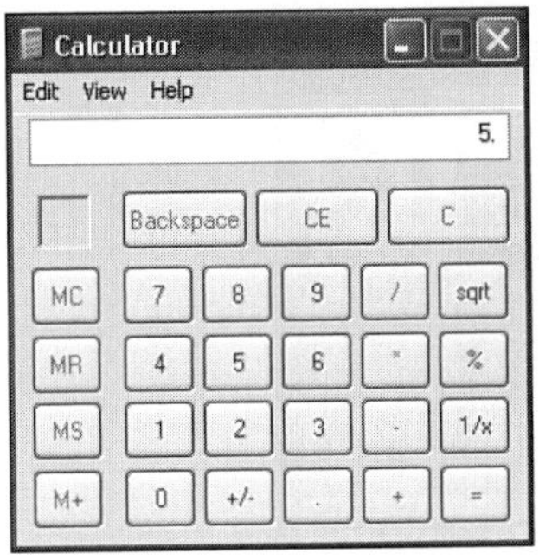

FIGURE 21.6

Use Calculator to perform basic calculations.

To use the calculator, type the first numeric entry. You can type values or operators on the numeric keypad (press Num Lock first) or on the number keys above the alphabet keys. You can also click the buttons on the calculator. Type the value, operator, value, operator, and so on until you complete your equation. You can use the following mathematical operators:

- Subtract

+ Add

* Multiply

/ Divide

To view the results of the equation, press the equals sign on the calculator. For instance, if you type 5 * 20 and then press the equals sign, you see the results of this equation—100.

Playing Games

Windows provides several games that you can play to break up your workday with a little entertainment. Playing games is also a good way to help you get the hang of using the mouse if you are a beginner. For example, playing Solitaire can help you practice clicking and dragging, if you're not accustomed to using a mouse. You can find the games by clicking Start, All Programs, Accessories, and then Games. Figure 21.7 shows the game Solitaire.

> **tip**
>
> The calculator also has memory and percentage features. If you routinely use a handheld calculator, you already know how to use these features. (If not, consult online help.) You can also use a more complex scientific calculator. Start Calculator and then click View, Scientific. You then can use any of these calculation features.

FIGURE 21.7

You can play one of many games, including the popular Solitaire.

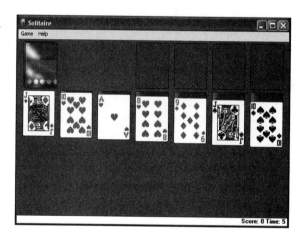

THE ABSOLUTE MINIMUM

Explore the many extra programs packed in with Windows XP, including the following:

- To create simple text documents, use WordPad.
- Paint is a great way to create simple drawings or graphic documents, such as party invitations. Kids also like to play around in Paint.
- For a quick mathematical problem, use Windows XP's built-in calculator.
- Playing games is a good way to practice using the mouse, as well as to take a break from work.
- Look elsewhere in this book for help with other accessory programs, including Fax, System Tools, and others.

22

SETTING UP WINDOWS XP FOR MULTIPLE USERS

If more than one person uses your PC, you might want to personalize certain Windows settings for each person. For example, you can customize the desktop, Start menu, Favorites folder, My Documents folder, and more. Each person can create a user account and then set up Windows the way he or she wants. Each time that person logs on, all of those settings are used. Accounts also provide some small measure of security because you can assign a password to each account. To log on (and access the computer), the user must type a password.

This chapter covers the basics of setting up accounts, logging on and off, and modifying accounts.

Setting Up a New User Account

When you first install and use Windows, you are prompted to set up the accounts for your PC. You can add names for each person using the computer (and then later go back and modify the accounts), or you can add the accounts later, as described here.

The purpose of accounts is to let each person customize how Windows works. The user accounts also save favorite Web sites, create My Documents folders, and more. You can customize Windows and then create a new account. In this case, the new account will use these settings. Otherwise, you can create a new account, and any changes you make to certain settings (the Favorites List, display, mouse, and so on) are saved with that particular account.

Follow these steps to set up a new account:

1. Click Start and then click Control Panel.

2. Click User Accounts in the Control Panel window. Any accounts you have created are listed (see Figure 22.1).

FIGURE 22.1

You can use this Control Panel option to modify existing accounts and to set up new accounts.

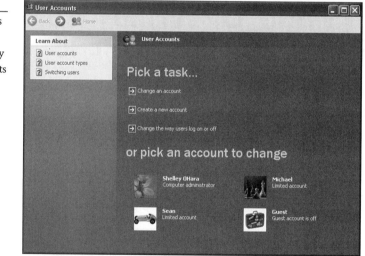

3. Click the Create a new account link. You are first prompted to type a name. As the prompt explains, "This name will appear on the Welcome screen and on the Start menu" (see Figure 22.2).

4. Type a name for the account and click the Next button. You are then prompted to select an account type.

FIGURE 22.2

The name identifies the account and is displayed when you start Windows XP.

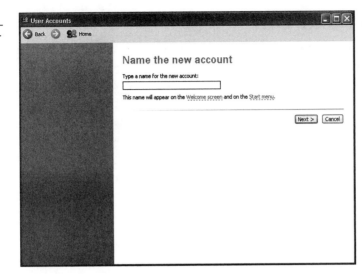

5. Select what type of account you want to create: Computer administrator or Limited. When you select an account type, you see a description of what that account can and cannot do. For instance, Figure 22.3 shows what you can do with a computer administrator account.

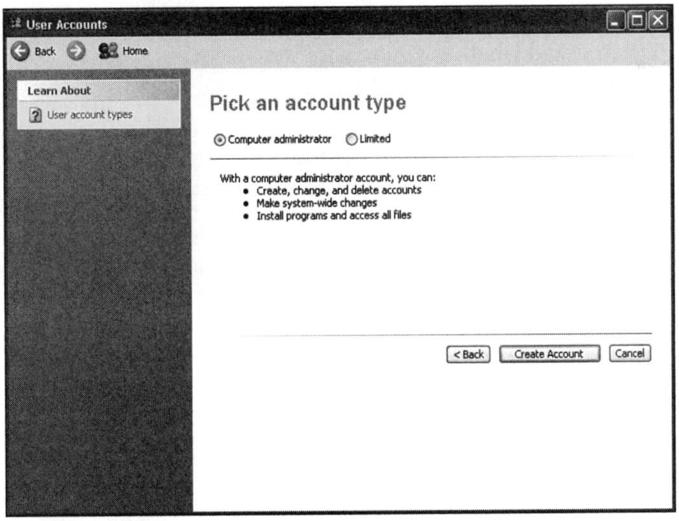

FIGURE 22.3

You can limit the types of changes a user can make to your PC using the account type.

6. Click the Create Account button. The new account is added.

Logging In and Out

If you have set up accounts, you see the different account names when you turn on your computer. You can click your account to log on. Any personalized settings, such as a customized desktop, wallpaper, Favorites list, and others, are loaded, and you see Windows XP just the way you left it. You can get to work.

You can also switch from one user account to another. For instance, if you are finished working, you can log off so that your child or spouse can log on. If you are going to be away from the computer for a short time, you can stay logged on, but simply switch users.

> **tip**
>
> Consider having one person as the computer administrator. This person can create new accounts and modify and delete existing accounts. Use limited accounts for those you don't want to have complete access to the computer. These users can perform all the basic computing tasks, but cannot perform system tasks such as installing programs.

Logging Off

To log off, follow these steps:

1. Click the Start button and click Log Off.

2. When asked whether you're sure that you want to log off, click the Log Off button. You are then logged off. Windows XP also saves any settings you changed, and you'll see the Welcome screen.

Switching Users

If you simply want to switch to another user account, you can do so without logging off. (However, it's best to log off to conserve system resources.) For instance, you may switch users if someone needs to check his or her email or use the computer for a short time. To switch users, follow these steps:

> **tip**
>
> You can change the way users log on or off. To do so, click Change the way users log on or off from the list of tasks in the first User Accounts window. You can use the Welcome screen (the default), or if you want to keep programs running and return to them as they are, you can also enable the Fast User Switching option. Make your choice and click Apply Options.

1. Click Start and then Log Off.

2. Click the Switch User button. You'll see the Welcome screen.

3. Click the account you want to switch to. (You'll also need to type the password if the account is password protected.) That account then becomes active.

Logging On

When you log off or when you first start Windows, you see the Welcome screen that lists all user accounts. To log on to one of these accounts, click the account name. If a password has been assigned to the account, type the password and press Enter. Once you are logged on, all personalized settings are loaded, and you can use your own personalized setup for Windows.

Modifying a User Account

You can make changes to existing accounts, such as specifying a password for that account, changing the picture, and so on. A picture appears on the Welcome screen, as well as at the top of the Start menu. You can, for instance, use one of the selected Windows pictures. As another example, you may assign a password so that no one can log on to the computer without first typing a password.

To modify an account, follow these steps:

1. Click Start and then click Control Panel.

2. Click User Accounts in the Control Panel window. Any accounts you have created are listed (refer to Figure 22.1).

3. Select the account in the User Accounts window. You'll see the available options for modifying this account (see Figure 22.4).

FIGURE 22.4

You can modify existing accounts as needed.

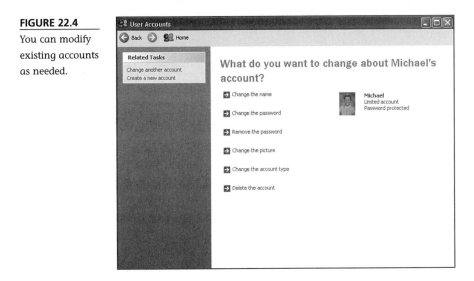

4. You can then make any of the changes covered in the following sections.

5. When you are finished making changes, close the Control Panel window.

Changing the Account Name

To change the name of the account, click Change the name. In the screen that appears, type a new name and then click the Change Name button. Again, this name shows up on the Welcome screen and Start menu.

Adding a Password

If you want to apply some security to using the computer, you can assign a password to an account. Then a user must type the password to log on to that account.

To create a password, click Create a password. You'll see several text boxes (see Figure 22.5). Type the password you want to use in the first text box. Type it again to confirm in the second text box. Finally, type a hint to help you remember the password. When you've completed all three text box entries, click the Create Password button. Now, this person is prompted to type the password to gain access to this account.

tip

You can also remove a password. To do so, display the account and then click Remove the Password. Click the Remove the Password button to confirm the deletion. Keep in mind that doing so also removes any passwords you have saved for your Internet browsing. If you have to type a password, Internet Explorer asks whether you want it to remember that password automatically. If you click Yes, the password is stored *with* your account. Deleting the account password deletes all of these passwords as well.

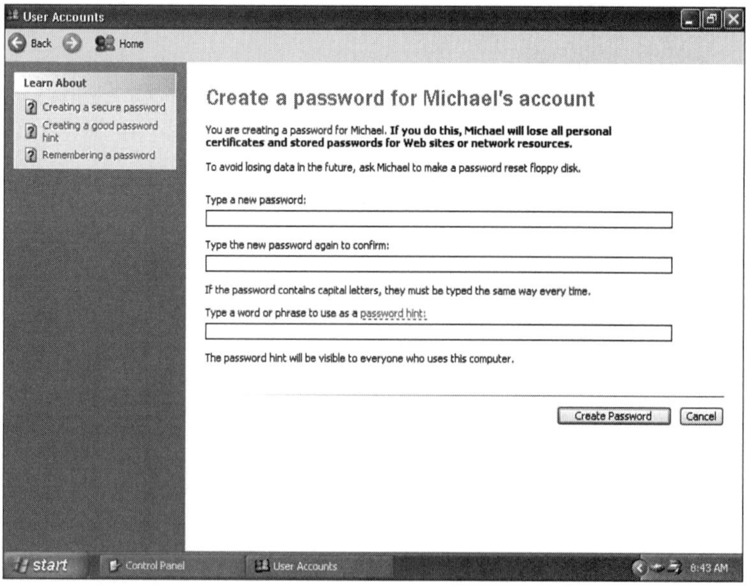

FIGURE 22.5

Assign a password for one measure of security.

Assigning a Picture

Windows XP assigns a graphic image to each account (including an airplane, butterfly, guitar, chess set, and others). If you don't like the graphics, you can use one of the other icons supplied with Windows XP. If none of these suits your fancy, you can use other graphic images. For instance, you might use actual pictures of each person for his or her account.

To use a different picture for the account, follow these steps:

1. Click Change the picture.

2. Select from one of the available pictures (see Figure 22.6).

FIGURE 22.6

You can select from several images included with Windows XP.

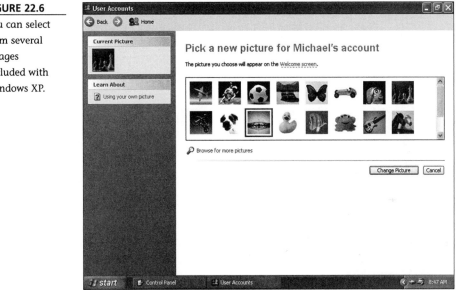

Or

Click Browse for more pictures to select another picture (for instance, a photograph) that is stored in another location. Open the folder that contains the image (see Figure 22.7). Select the image and then click Open. The image is then used for this account (see Figure 22.8).

FIGURE 22.7

To use another image, browse to that drive and folder.

FIGURE 22.8

You might, for instance, use a photograph of each person.

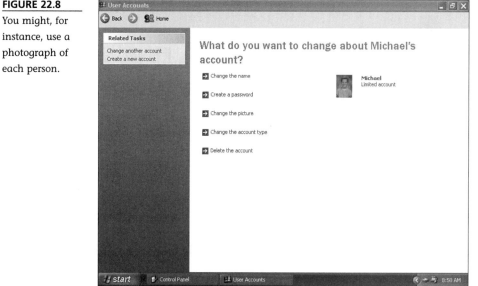

Changing the Account Type

If you want to set limits (or lift the limits) on a user account, change the account type. To do so, click Change the account type, select the account type, and then click the Change Account Type button. You can view the specifics for the different account types by checking the screen. When you select an account type, you see a description of what that person can (and cannot do).

Deleting an Account

If someone no longer uses the computer (perhaps he got his own!), you can delete accounts. Doing so frees up the disk space taken by this person's user account settings and documents. (You do have the option of saving the documents or deleting them.)

To delete an account, follow these steps:

1. Select the account you want to change.

2. Click Delete the account. You are then prompted to keep or delete the files (see Figure 22.9).

FIGURE 22.9

You can delete outdated or unused accounts.

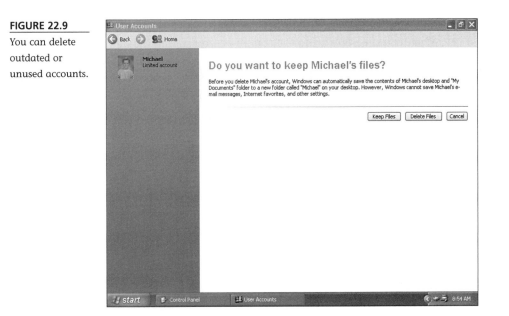

3. Select whether to keep or delete the account files by clicking Keep Files or Delete Files. Next you are prompted to confirm the deletion.

4. Click the Delete Account button.

THE ABSOLUTE MINIMUM

User accounts provide a handy way to let multiple users have personalized versions of Windows XP that suit how each person uses the computer (including how the desktop appears, the list of favorite sites, and so on). For this purpose, Windows enables you to create user accounts. You can use this feature to do the following:

- You can set up accounts for each person who uses the computer by selecting an account name, picture, and type.

- When you turn on the computer, all user accounts are displayed. You can then log on to your account.

- When you are done using the computer, you should log off. Then another user can log on. You can have several people logged on at the same time and simply switch users, but it's best to conserve system resources by logging off. Use the Log Off button on the Start menu to log off.

- Any changes made to Windows settings are saved each time a person logs off.

- You can modify a user's account as needed by changing the name, type, or picture. You can also assign passwords and delete unneeded accounts.

23

USING ACCESSIBILITY OPTIONS

Microsoft created Windows XP's Accessibility Options for people with special needs, but they can be useful for everyone. Windows XP includes two sets of accessibility tools: those listed on the Accessories menu plus a set of Control Panel options. These features make using the computer easier for those with special needs. For instance, you can magnify the screen so that one area is larger and easier to see. Likewise, you can display visual warnings for system sounds if you have special hearing needs. Furthermore, you can customize the keyboard, as well as type, using an onscreen keyboard and your mouse or other pointing device.

This chapter covers these special-need features of Windows XP.

Using the Accessibility Accessory Programs

In addition to the accessory programs covered in Chapter 21, "Using Windows Accessory Programs," Windows XP includes a set of accessibility accessory programs. These programs make it easier for those with disabilities to use the operating system and include the following:

- Magnifier magnifies the contents of your screen.
- Narrator reads the contents of your screen aloud.
- On-Screen Keyboard enables users who have limited mobility to type onscreen using a pointing device.

To start any of these accessory programs, follow these steps:

1. Click the Start button, select All Programs, choose Accessories, and then click Accessibility.

2. Click any of the programs: Magnifier, Narrator, or On-Screen Keyboard. The particular program is then started.

When you start each program, you see a dialog box that provides information about the program you opened. When this appears, read over the contents of the dialog box and click OK to close it.

You can also use the Accessibility Wizard to set up and turn on any of the programs. The wizard is covered later in this chapter.

Finally, to keep the program open but remove the program's dialog box from view, click the Minimize button in the top-right corner of the dialog box.

The following sections discuss how to use each of the accessibility accessory programs.

Using Magnifier

Magnifier magnifies part of your screen so that you can see it better. The top part of the screen shows the location of the mouse pointer. The rest of the screen shows the "regular" view of the window. In Figure 23.1, for instance, you see the Display Properties dialog box open. The magnification area shows the location of the mouse pointer. You can use this tool to better see and select options.

To fine-tune this program, you can use the Magnifier Settings dialog box, shown in Figure 23.2. This dialog box appears when you start the program. From this list of options, you can do any of the following:

- To change the magnification level, display the drop-down list and select a different level. The higher the level, the bigger the current pointer location appears.

FIGURE 23.1

You can magnify the current location of the mouse pointer so that you can better see and select options.

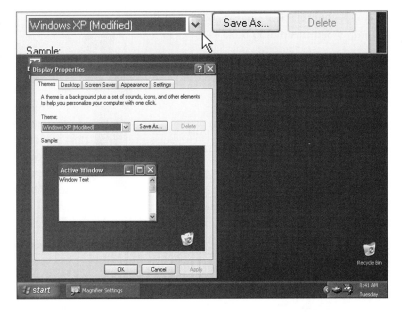

- By default, Magnifier automatically follows the mouse cursor, keyboard focus, and text editing. To turn off any tracking options, uncheck them.

- By default, the Magnifier Settings dialog box is displayed. You can choose to start the program minimized. You can also invert the colors. To do so, check any of these options in the Presentation area of the dialog box.

FIGURE 23.2

Use the Magnifier Settings dialog box to make changes to how this program works.

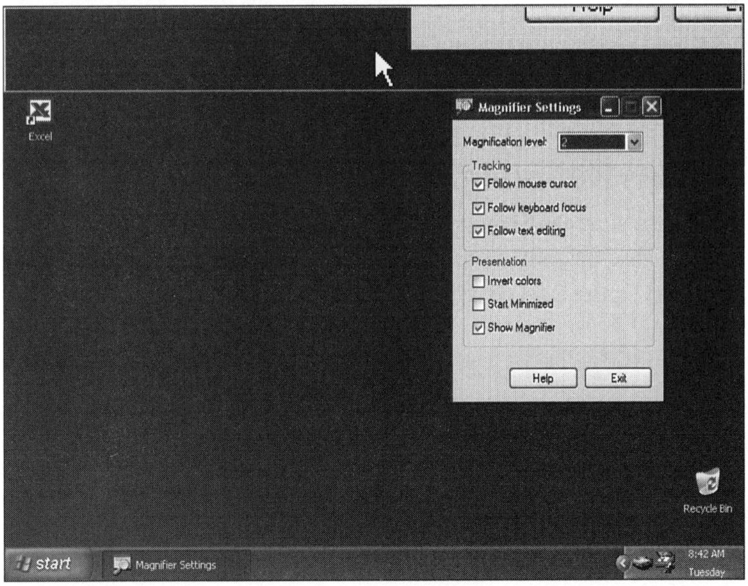

To exit Magnifier, click the Exit button in the Magnifier Settings dialog box.

Using Narrator

When you start Narrator, you see the opening screen. Click OK and you'll see the Narrator dialog box, shown in Figure 23.3. The Narrator reads onscreen events and typed characters.

tip

Another option for making your screen easier to read is to change the display size of text and other onscreen elements. You can do this with the wizard or with the Accessibility Control Panel options, which are covered later in this chapter.

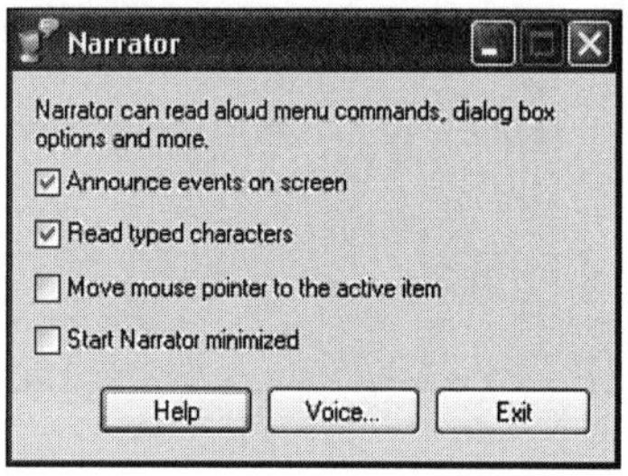

FIGURE 23.3

Use Narrator to have the program announce events, including dialog box options and typed characters.

You can also have Narrator move the mouse pointer to the active item. As another option, you can start the program minimized. Check any of the desired options in the Narrator dialog box.

You can select a voice you want to use for Narrator, as well as the speed, volume, and pitch of that voice. To do so, click the Voice button in the Narrator dialog box. At that point, a Voice Settings dialog box opens. Select your settings and then click OK.

To exit the program, click Exit. Then click Yes to confirm that you want to exit.

Using On-Screen Keyboard

When you start On-Screen Keyboard, you see the welcome screen, which describes its use. Click OK to close the dialog box. You can then use the On-Screen Keyboard, shown in Figure 23.4, to type.

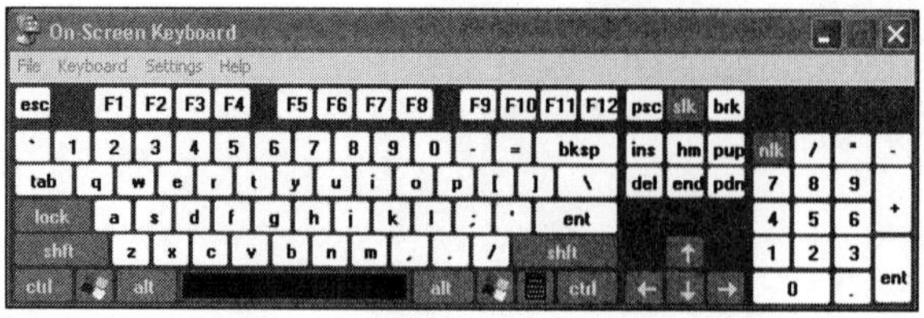

FIGURE 23.4

You can use On-Screen Keyboard to type using your mouse.

You can type by clicking the onscreen keys with your mouse pointer. If you prefer a different method, you can click Settings and then Typing Mode to select another method: hovering or scanning. In hovering mode, you use a mouse or joystick to hover the pointer over a key; the selected character is then typed. In scanning mode, On-Screen Keyboard scans the keyboard, highlighting letters; you then press a hot key or use a switch-input device whenever On-Screen Keyboard highlights the character you want to type.

Using Accessibility Control Panel Options

In addition to the accessory programs, you can use one of several Control Panel options. For instance, you can adjust settings, such as the size of the text display. You can also use the Accessibility Wizard to select options suited for particular needs. This section covers both.

Using the Accessibility Wizard

To start the Accessibility Wizard, follow these steps:

1. Click Start and then click Control Panel. You'll see the various Control Panel options.

2. Click Accessibility Options. You'll see the options available for this Control Panel group (see Figure 23.5).

FIGURE 23.5

Use the Accessibility Options Control Panel to set options and use the Accessibility Wizard.

3. Click Configure Windows To Work For Your Vision, Hearing, and Mobility Needs to start the Accessibility Wizard.

4. Click Next to move past the welcome screen. You'll see the first screen, which lets you select the text size. If larger text would, for instance, make the computer easier to use, select one of the various text size options (see Figure 23.6).

FIGURE 23.6

Select a different text size to make the text easier to read.

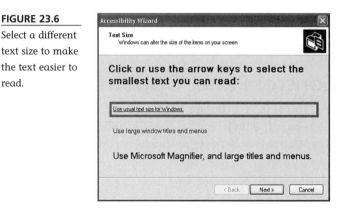

5. Select a text size option and then click Next. You'll see additional options for the display, including changing the font size, using Magnifier (covered earlier in this chapter), and disabling personalized menus (see Figure 23.7).

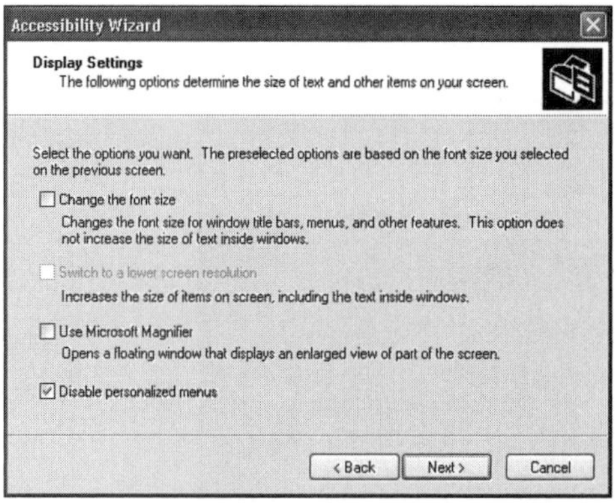

FIGURE 23.7

You can select additional display options.

6. Select the display options that control the size of text and other items and click Next. You'll see additional special needs (see Figure 23.8).

7. Complete the wizard, turning on various features for a particular special need and clicking Next to move through the options. For instance, if you have problems with the keyboard, the wizard prompts you to turn on StickyKeys (covered later).

8. After making your selections, click Finish.

The options you selected are then put into effect.

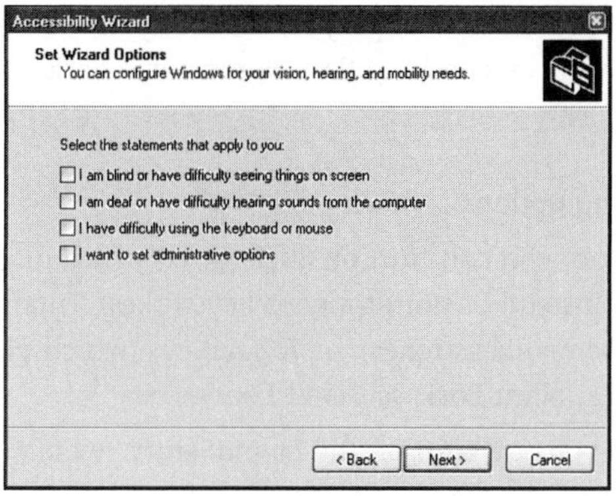

FIGURE 23.8
Select display options in the Accessibility Wizard.

Modifying Accessibility Options

In addition to the wizard, you can view and select other accessibility options. These are the same options that appear in the wizard when you select your special needs in step 6. The wizard simply selects the most appropriate options for you. With the dialog box method, you can select from all the options.

To view and select these options, follow these steps:

1. Click Start and then click Control Panel.
2. In the Control Panel window, click Accessibility Options.
3. In the Accessibility Options window, click Accessibility Options again. You'll see the Accessibility Options dialog box (see Figure 23.9).

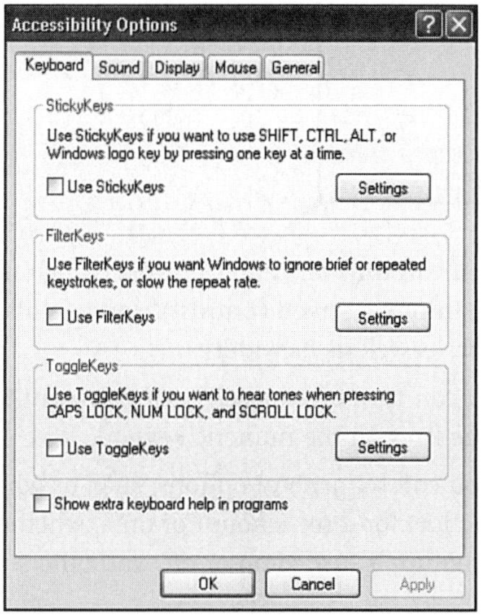

FIGURE 23.9
Select the tab and then turn on the options you want to use.

4. By default, the Keyboard tab is displayed. Click any of the tabs and turn on any additional options by checking the appropriate check boxes.

5. Click OK.

You can select the following options:

■ On the Keyboard tab, you can turn on StickyKeys (which allows you to press one key at a time, instead of simultaneous keystrokes), FilterKeys (which ignores brief or repeated keystrokes), or ToggleKeys (which plays tones when you press Caps Lock, Num Lock, or Scroll Lock).

■ On the Sound tab, you can turn on the SoundSentry (which displays visual warnings in conjunction with playing system sounds) or ShowSounds (which instructs programs to display captions for sounds). Figure 23.10 shows these options.

FIGURE 23.10

Use this tab to select sound options.

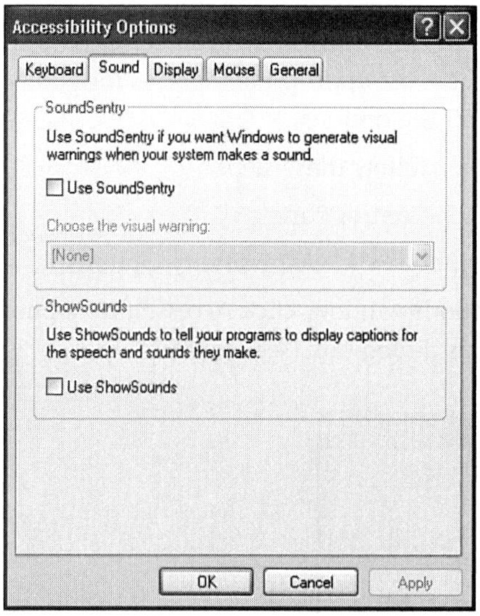

■ On the Display tab, you can turn on High Contrast (which uses alternative colors and font sizes to improve screen contrast). You can also select the blink rate for the cursor, as well as its width.

■ On the Mouse tab, you can turn on MouseKeys if you want to control the mouse pointer using the keys on the numeric keypad.

■ On the General tab, you can set general options, such as whether a feature is turned off after being idle for a set amount of time, whether you see or hear a sound when a feature is turned on or off, and others (see Figure 23.11).

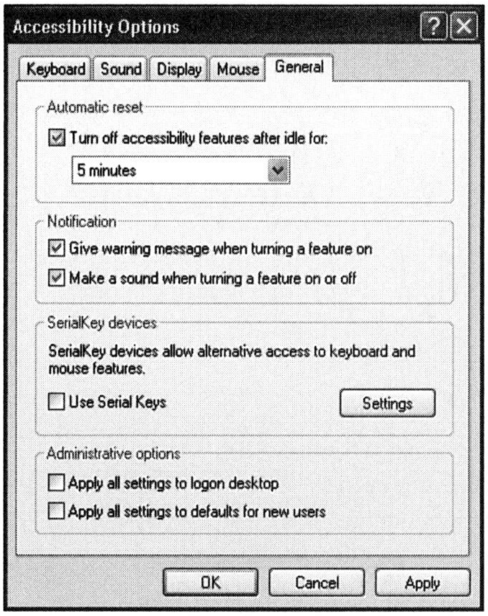

FIGURE 23.11

The General tab controls options such as when notification warnings sound.

THE ABSOLUTE MINIMUM

If you have special needs, it's worthwhile to explore the many features designed to make the computer as accessible as possible. You can use any of the following features:

■ Windows XP includes several accessibility programs including Magnifier (which enlarges the view of your screen), Narrator (which reads the contents of your screen aloud), and On-Screen Keyboard (which enables you to type onscreen using a pointing device).

■ You can use the Accessibility Wizard to turn on additional features, such as enlarging the text size.

■ You can also access accessibility options that control your hardware (sound, keyboard, mouse, and display) from the Control Panel. You can use these options to make these components more suited to your needs.

24

SETTING UP WINDOWS XP ON A HOME NETWORK

It used to be that setting up a network was a stupendous task, requiring all kinds of special wiring and special devices. A network still requires these basic features (some type of connection, some networking hardware, and a network card), but the processes of setting up and using a network are dramatically easier. This chapter touches on the basics of home networking.

Home Networking Basics

If your household contains multiple computers (one equipped with Windows XP and Internet access and at least one more equipped with Windows XP, Windows ME, Windows 98, or Windows 95), you can connect them to create a home network. Doing so enables you to share an Internet connection, hardware (such as a printer, scanner, and so on), and files and folders. Networking the computers in your home also enables members of your household to play multiplayer computer games.

Setting up a home network involves three basic steps:

1. Planning your network.
2. Installing and configuring the appropriate network hardware on each computer on the network.
3. Running the Windows XP Network Setup Wizard.

This section provides a brief overview of steps 1 and 2. You also learn about using the wizard (step 3). Keep in mind that an in-depth discussion of the first and second steps is beyond the scope of this book, but you can find ample information about them in Windows XP's online help.

Planning Your Network

When planning your network, you must decide what type of network you want to build. Your options are mostly determined by how the computers are connected. You may use telephone cabling, for example, or as is more common in recent years, you may set up a wireless network. (Wireless connections are the topic of Chapter 6.) This type of network has a hub, and as its name indicates, the other computers communicate without wires.

You also need to decide which machine will serve as your host or main computer. This main computer is usually called the *network server*. The computer you designate as the server should run Windows XP and be connected to the Internet.

Installing and Configuring Network Hardware

In terms of installing and configuring the appropriate network hardware, you must have a computer with built-in network ports. If you have an older computer, you need to equip each computer on your network with a network interface card (often referred to as an NIC or a *network adapter*).

Additionally, if you want to network more than two PCs, you will need a *hub*, which is a separate box into which cables from each network card connect. The hub acts as a go-between among all the computers and printers connected to the network. Many retail home networking kits contain the cards and the hub, as well as setup instructions. Note that a router doesn't function as well as a hub; it's best to route the Internet connection to the hub and let the hub take care of routing the Internet to all PCs on the network.

Again, the details for installing and configuring vary depending on the type of setup, the number of computers, and many other factors.

Running the Windows XP Network Setup Wizard

After you have installed the necessary networking hardware, you can configure each computer to use the network by working through the Network Setup Wizard. This wizard automates several procedures that were once done manually in earlier versions of Windows, including configuring your network adapters, configuring all your computers to share a single Internet connection, naming each computer, setting up file and printer sharing, installing a firewall, and more.

Follow these steps to run the Network Setup Wizard:

1. Click Start, All Programs, Accessories, Communications, and finally Network Setup Wizard.

2. Click Next to begin setting up your home network. Make sure that you've installed all network cards, modems, and cables; turned on all computers, printers, and external modems; and connected to the Internet (see Figure 24.1). Then click Next.

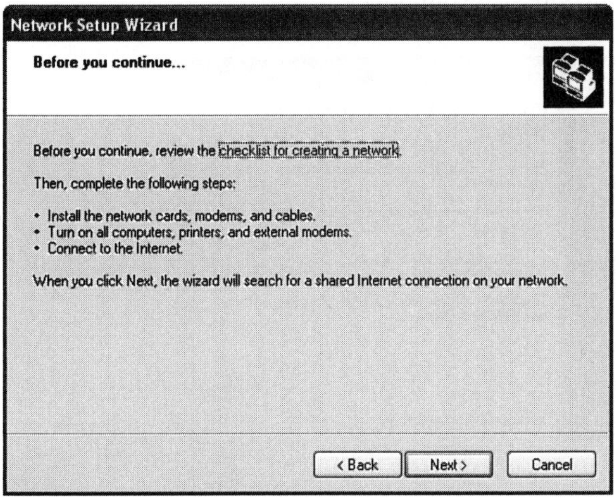

FIGURE 24.1

Make sure that the network hardware is set up.

3. Complete each step in the wizard, answering the questions based on your particular setup and clicking Next to move to the next step. You can expect to select the type of computer you are configuring, to enter a name and description of the computer, to name the network you are creating, to

confirm the settings for the network, to set up the Internet connection (see Figure 24.2), and then to configure all other computers hooked up to the network.

FIGURE 24.2

As one step for setting up the network, select your Internet connection type.

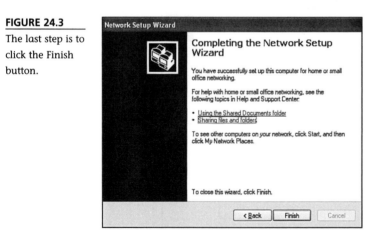

4. When the setup is complete, click the Finish button (see Figure 24.3). You then need to restart to finish the setup and start the configuration setup for all other connected computers.

FIGURE 24.3

The last step is to click the Finish button.

Sharing Resources on a Network

The purpose of a network is to make sharing information and hardware components (such as a printer) easier. This section focuses on common networking tasks including sharing files, sharing printers, and setting up network security.

Enabling File Sharing

By default, certain folders are made available to all computers on
your network. To make other folders available to other computers
on your network, you must enable file sharing for
those folders. (You'll also need to perform this
task on all networked computers that contain
folders that you want to make available over the
network.)

To enable file sharing, follow these steps:

caution

Enabling file sharing
could make your com-
puter vulnerable to out-
side users unless you
have a firewall. Be sure to
turn on firewall protection, as covered in Chapters 8 and 17.

1. Right-click the folder you want to share
   on your network and click the Sharing
   and Security command. The folder's
   Properties dialog box opens, with the
   Sharing tab displayed (see Figure 24.4).

FIGURE 24.4

Use this dialog
box to enable file
sharing for the
selected folder.

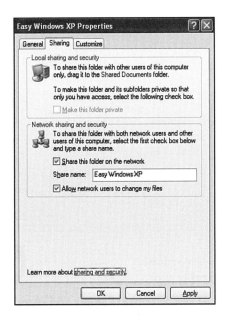

2. Check the Share this folder on the network check box.

3. If you want users on other machines to be able to change the contents of
   this folder, check the Allow network users to change my files check box.

4. Click OK.

Browsing Shared Files

You can browse shared files on the network through My Network Places. It works just like My Computer, except that it shows you files on the other network computers.

To view these files, follow these steps:

1. Click the Start button and My Network Places. The My Network Places window is displayed, listing all shared folders on the network (see Figure 24.5).

tip

In addition to sharing folders and files, you can share drives and devices, such as printers, scanners, and so on. Follow the same steps, but instead of right-clicking a folder, right-click the drive or device.

FIGURE 24.5

You can open any shared folders on the network.

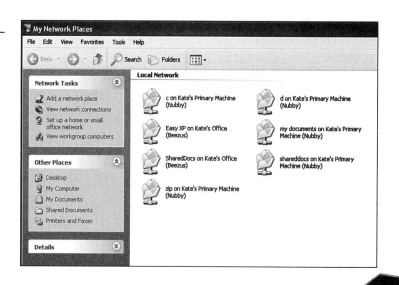

2. Double-click a folder icon to open that folder. You'll see the contents of that folder.

3. To open a document, double-click the document. You can then edit, print, and save the document as needed.

Sharing Printers

You can connect and set up a printer to the main network server. When you add the printer using the Printer Wizard, you can

caution

Depending on the file-sharing properties, you may only be able to view certain files. To make changes, the Allow network users to change my files check box for this folder/file must be checked.

select network printer as the type. Once set up and set as a shared device, you can print to this printer from any of the other networked computers.

To do so, select Network the printer from the Print dialog box in whatever program you are printing from. For more information about printing, refer to Chapter 2, "Saving and Printing Your Work."

Sharing Internet Connections

You can also share an Internet connection. You set up your Internet access for the main computer (server) using the Network Wizard. You can then connect to the Internet from any of the networked computers.

You have several options for how the connection is made. You can use one of the machines as the gateway, you can use a special Windows XP feature (Internet Connection Sharing or ICS), or you can purchase and set up a broadband router.

If you use one of the machines on the network as the gateway, the network's performance will be slowed based on the amount of traffic you're sending through it.

You can share a modem connection on a single machine with others on the network using ICS (Internet Connection Sharing). This, again, is not the fastest method, but it does work transparently.

Finally, you can purchase and install a broadband router instead. This component allows you to share the connection without having one of your machines do the job. The router also can act as a firewall for your network.

Controlling Network Security

If your home network is connected to the Internet, you suffer an increased risk of hackers obtaining access to the computers on that network. One way to obstruct unauthorized users is to erect a *firewall*. Windows XP ships complete with a firewall that is installed automatically when you run the Network Setup Wizard on a machine with a direct connection to the Internet.

You can also view and change security options as needed. Follow these steps:

1. Open the My Network Places window.

2. Click the View network connections link in the task pane (see Figure 24.6).

> **tip**
>
> The network properties dialog box includes many more features for controlling your connection, network use, security, and other settings. Consult online help or consider purchasing *Absolute Beginner's Guide to Computer Basics* (ISBN 0-7897-2499-6), which has some coverage on home networking.

FIGURE 24.6

To set security options, first display the network connections.

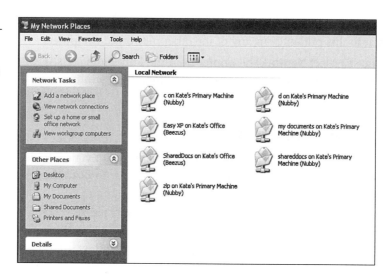

3. Right-click the icon for your network and then click the Properties command. You'll see the General tab of the network properties dialog box (see Figure 24.7).

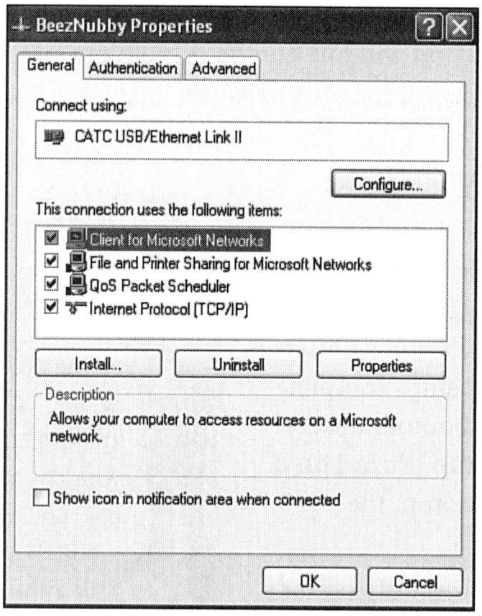

FIGURE 24.7

The network properties dialog box provides several tabs with useful connection and security options.

4. Review or make any changes to the General options.

5. Click the Advanced tab to check that firewall protection is on (see Figure 24.8).

6. Click OK.

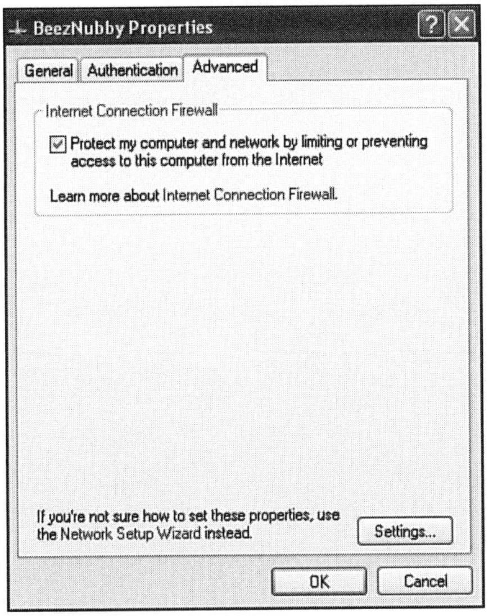

FIGURE 24.8

You can use the Advanced tab to check your network's firewall protection.

THE ABSOLUTE MINIMUM

If you have more than one computer, it's worthwhile to set up a home network so that you can more easily share data and hardware components (such as a printer or an Internet connection). Setting up a home network has been greatly simplified in Windows XP. In particular, look into the following features:

- To set up a network, you need a main computer (usually called the server or host). You also need a connection type; common connection types include phone lines or wireless connections. Furthermore, each computer on the network must have a network card. Setting up and installing the individual hardware components of a network are beyond the scope of this book. Try online help for more detailed information.

- Windows XP includes a Network Setup Wizard that guides you step by step through the process of setting up a home network.

- After a network is set up, you can share files. To do so, you must enable file sharing. After you have done so, you can open and work with any shared files on the network.

- You can also share a printer (thereby printing to the network printer) and an Internet connection.

- Security is a big issue for networking. Make sure that you turn on and keep on firewall protection. You can also investigate additional security and network options from the network properties dialog box.

Index

How can we make this index more useful? Email us at indexes@quepublishing.com